MAKERS AND BREAKERS OF CHICAGO

BOOKS BY JAY ROBERT NASH

Fiction
ON ALL FRONTS
A CRIME STORY

Nonfiction
DILLINGER: DEAD OR ALIVE?
CITIZEN HOOVER
BLOODLETTERS AND BADMEN
HUSTLERS AND CON MEN
DARKEST HOURS
AMONG THE MISSING
MURDER, AMERICA
ALMANAC OF WORLD CRIME
LOOK FOR THE WOMAN

Poetry
LOST NATIVES AND EXPATRIATES

Theatre
THE WAY BACK
OUTSIDE THE GATES
1947 (Last Rites for the Boys)

Jay Robert Nash

MAKERS AND BREAKERS OF CHICAGO

An Anecdotal History

Originally published in hardcover as *People to See*

Academy
Chicago
Publishers

Published in 1985 by

Academy Chicago Publishers
425 N. Michigan Ave.
Chicago, IL 60611

Copyright © 1981 by Jay Robert Nash

Printed and bound in the USA

Library of Congress Cataloging in Publication Data

Nash, Jay Robert.
    Makers and breakers of Chicago.

    Reprint.   Originally published: People to see.
Piscataway, N.J.: New Century Publishers, ©1981.
    Bibliography: p.
    Includes index.
    1.   Chicago (Ill.) —Social life and customs.
2.   Chicago (Ill.) —Biography.   I.   Title.
F548.3.N39   1985   977.3'11   85-1369
ISBN 0-89733-133-8

Contents

1
NEWS MANIACS   1

2
IT'S A WONDERFUL WORLD   27

3
UNDERWORLD, 1858   57

4
KING CRIME   75

5
BALL PARK AFTERNOONS   99

6
THE GAME'S THE THING   143

7
THE MAD MONEY MERCHANTS   163

8
ELEGANT EGOMANIA   193

9
AUTHOR, AUTHOR   205

10
THE BULLY BOYS   227

BIBLIOGRAPHY   247

INDEX   257

Preface

The reason for this book is simple: nothing like it has ever been done in the sense of a social history based solely upon personalities. Chicago, unlike the great cities of the East, has a wholly unstructured and "unofficial" history. Its existence, from swamp to metropolis, is sketchily recorded in fragments and those fragments have been created out of its personalities, living and dead, the very reason why Chicago is known elsewhere by slender but hot images that deal exclusively with its most outstanding citizens. The rest is crowd.

The individuals who lionized, defamed, and exalted the image of Chicago did so generously (and greedily) to immortalize themselves, for they struggled out of the crowd to *become* Chicago. There is no strict caste system in Chicago as in New York and Philadelphia and Boston; Chicagoans are innocent immigrants, no matter what their economic level. To be sure, there are the haves and have-nots, but socially, Chicago remains as it has always been—a polyglot mass from which a few in each generation emerge to establish reputations, either for good or evil, fiercely, desperately different than the crowd. That emergence is the heart of this book.

Chicago is, indeed, Horatio Alger with brass knuckles, indefatigable dreams, murderous passions, a city essentially like its weather, without compromise, its residents clinging to the image of *any* fellow citizen who has punched, pushed, or persuaded his way free of the crowd, from the posturing multimillionaire insurance tycoon W. Clement Stone, to the gesturing multimillionaire crime czar Al Capone, both great success stories. Success, infinitely more than noble or artistic failure, is the fabric of Chicago's trench coat.

It is a cruel city, but not heartless or anonymous as is New York. It enjoys being tough and insists upon winning. Ironically, its sports teams do not win yet receive fanatical support, a loyalty that lingers by virtue of only one hope—winning, and to hell with the game!

Many a winner leaves Chicago, strutting off to New York, or slinking with

xi

fat bankrolls earned in Chicago to the hazy heat of the West Coast. Those who stayed did so because they were rooted by ongoing empire exclusively generated in Chicago. And many who stay live as hermits, incognito from the crowd, husbanding their fortunes as did their grandfathers, hiding in the shadows of their achievments. The businessmen mostly stay in Chicago, the artists invariably flee. Chicago, it tells itself in ritual chant each dawn, is business, commerce, industry, money. Art, the city carps at dusk, is that nagging, dirty-faced, and unemployable stepchild babbling ridiculous ambitions.

Ben Hecht, who chronicled Chicago's wild and willful ways for a boisterous decade, knew this to be true. He departed the city permanently for Broadway fame, yet always uttered fond nostalgia for the city, once lamenting; "We should have never left Chicago." However, when the author questioned him on this in 1959, he blurted; "Are you kidding? I had to get out—I had to survive!"

In Chicago the insurance companies, the banks, the food processors survive and flourish. The city government, the last true vestige of real Chicago as most love to remember it, continues to stumble happily into blatant corruption and idiotic management, preserving for the world the stereotyped profile of cigar-chomping bossism. The crowd has always given an approving wink at the personalities of this bellowing realm, demonstrating a perverse pride in the shoddy reputations of its lawmakers and managers, quoting those immortal words of the late alderman Paddy Bauler, "Chicago ain't ready for reform!"

For years Richard J. Daley was staunchly supported because "he made Chicago the city that works," a thought that brings to mind the line about how "Mussolini made the trains run on time!" It was the same enlightened Mayor Daley who once enthusiastically suggested that the city tear down the Water Tower on Michigan Avenue, that great surviving edifice of the Chicago Fire of 1871, and replace it with a parking lot.

There is (The cretinous inclinations of Babbitt aside) much to love in the city of Chicago. Its physical appearance, its architecture, its parks are distinctive glories reflecting the city's stubborn individualism in spite of the crowd. For all its predictable Capones, Chicago continues to produce from the crowd spectacular Louis Sullivans and marvelous Helen Kellers, larger in life, more vital and important than a city seen through a museum case displaying its convenient reputation. These are the memorable ones who make up the actual history of America's giant inland city, perpetuate its name, pump its blood, think its thoughts—bronze statues that move.

Jay Robert Nash
Chicago, 1981

Acknowledgments

I would like to thank Judy Anetsberger for her great help in research and in the overall production of this book. My deepest gratitude also goes to my tireless typist Sandy Horeis.

Great help in my search for graphics for this book was provided by Bill Kelly of the Associated Press (Wide World), Arthur S. Levine, Bernard Van Marm, and Thomas Buckley.

For special collections of records, correspondence, and memorabilia, I would like to thank Edgar Krebs; Phil Krapp; Neil H. Nash; Jack Jules Klein, Jr.; Hand Oettinger; Art Kluge; Bruce Spivey; Jim and Edie McCormick; Neal and Joan Amidei; Curt Johnson; Marc Davis; Bob Abel; and Mike LaVelle.

In addition to my own library of fifty-thousand books, plus more than a quarter of a million files, I consulted Chicago's many fine libraries, where the staff personnel proved most helpful. These include Joseph C. Lutz of the Chicago Public Library (downtown branch), the staff of the Newberry Library, the staff of the Joseph Regenstein Library of the University of Chicago, the staff of the Northwestern University Library, the staff of the John Crerar Library of IIT, and the Chicago Historical Society.

1

News Maniacs

"Low, filthy, and disgusting, displaying not the least trace of comfort." With these stinging but apt words visiting geologist William H. Keating described the boggy village that was Chicago in 1823. The boom town's first newspapermen—Chicago was and is fundamentally a newsman's newspaper city—did their utmost to retain the repugnant image set forth by geologist Keating. Far from the lofty motives and ideals prodding the founders of most newspapers in the East, Chicago's press was almost always self-serving, nepotistic, and downright greedy, not to exclude dangerous, libelous, and ofttimes treasonable.

The "me first" posture of Chicago's fledgling newsmen was wholly in keeping with a frontier town that danced in the mud of its swamps, prided itself on having more saloons than homes at its founding, and reveled in corruption, proving that the real heathens in this unsanitary marsh were those white settlers who trekked to the shores of Lake Michigan to make, borrow, or steal their future fortunes. The ambitions of twenty-five-year-old John Calhoun, who had apprenticed in New York as a printer's devil, were wholly in keeping with the 200-odd husky souls who had erected by 1833 forty-three makeshift cabins along the Chicago River. When he arrived that year with a small press and battered boxes of type, Calhoun was determined to begin Chicago's first newspaper. His was not the concern of bringing the national news to Chicago's inhabitants; the tardy mails from the East would eventually provide that. Calhoun's sole purpose for publishing his *Weekly Democrat* ostensibly was to promote the cause of his idol President Andrew Jackson and fanatically further his own political career.

O Strutting Pioneers

Calhoun's *Democrat*, published in a one-room shack at the corner of what is now South Water and Clark streets, was a six-column, four-page infant that

1

Long John Wentworth who ran Chicago's first newspaper for his own political ambitions.

screamed into birth on November 26, 1833. The publisher hooted Jacksonian philosophy from the first, but the residents didn't seem to mind. By the following year, the office-seeking Calhoun had 700 of the 800 inhabitants of the city subscribing to his paper at $2.50 a year, a mean price for those days. The sledding was rough. Calhoun's wife was pressed into service when the help ran off to trap beaver, and that good woman spent much of her time reading proofs and smoothing out the deep impressions in the paper with an iron.

Chicagoan Thomas O. Davis cried enough at Calhoun's monopoly of the press and began his own newspaper, the *American*, in 1835, mostly to combat the Jackson organ with one that stumped the politics of Henry Clay and the new Whig party. The press competition grew so stiff that to support himself, Calhoun finally decided to run for public office after offering his paper for sale. His successor, at about the time of his decision, was sleeping in the forests outside of Michigan City, Indiana, sixty miles distant from brawling Chicago.

It was October 1836 and a 6-foot-6 inch Bunyanesque fellow named, quite naturally, Long John Wentworth decided that he could not rest in the stage-coach that had rattled him unmercifully during the long trip from his native New Hampshire. He yelled up to the driver to halt and alighted to curl up inside the wilderness for a long sleep. Awakening, Wentworth, whose lanky frame would some day fill out to a behemoth 300 pounds ("My tailor doesn't measure, he surveys me," he would later chuckle), took off his shoes— fourteen inches in length, five inches in width—and slung them over his shoulder. He began to walk the final sixty miles to Chicago along the marshy beaches of Lake Michigan carrying a jug of whiskey with him, not for his stomach, but to massage his burning feet.

Long John entered Chicago in legend—the twenty-one-year-old went immediately to the Sauganash Tavern where he devoured six complete dinners and drank two gallons of beer. Brandy, however, was soon to become Wentworth's favorite spirit and he downed from a pint to a quart every day for the remainder of his robust life. The young giant's life-style was in keeping with the nomadic, unregulated pioneers roaming early Chicago. He would never live by the bells. He roared, "I never did and never will live on time. Got no use for call bells, dinner bells, or alarm clocks. My doctrine is this: eat when you're hungry, drink when you're thirsty, sleep when you're sleepy, and get up when you're ready." Wentworth lived up to that credo with a vengeance, preferring the luxuries—such as they were—of Chicago's rough hotels rather than those afforded him in his later-constructed Summit home. Time being money and opportunity was emphasized by Wentworth in the horrendous meals which he planned in advance every day of his life, checking off those dishes—sometimes as many as forty different servings— he preferred from hotel menus. He considered any time spent waiting to be served as inexcusably wasteful.

Dartmouth trained for law, Wentworth was no sooner the star boarder in Murphy's rooming house than he was approached by a fellow New Hampshire man, one Horatio Hill, who had purchased the shaky *Democrat* from John Calhoun for a mere $2,800. Since Hill was returning East, would Long John deign to take over the role of acting editor of the paper? Would he!

Wentworth hurled himself into the back-breaking work of running the *Democrat* without hesitation, promoting himself, as had Calhoun, into a powerful political position that would eventually vault him into the office of mayor. Although a stickler for gathering newsworthy items for his paper and a lobbyer in editorials for improved living and harbor conditions, Wentworth's chief news topic was Wentworth. So much print did he squander on his own activities that rival newsmen grew disgusted with him. Carped William Walters editor of the *Illinois State Register* in one editorial directed to the ambitious giant, "Nearly one half of your paper is occupied with your own movings and doings."

Long John's reactions to such criticism was no different than his response to those who took issue with his press statements even to the point of threatening the still-fashionable duel. When Wentworth wrote an editorial defending the local Indians, a certain Captain David Hunter stomped into the *Democrat*'s offices where he slammed two pistols onto the editor's desk and bellowed, "I challenge you, John Wentworth!" Long John leaned slowly back in his chair, stretched his enormous frame, and, much to Hunter's red-faced chagrin, let loose a gut full of laughter. (Hunter's version of the confrontation had it that he had placed empty pistols on Wentworth's desk and that the self-serving editor cringed and begged off, a tale which tickled Tom Davis of the competing *American* so much that he labeled Long John a "laughable dupe of full fears and empty pistols.")

Job printing was more lucrative for Long John than revenue generated by his *Democrat;* he grew rich and powerful as Chicago's official printer, gleaning hefty payments for all of the city's printing needs as well as being paid by the county for publishing tax bills and receiving handsome payments from the federal government for listing all mail at the post office awaiting pick up by residents. Shrewd as he was affable, Wentworth's policy was to obtain payment for all his services, the least of which was his advertising space, before bestowing any favors upon grubbing politicians. In this way, he built up his power among the jostling political ranks until, in 1857, he muscled his way into City Hall as the mayor. Wentworth, in July 1861 while he was enjoying his second term as Chicago's chief executive, grew tired of his newspapering and sold the *Democrat*, a thriving daily since 1840, to the already powerful *Tribune* which had been publishing since June 1847, the sixth daily to be founded.

Exactly *what* the *Tribune* had been publishing was open to gun-toting debate. Run by several merchants at its inception, the *Tribune* was originally a Know-Nothing rag (subscribing to the Know-Nothing party philosophy, which was sort of an America-first credo; its members, operating secretly for fear of reprisal, answered, "I know nothing," to all inquiries about their beliefs). Its columns oozed xenophobia, and, in addition to spewing out hate for all foreigners, the *Tribune* was unswerving in its opposition to all Roman Catholics.

When Joseph Medill and five partners took over the *Tribune* eight years after its founding, the new editors eased away from the antiforeign and anti-Catholic stances, but retained, since Medill was a teetotaler, the paper's unflinching battle for temperance. The Canadian-born Medill sold his *Cleveland Leader* and used the proceeds to buy into the *Tribune* which was then printed on a horse-powered Adams press driven by an old blind horse plodding around a revolving shaft to which it was yoked.

The thirty-two-year-old Medill was an unbending, taciturn type who sported a grandfather's beard early in life and never shaved it off. His appearance could best be described as somber. Tall, stoop-shouldered, this dynamo of early Chicago journalism was always seen in the same apparel: a black frock coat, spring tie, and black fedora. He always wore knee boots during the daytime and carpet slippers in the house.

According to his own paper, Medill "hated drunkenness because he hated

Archconservative owner of the *Tribune*, Joseph Medill almost single-handedly put Lincoln into the White House.

Tribune humorist and creator of "Mr. Dooley," Finley Peter Dunne complained of Medill's teetotaling.

anything that was stronger than a man." Such was Medill's disdain for drink that he became an ardent sponsor of what was then known as the Keeley Cure, an early day alcoholic recovery program located in Dwight, Illinois, for which the abstemious editor did free advertising. According to historian Ernest Poole, Medill "told his managing editor to send any drunks on the staff down to Dwight to take the cure." The creator of Chicago's memorable Mr. Dooley, Finley Peter Dunne, afterwards a guiding light for the *Tribune*, once complained that "the only way to keep your job on the *Tribune* is to go to Keeley's!"

Medill's rabid crusade against booze often backfired. In the early 1880s, the editor attempted to get the saloons of Chicago closed on Sunday which created so much public furor that the Sunday-open saloon was permanently established. The sanctimonious Medill was responsible for one of the most ostentatious flexing of religious muscle when, on Sunday, May 21, 1887, the *Tribune* printed, in addition to its regular issue, a "revised edition" of the New Testament, complete. (The revisions to Holy Scripture undoubtedly sprang from the bubbling wellsprings that inspired Joe Medill.)

Faithfully, Medill's lips never touched spirits until physicians insisted he take a thimbleful of digitalis to speed up his heart in later years. By then, states Wayne Andrews in *Battle for Chicago*, Medill was easy prey for doting doctors, a last-legs period when "he was stone deaf and never without his ear trumpet."

Any of Medill's reporters who smoked sparingly or not at all—the stern-faced editor's tobacco intake was limited to one cigar a week—or fought off the stomach-quivering compulsion to gamble, remained within the good graces of the chief. Medill violently opposed card playing and saw no use in the stock market or Board of Trade, as "it only encouraged gambling," according to his grandson and eventual successor Colonel Robert R. McCormick. A man of no hobbies, a rather curious curmudgeon who never exercised, Medill also scorned all athletics and only while he was away on trips could his editors manage to sneak copy into the *Tribune* regarding sports activities of any kind; thus did the paper surreptitiously build up its sports page. (Fine arts in Chicago also struggled for space in the *Tribune;* its first music critic George R. Uptmas disguised himself from both readers and Medill by writing under the name Peregrine Pickle.)

Much can be said of Medill as a scrupulous newsman and innovator in his mercurial profession. He was one of the first editorial lights in the country to openly oppose slavery. Almost single-handedly he formed the Western Associated Press and compelled the AP of New York to provide better service to midwestern dailies. But his driving ambition was to be the leading political voice in Chicago and throughout the Midwest.

Through Medill an obscure back country lawyer named Abraham Lincoln was promoted into a national political figure and the subsequent birth of the Republican party was largely spanked into existence by the archconservative editor. The *Tribune* supported almost every measure Lincoln took during his administrations, Joe Medill only once exploding at a Lincoln edict. During the Civil War, Chicago, beyond any other city of its size in the land, contributed more men to the Union army. Yet Washington upped the city's quota halfway through the conflict. Medill's response was one of wrath. He went to Washington to thunder at Lincoln that the quota was too high.

"This is coward's talk, Medill," Lincoln told the publisher. "Your *Tribune* has done more for recruiting than any other paper in the West, yet now you cry that your city be spared when our whole cause is in desperate need! Go home and send me those men!" Medill went home and the *Tribune* let loose an avalanche of appeals, directives, and screams for more recruits. Lincoln got his men, 28,000 all told from Chicago's population of 156,000.

Public loyalty to Lincoln and the cause of the Union did not interfere with Medill's private dreams of grandeur, thoughts he put to paper that revealed him to be no less than a spectacular warmonger and racist. In one letter to his brother William, who was then serving in the Union army, Joe Medill gushed out his thoughts of an American empire.

War and more war was the only answer to America's future, Medill thought. Medill wrote, "It is very possible that we shall have two wars when this one is ended—one to clear the British out of Canada and the other to clear the French out of Mexico. This continent belongs to the Free American Race and they are bound to have it, every inch of it, including the West Indian islands. We have got a taste of blood and learned the art of war and our tremendous strength and exhaustless resources. Our navy will domineer the seas and our army the continent. The insults received from England must be wiped out. . . . And as to France, she has taken a mean and cowardly advantage of this nation to crush poor Mexico. . . . We shall permit no nation to abuse Mexico but ourselves. We claim the right to turn her up on Uncle Sam's knee and spank her bottom for not behaving herself. . . .

"In future wars black and yellow men will be used freely to fight. We will not be so careful about spilling the blood of niggers. . . . How easy for us to hold the South with black troops who love the North and are devotedly loyal. . . . The tree of liberty must be watered by the blood of patriots at least once in every three generations."

William Medill, a few weeks after receiving his brother's letter, watered that tree with his own blood, killed by a minié ball at Williamsport, Maryland.

Medill's devotion to Lincoln and the Union cause indirectly benefited the editor's scribbling minions. It was no secret to the bickering journalistic fraternity in Chicago that many correspondents of the city's press covering the war near the front lines found favor and funds by writing complimentary articles about certain Union officers. Of these enterprising scribes, according to *New York Times* correspondent Franc B. Wilkie, the most exceptional was Medill's hand-picked reporter, one Albert H. Bodman. Though he received only $16-a-week salary, Bodman heaped praise on several Union commanders at the front around Memphis, Tennessee, in dispatches that appeared in full gloat in the *Tribune*. For such marvelous publicity, this *Tribune* man was paid off by being allowed to purchase cotton dirt-cheap and sell it in the North for enormous profits. One such deal netted Bodman $22,000.

Paradoxically, where Medill appeared to be the shining abolitionist, he was also the front man for big business. The common worker was a subject guaranteed to throw Medill into instant fits of distemper. By the 1880s, when the *Tribune* was about the most powerful paper in the city and the dominant Republican voice in the Midwest with a whopping 67,000 Sunday readers alone in 1887, Medill busied himself with unflagging attacks against the eight-hour day. He directed his editorial writers to label labor strikers as the "scum and filth of the city."

The unemployed were simply classified as tramps in Medill's lexicon of labor. These out-of-work be   ...oned the *Tribune* in 1884, could be easily dispatched. In a   ...ible editorial, which would certainly have
                    ...propagandists looking for ways to dispose of "undesirables" some fifty years later, Medill wrote, "The simplest plan probably, where one is not a member of the Humane Society, is to put a little strychnine or arsenic in the meat and other supplies furnished the tramp. This produces death within a comparatively short time, is a warning to other tramps to keep out of the neighborhood, puts the Coroner in a good humor, and saves one's chickens and other portable property from constant depredation."

The paper's own official history booklet of 1922 admitted that the *Tribune* "tried cases and imposed sentences in its news columns" during the Medill editorship. A sample of Joe Medill's early day news coverage, colorfully headlined "A BRUTE," offered a mixture of fact and opinion. "James Wheeler was yesterday fined $5 for abusing his wife. Mrs. Wheeler is the woman who has twice attempted to commit suicide, once by throwing herself into the lake and again by taking laudanum. Both those attempts resulted from injuries inflicted upon her by her husband. A few month's experience in breaking stones in the Bridewell [the local jail] would do this Wheeler 'a power of good,' and he ought to have been sent there."

Any organization or person who opposed the established American political system, chiefly the *Tribune*'s concept of that system, was also condemned in print. Medill saved his special venom for Communists. Said one of his editorials in the fall of 1875: "If the Communists in this country are counting upon the looseness of our police system and the tendency to proceed against criminals by due process of law, and hope on that account to receive more leniency than in Europe, they have ignored some of the significant episodes in American history.... Judge Lynch is an American by birth and character.... The Vigilance Committee is a peculiarly American institution. Every lamp-post in Chicago will be decorated with a communistic carcass if necessary to prevent wholesale incendiarism . . . or any attempt at it."

Anyone who sided with the underpaid, overworked employee of the day

was subject to Medill's rage. This included no less a humanitarian than the
near saintly Governor John P. Altgeld. When Altgeld pardoned three of the
anarchists convicted in the Haymarket Square bombing, Medill's editorial
cannonade was deafening and Altgeld was forever after referred to as The
Viper and was mercilessly pilloried in *Tribune* headlines and cartoons.

Labor leader Eugene V. Debs fared no better. In 1894, the crusty news
arbiter ordered his editorial hatchet men to refer to Debs at all times as
Dictator Debs, but by then, Medill's son-in-law Robert W. Patterson held
enough control at the paper to countermand the order.

For all his spattering prejudices and hates, Joseph Medill remained the idol
of many a newsman until his death in 1899 at age seventy-six. The editor died
with the bark on a dogged question, perhaps apocryphally reported, that
summed up his journalistic career. From his sickbed, Joe croaked his last
words, "What's the news?"

The Lunatic

When it came to news in the zany world of Wilbur F. Storey, editor and
publisher of the irascible *Times*, anything was grist for his bubbling mill,
from boulevard brag to back-alley whispers. The *Times* had been, since
1854, a political vehicle for Stephen A. Douglas, the "Little Giant" (exactly

Wilbur Storey, Chicago's first unbridled yellow journalist.

five feet tall), and had been a losing proposition even when Cyrus H. McCormick, inventor of the reaper, bought it in 1860. McCormick, a Virginian, used the paper to seek a compromise on the slavery question. Medill's *Tribune* heaped scorn upon the inventor, calling him a rebel and a slave-driver. McCormick retorted that the *Tribune* was a dirty sheet. It was all too much for the founder of the harvester machinery company who was edified at the sudden appearance of a hell beater named Wilbur F. Storey, a fiery Democrat who adored the memory of Stephan Douglas (the Little Giant having died after Lincoln's inauguration), and who had newspaper ink swimming in his blood since he had become a printer's devil at age twelve.

Storey had tried his hand at running newspapers in Indiana and Michigan with little success. In his spotty career, before arriving in Chicago at forty-two with premature white hair and beard, Wilbur had operated a bookstore and had been a postmaster and a druggist. None of these professions suited him; Storey was a temperamental man who took orders from no one. When his minister hinted that he stop selling liquor in his drugstore, Storey quit the church in a lung-yelling rage.

Selling the *Detroit Free Press* for $30,000, Storey moved to Chicago where Cyrus McCormick was more than gleeful to unload the *Times* on him for $13,000. The *Times* had then less than 1,000 paid subscribers. Challenge, however, was a sweet bugle call to Storey whose editorial philosophy quite simply was "to get the news and raise hell." This he accomplished for twenty-three years of storm and assault upon the senses of an already hardened Chicago populace, deftly wielding sensation and scandal with either hand. Long before the *New York Herald* in the reign of James Gordon Bennett I outraged its readers, Wilbur Storey scandalized all that was living in the Windy City. "It was the part of the *Times*," commented Willis J. Abbott, "to create discord in a journalistic orchestra which otherwise was joined in perfect harmony."

Wilbur's brand of journalism was unlike anything Chicago had ever seen. As one of his own staff members later recalled with a shiver, "Scandals in private life, revolting details from the evidence taken in police court trials, imaginary liaisons of a filthy character, reeked, seethed like a hell's broth in the *Times'* cauldron."

Henry Justin Smith, a great Chicago newspaper editor of another century, in a 1930 lecture was much kinder to the irrepressible Storey in saying that "he was obsessed by news values; if he saw news in a story he ignored the fact that it might deal with life at its shadiest." He would "go to hell for news" and often did. That hell was created in the bowels of the *Times* offices, in the composing room where Storey, one of the few editors of Chicago venerated by printers, would religiously spend endless hours through the night doting over galleys of type. He would meticulously point a long, bony index finger at a column of type and indicate exactly where it was to be locked into a form.

One of Wilbur's devoted printers was a colossus compositor called Big Jim who so respected his boss that he saved the volatile editor's life. A gambler, scathingly attacked in a *Times* article, tracked Storey to his nocturnal lair and, amidst spilling type and crashing galley trays, viciously punched and kicked the editor. Stripping off his leather apron, Big Jim roared a stream of curses and fell upon the gambler beating him senseless. Storey, as was his usual manner, never bothered to thank the printer. Big Jim, however, appeared grime-smeared the next morning in Wilbur's office, asking for five dollars. "A bonus," some said, as they watched the skinflint editor fork over the five-spot. "A hold-up," howled critics. Yet Big Jim got his five dollars extra each week as long as he and Wilbur Storey were alive.

The surplus cash picked up by the compositor each week was no sign of friendship, for editor Storey had no friends; he wanted it that way. The six-foot, muscular Wilbur, his wiry beard jutting, his hazel eyes permanently fixed with a frightening gaze, was not a man who inspired camaraderie. Always brusque and cold, the aloof Mr. Storey was never known to put his arm about his loyal newsmen for news well scooped, or to chat with any of his dogged crew inside his private offices. "Brutal," some said of Storey, who received his writers' copy without a murmur and then proceeded to print what he liked, neither giving praise nor reason for his selection, and cavalierly dumping what displeased him into a towering deskside wastebasket.

The Civil War appeared to Storey as the greatest scandal going. A devout Democrat with the backing of the heavily Democratic city council and a Democratic mayor, the editor freely let loose his broadsides against Republican Lincoln, his cabinet, and especially his Army field commanders. Warren P. Isham, Storey's ace correspondent at the front, was never above faking war reports that showed Union generals in a bad light to liven up the *Times* columns. (This was totally within the directives of editor Storey who ordered all his war correspondents to "telegraph fully all news and when there is no news, send rumors.")

Isham once dreamed up a Confederate flotilla about to destroy Union ironclads along the Mississippi waterways, a story so exaggerated that the correspondent was publicly denounced by General Ulysses S. Grant. Hearing that some reporters had been killed in the battle for Vicksburg, General William Tecumseh Sherman, Grant's right-hand man and a hater of newsmen in general and the *Times* newsmen in particular, quipped, "Good! Now we'll have news from hell before breakfast!"

Later, Sherman, under Grant's orders, arrested the imaginative Isham for printing a story that a Union general had been surprised in a Memphis whorehouse by some roving Confederates and escaped out a window clad only in his underwear. The *Times* correspondent was jailed for "the duration of the war unless released by competent authority." That authority was, of course, Ulysses S. Grant. Wilbur Storey reached Grant through another

General U.S. Grant was a favorite target for Wilbur Storey and his scandal-mongering *Times*.

General William T. Sherman arrested Storey's libel-scribbling correspondent Warren P. Isham.

emboldened reporter, one Sylvanus Cadwallader, a Milwaukee scribe who replaced Isham on the Vicksburg front. Twice in a short period of time Cadwallader found Grant drunk—once about to fall off a riverboat and another time riding uneasily on horseback, again about to fall off. The reporter, on both occasions, took the General's bottle away and carted him off to bed. In return for such extraordinary services, Grant allowed Isham to return to the *Times* office in Chicago and gave special reporting privileges to the honorable Mr. Cadwallader, allowing him to file reports before any other correspondent in the Western Theater of Operations which gave Wilbur Storey the biggest war scoops in Chicago and shot circulation profitably upward. (Isham drowned a year later in a Lake Michigan shipwreck; Cadwallader kept his mouth shut about Grant's dipsomania until the general's death.)

Wilbur Storey's attentions, however, were not centered about Union field commanders but upon Old Abe and Washington bigwigs. Although he supported the war effort of the North, albeit a feeble gesture, Storey reserved his special invective for the seat of government, charging that "the war, as waged by military satraps of the administration, is a subversion of the Constitution and the people's rights under law."

When Lincoln bowed to antislavery forces and delivered his Emancipation Proclamation, Wilbur Storey exploded, writing on the front page of the *Times* that "the cheek of every American must tingle with shame as he reads the silly, flat and dishwatery utterances of the man who has to be pointed out to intelligent foreigners as the President of the United States." This attack, of course, was directed also at Medill, and his *Tribune*, who Storey felt owned the administration; Lincoln was Medill's man. The reference to "intelligent foreigners" was an open blast against the *Tribune's* antiforeigner philosophy. What earned Storey and the *Times* the wrath of Union soldiery was the editor's penchant for pointing out the good manners of Confederate President Jefferson Davis and the sterling military qualities of General Robert E. Lee.

In 1863, four soldiers, drunk and raving, burst into the *Times* office and shouted for that "damned old secesh [secessionist]" to come out of his office. Wilbur Storey came out running, selected a corporal from the sodden group, and hurled him through a window. The others fled in panic. A devout *Tribune* subscriber encountered Storey sometime later and knocked him down in the street "for his Johnny Reb sympathies." The *Tribune* took to calling Storey a Copperhead, the sobriquet applied to Northerners who were against the war.

After Jim Goodsell, Storey's city editor, was found beaten into unconsciousness in an alley, the editor fortified his premises. The *Times* became an armed camp. Muskets were stacked along the walls of the editorial rooms and the printers wore as many as three pistols each while making up the

Union General Burnside was so incensed by Storey's copperhead attacks upon him that he ordered the editor arrested and his newspaper closed down.

paper. Further, Storey ordered a special system of pipes connected to the boiler; these were then routed to various outlets on the street so that bursts of scalding steam could be unleashed upon any invaders.

Those invaders came in the shape of soldiers in blue, sober and in marching order. They arrived to close Wilbur Storey's newspaper under direct orders of General Ambrose E. Burnside, who was known for his bushy sideburns, his innovations in weaponry, and his colossal militaristic blunders. Burnside had brought about the catastrophe at Fredericksburg, Virginia, in 1862 by ordering a frontal attack against Lee's impregnable position at Mayre's Heights, an order that turned into a slaughterhouse suicidal uphill charge that all but wasted the entire Union army. For that unforgivable error, the pathetic Burnside was demoted from Commander in Chief of the Potomac Army to a military district commander in an area that included Chicago and Wilbur Storey. The editor never failed to level attacks at the general, and took special delight in skinning him editorially after Burnside ordered the arrest of a onetime congressman who had criticized the moral purposes of the war.

Burnside retorted by immediately ordering General J. B. Sweet in Chicago to shut down the *Times*, charging that the paper was guilty of "repeated expression of disloyal and incendiary sentiments." Storey got wind of the forthcoming suppression of his newspaper and sent a rider to wait outside

Sweet's headquarters and gallop back to report when he learned the troops had received their marching orders. Meanwhile, like a man possessed, Storey tore about the *Times* building racing from editorial rooms to printing areas to get out a final edition which barely managed to escape the military cordon thrown around the building.

News of the suppression of the *Times* electrified the city and in the proverbial words of Wilbur Storey, "All hell broke loose." Burnside's idiotic order caused enormous pro-Storey crowds, most of them Democrats, to gather until more than 20,000 screaming Chicagoans swelled into Courthouse Square at Randolph and Clark streets. The Democrats yelled that "if the *Times* is not allowed to publish, there will be no *Tribune!*"

The *Tribune* replied in a hastily-written editorial that the Democrats would never resort to violence because "they know too well the stout-hearted quality of *Tribune* men." Life-squandering riot seemed inevitable, especially when the eccentric "Colonel" Charles Jennison, who had once been one of John Brown's henchmen in the fiery abolitionist's murdering Bloody Kansas days, announced that he and his armed thugs would protect the *Tribune* from the mob. Jennison was, in the words of Chicago historian Emmett Dedmon, "a poseur who dressed cowboy fashion and was usually to be found swaggering down the street with a retinue of admirers." Jennison lost no time in placing his armed ruffians in the lofts of the *Tribune* plant and surrounding buildings, all ready to shoot down any storming invaders.

All through the chaos, while fire-eating crowds assembled to denounce Republicans and Democrats alike, Wilbur Storey sat smiling in his office. Repeatedly, throngs assembled beneath his window but he refused to show himself, smug with the certain knowledge that Burnside's rash order would be repealed. He thoroughly enjoyed the frenzy, believing that such an upheaval would permanently divide the abolitionist groups.

After three days of rage when Chicago bordered upon riot and civil war within the city precincts, President Lincoln wisely rescinded Burnside's order and the *Times* was back in business. The entire fiasco resulted in vaulting Storey to hero status and made of the *Times* the most popular newspaper in the city, a development which, some wags claimed, was planned all along by the shrewd Storey as a circulation booster. Whatever, the *Times* immediately prospered but, in an unusual move, Wilbur Storey backed away from his ardent antigovernment stance, declaring to a few intimates that "after this, the *Times* will support all wars the country will undertake."

What Wilbur especially supported was highly profitable scandalmongering. No story was too sleazy for his newspaper. He and his scurrying reporters particularly enjoyed love triangles which brought about a plethora of libel suits, twenty-four of them pending in the courts in one week alone. Lurid sex and crime became Wilbur's strong hand. When he ran an article about a naked prostitute performing a lewd dance in one of Chicago's many brothels, a criminal action was brought against the paper charging it with publishing obscene matter. One of Storey's conniving reporters discovered that several influential residents had been present during the dance and the editor lost no time in letting it be known that, unless the criminal charge was dropped, those resplendent citizens would discover their names in *Times* headlines. The literary blackmail worked; the charges were dropped.

Sale by Headline

Storey charged 5¢ per copy for the *Times*, an unheard of price for a newspaper following the Civil War, when most sheets cost about 3¢. Wilbur got his price and handily. The headlines he and his fellow scribes dreamed up were worth the entire edition. Typical was his inspired one-word headline for an important wedding: "Welded." For a train wreck, Wilbur offered, "Death's Debauch." In covering the report of a Vanderbilt will, Storey's headline read, "The House That Vanderbilt."

Gory crime and explicit sex captured most of the *Times* massive black headlines with Wilbur and his delightfully deranged chief headline writer Horatio W. Seymour offering up such banners as "Frail Females" and "Sexual Skulduggery." Hangings simply enthralled Storey and Seymour, and, judging from the paper's soaring circulation, more than edified *Times* readers. "A Drop Too Much" bannered one hanging report. Another read "Feet First" with the deck beneath screaming, "That's The Way They Shoved Bill Green Down Among the Fireworks."

Even a murder conviction before the hangman performed his duty provided classic headline grist for the paper such as the time when a cop killer was given a death sentence.

SHUT OFF HIS WIND
A Satisfactory Job For Jack Ketch At Last
The Hangman's Rope Awarded To
Christopher Rafferty
Now, Do Not Reprieve Nor Pardon Him,
Nor Give Him A New Trial
And In The Name Of All That's Decent,
Don't Commute His Sentence
The Jury Concludes, In Just Twenty Minutes
To String The Ruffian Up

The most inspired headline Storey and Seymour ever produced from their nightmare noddings dealt with energetic hangmen in the Deep South. Over one wrap-up story, the *Times* blared stupendously:

JERKED TO JESUS
Four Senegambian Butchers Were
Wafted To Heaven On
Yesterday From Scaffolds

Two Of Them, In Louisiana, Died With
The Sweet Confidence Of
Pious People
While Yet Two Others, In Mississippi, Expired
Exhorting The Public To Beware Of
Sisters-In-Law

In 1870 Wilbur's impossible headline writing brought about more than public guffaws, creating a street brawl with the illustrious Mr. Storey on the receiving end of lashing whip. No doubt the whipping, an incident that proved to the world that Chicago was the wildest "civilized" town in America, was the direct result of Wilbur's oft-shouted directive to his editors and writers in dealing with any of his many personal enemies: "Go for his [or her] gut fat!" One such enemy of Storey's was the impresario Uranus H. Crosby who owned the sprawling Crosby's Opera House, a 3,000-seat auditorium where Ulysses S. Grant had been nominated for the presidency in 1868.

Storey's feud with Crosby boiled over into printed spleen in February 1870 when Lydia "Black Crook" Thompson brought her British Blondes to Chicago, introducing burlesque to the city for the first time, where, Lloyd Lewis commented later, "their bare bosoms and hips, outlined in tights, stirred the wrath of the Puritans."

Assuming the role of the leading and most offended Puritan was the inimitable Wilbur Storey. The girls, raged the *Times*, were nothing more than "large-limbed, beefy specimens of the barmaid class" whose act consisted of "capering lasciviously and uttering gross indecencies." Lydia Thompson, the paper added, was not much better than a common whore and should depart Chicago along with her immoral company. Bellowed Storey in his headline: "Bawds at the Opera House! Where's the Police!"

A few afternoons later the incensed Miss Thompson, accompanied by Mr. Henderson, her manager; Pauline Markham, one of the now notorious Blondes; and a free-lance press agent Archie Gordon sat in an elegant carriage at the corner of Wabash Avenue and Peck Court in wait for Wilbur Storey whose daily constitutional invariably took him past this spot. Miss Thompson's intentions were clear; she clutched a long, black whip with which to attack the editor.

Suddenly Wilbur strolled into view. Henderson squinted and then turned to the eye-blazing Lydia. "He's with his wife. I think this should be postponed."

"Not at all," hissed Miss Thompson. "So much the better. She will get an idea of what it means to attack out of her sex."

As Storey came abreast of the carriage, Lydia leaped out shouting, "You dirty old scoundrel!" She brought her whip cracking downward on the white-bearded Wilbur. He received the blow on his left arm. His right hand instinctively clutched the burlesque queen's throat.

"Draw your pistol, Wilbur!" shouted the aghast Mrs. Storey.

Wilbur, however, was fully engaged, for at that moment Lydia Thompson was striking him with her whip and her lover-press agent Archie Gordon had jumped upon his back and was scratching his face. Henderson attempted to restrain Miss Thompson but the amazon was too much for him. Then Henderson tried punching Wilbur. The tangled foursome (Pauline Markham sat out the fracas in the carriage laughing hysterically) suddenly toppled to the ground, "Mr. Storey *uppermost*," the *Times* was quick to point out when reporting the incident.

Before Judge Augustus Banyon the following day, Storey turned in court and aimed a bony finger in the direction of the towering, glowering Lydia. "That creature, there," he intoned, "undertook to strike me with a whip. I caught her by the throat and would have choked out her life, when that little chap [Archie Gordon] jumped on my back, and that ruffian [Henderson] attacked me from the front."

Judge Banyon smirked at defendants and plaintiff alike and promptly fined the attackers $100 each. Before Wilbur could manage a victory grin, the judge suspended the sentences, making it clear that he sided with the theater people.

Storey quickly forgot the affair, busying himself with more scandal. He was never quite to forget the incredible event occurring the next year when the Great Chicago Fire destroyed most of the city, including the *Times* building. Wilbur was as spiritually flattened as the city was after it was incinerated, moaning disaster from a prostrate position on a couch in his marble mansion which had survived the fire.

"I shall not resume publication of the *Times*," groaned Storey to Franc Wilkie and other newsmen from his paper. "The city is destroyed. I am now an old man. [He was only 52.] I have about $80,000 with which I can live comfortably for the rest of my life. If I put that into a new paper, I would be a pauper in less than a year."

Wilkie and company would have none of it; they bodily lifted the publisher from his couch and carried him into the backyard over burned timbers to the barn where they found some old type and a small press. The *Times*, irrespective of Wilbur's theatrical despondency, was back in business ten days later. Storey was revitalized into a journalistic dynamo and within ten years he had pioneered new techniques in modern stereotyping. He opened a London bureau and displayed his genius by scoring great "beats" by telegraph.

Wilbur's personal life was as colorful and unpredictable as ever. He divorced his wife and married his longtime mistress Harriet Dodge, whose husband was a convict. The incarcerated Mr. Dodge did not object to being divorced, and shortly after Wilbur and Harriet were "welded," the convict was paroled through Storey's influence. The Storeys became social gadflies as Wilbur attempted to make his wife queen of Chicago society; if the couple received an invitation to an important party, news-conscious hostesses learned, the *Times* would give the affair front-page coverage listing, of course, the complete guest list with Mr. and Mrs. Wilbur Storey at the head, their names in capital letters.

The love of Wilbur's life died three years after the marriage. The tragedy-engulfed publisher naturally blamed the doctor for Harriet's death and began a bitter editorial crusade to destroy him. "The world will set me down as a dog if I do not ruin the man who killed my wife," gritted Storey to one crony. The physician retaliated by going to Wilbur's nemesis, the *Tribune*, and giving out the story that Mrs. Storey's death was caused by a dissolute life-style, also alleging that Wilbur was impotent.

Storey exploded and immediately printed a broadside aimed at the senior *Tribune* editor who had shepherded the doctor's charges into print. Though the editor was afflicted with a mild skin disease, Storey claimed that his mind was deranged, that he was suffering the ravages of dreaded syphilis picked up from a red-light madam who was his mistress and ran the most disgraceful brothel in Chicago.

It was Wilbur Storey's mind, however, that began to crack wide open. By the early 1880s, Storey, desperate to contact his beloved Harriet somewhere in the beyond and already having endured paralytic strokes, fell prey to a gang of spiritualistic quacks who established Wilbur's "control" as Little Squaw, the ghost of an Indian girl. Little Squaw advised Storey on all investments, money that was eventually channeled into the pockets of the spiritualist charlatans bilking him. His fortune was slowly bled away.

He went to the newspaper offices no more. Instead, he dreamed his life away in his unfinished $500,000 marble Gothic palace on Grand Boulevard on the South Side. At the suggestion of his Indian ghost, Wilbur leaped into the bathtub each dawn splashing down into icy water. The remainder of his day consisted of toying with expensive jewels and antiques and telling visiting employees that his place in American history was similar to that of German kings of old; he too would expect a personal Götterdämmerung: "I don't wish to perpetuate my newspaper. I am the paper. I wish it to die with me so that the world may know that I was the *Times*." He then wistfully added; "Little Squaw tells me that I shall live as long as Commodore Vanderbilt." He did not.

Wilbur Storey died a blind lunatic on October 27, 1884. The *Times*, mercifully, went on without him.

"A Matter of Conviction"

Wentworth's ruthless political ambition, Medill's obsession with power, and Storey's love of corruption vexed one Chicagoan to the point of newspaper rebellion. Melville E. Stone was dead broke but he was slavishly devoted to newspapers and, as managing editor of J. Young Scammon's

The truculent co-founder of the great *Daily News*, Melville E. Stone.

The great newspaper publisher Victor Lawson, who founded the *Daily News* with Melville E.
Stone.

Republican and as editor of the *Post and Mail*, had earned a reputation as a pile-driving, utterly honest journalist. His brainchild was the *Chicago Daily News* which was given birth on Christmas Day 1875, funded with $5,000 from an English publishing dilettante named Percy R. Meggy. Assisting Stone was his friend William E. Daugherty.

It was Stone's dream to publish a newspaper that was apolitical and devoid of pressure from large advertisers. His paper would carry "pure news" only and it would sell for 1¢. The *Chicago Daily News* ran into stiff competition from four other evening papers, its chief adversary being the *Journal*. The almost fanatical independence displayed by Stone, however, soon had readers turning more and more to his newspaper. He would never sacrifice news space for advertising, a suicidal course most news bigwigs thought. On one occasion, a large department store attempted to force a full-page ad into a special edition of the *News*. Stone flabbergasted the store and his colleagues by returning the ad.

Moreover, the dedicated newsman refused to print "reading matter puffs" stemming from advertisers looking for free space. "We will be owned by no one," declared Stone, and announced that he would never purchase interest in and be obligated to any utility company. Stone's view of newspaper coverage was summed up by his idealistic declaration that "there must be no publishing of so-called sensational or exaggerated or scandalous material for the purpose of making sales."

Such high-minded aims were not economically feasible and within seven months Stone had divested himself of his partners and turned to his landlord, a young Norwegian named Victor Fremont Lawson, who was a wealthy printer of foreign-language publications and owner of the *Skandinavan* the only daily newspaper in the Norwegian language in America. Lawson's father had made a fortune in Chicago real estate; his son was a prudent, God-fearing man who saw a great future for the *Daily News*. He backed Stone, making him editor and general manager in addition to giving him a third of the paper's future profits.

Lawson was as lofty a man as Stone and devoted to his religion. Shortly after the *News* began publishing under his aegis, Lawson received an invitation from a congressman to dine on a Sunday. His written regrets stated; "I never attend a general social function, entertainment, or amusement on the Christian Sabbath as a matter of conviction."

In comparison with other Chicago newspaper moguls, Victor Lawson was an outright saint. Sympathetic to immigrants—his father had immigrated from Norway enduring hardships—Lawson provided his own money for free lectures and language courses in public schools. To help the workingmen Medill scorned, the benevolent Lawson sought to encourage their savings by urging the government to set up the postal savings banks. He poured money from his own coffers into special health programs for the city's children.

Where Chicago's glut of papers were largely devoted to character assassination of all kinds at all levels, the *News* would have no dealings with spurious prose. Lawson and Stone published a declaration of principles (exemplified decades later in Orson Welles' study of newspaper czardom *Citizen Kane*) which stated that the *News* would be "*Candid*—That its utterances shall at all times be the exact truth. It is independent but never indifferent; *Comprehensive*—That it shall contain all the news; *Concise*—The *Daily News* is very carefully edited, to that end that the valuable time of its patrons shall not be wasted in reading of mere trifles; *Clean*—That its columns shall never be tainted by vulgarity or obscenity; *Cheap*—That its price shall be put within the reach of all."

Lawson was a shrewd businessman, his envious competition soon discovered. He encouraged retail stores to hold 99¢ sales, having thousands of copies of his paper nearby to collect the extra penny from a thrifty shopper. Lawson was full of surprises. He was the first publisher to print his exact circulation, supported by affidavits, on the front page every day. It was also Lawson who dreamed up the idea of using schoolboys as news carriers, a system still heartily in use. The dogged publisher was always looking for new technical methods by which to improve the *News* and was the first in Chicago to install the then modern Mergenthaler linotype machines. The *News* quickly became a powerhouse, its readership soaring to 70,000 daily during the late 1870s; it became the leading paper in the city and remained so until the turn of the century.

Ingenious methods abounded at the *News*. Stone was an unrelenting editor who never gave up on a story. When Chicago was crippled by the city-wide strike of 1877, a strike which most other publishers considered an act of anarchy, the *News* gave wide coverage to the workingmen, sending squads of reporters into the thronged streets on horseback. They galloped back to the offices hourly with dispatches, and Stone and Lawson issued many extras which were gobbled up by a news-starved public.

On July 23, 1877, the most powerful merchants and business men of Chicago, headed by the banker Levi Z. Leiter, stalked into Victor Lawson's offices. They demanded that the paper suspend its operations for the time being.

"Why should we?" challenged the feisty Stone.

"These extras are inflaming the masses," thundered the illustrious Mr. Leiter. "They must stop."

Lawson folded his hands on his desk, stared at the group intently, and calmly said, "We refuse."

Stone hooked his thumb toward the door and the merchant princes departed in grim silence. The *News* continued to produce its extras.

The paper became the highest standard for newspapermen. Editor Stone led the way. D. D. Spencer, president of the State Savings Institution of

Chicago the largest bank of its kind west of New York City, had closed the institution's doors and fled without arousing the suspicions of local authorities. When Stone learned of the banker's flight with satchels full of his depositors' money, he packed his own bag and went in pursuit. Stone trailed the errant financier through Canada, to England, and through France, filing stories for spellbound readers, finally overtaking the man in Germany where he was arrested. Stone became the first great newspaper detective by this act. (In 1888, Stone sold his interest in the *News* for $100,000 and departed for New York where he became the chief architect of the Associated Press as it is known today.)

In addition to Stone, the paper was rich in human resources. One enterprising, though somewhat devious, reporter Clarence Dresser gave the paper one of its most memorable quotes. Railroad magnate William H. Vanderbilt was en route to Chicago on his own line, the Michigan Central, in his own ornate railroad car on October 8, 1882. Vanderbilt was, at the time, trying secretly to buy the Nickel Plate Railroad for the lowest possible price to add to his empire. The magnate therefore made it appear that the Nickel Plate was really worthless. Dresser boarded the Vanderbilt train at Michigan City, Indiana, sixty miles outside of Chicago. The dogged reporter demanded an interview with the Great Man and was shocked when he was told he could ask all the questions he wanted. Seconds after the train halted in Chicago, Dresser sprinted to the *Daily News* offices where he began to write the interview for the morning edition.

Looking up from his desk, the reporter shouted to managing editor Colonel Nate Reed, "Colonel, shall I write it just as he said it?"

Reed, a strange bird with a flowing beard and a top hat that he never removed perched on his head, spun about in his chair. "Yes, exactly."

Dresser turned in the story some minutes later. "Colonel, you told me to write just what he said," he told Reed, "but he said one thing that I didn't put in."

"What was that?"

"When I asked him whether he ran his express trains for the public's benefit, he said, 'The public be damned!' I didn't put that in."

"What!" yelled Reed, his high hat almost toppling from his head. "You left that out? That's important. Put it in."

Dresser rewrote the story and Vanderbilt's notorious "Public be damned!" statement reverberated across the nation thanks to the *News* and the quote-smelling Reed.

Although Lawson required his reporters to work seven days a week, his scribes were utterly devoted to him, Stone, and the newspaper. To his banner flocked such journalistic stalwarts as William E. Curtis, Dr. Albert Shaw, William Morton Payne, the light-opera librettist Harry B. Smity, Colonel George Harvey, and Paul Hull. It was Hull who became distinguished by being the only reporter to be present during the Haymarket Riot of 1886, narrowly escaping death by police bullets when officers opened fire upon the mob after a bomb killed seven of their number. Hull's account, the only minutely detailed report on the event, was printed in a large edition by a Chicago publisher but the night before the books were to be distributed, the plant burned down (some whispered arson) and the narrative was lost to posterity.

The short-story writer George Ade joined the *News* staff. So did Peter Finley Dunne and John T McCutcheon. By then Lawson was the sole proprietor and editor of the paper, a guiding light to his writers with a surprisingly understanding heart. He knew his reporters drank although he campaigned against booze in a quiet manner. When one scribe enthusiastically protested that he had not been drunk while doing a story, Lawson took him to lunch and ordered for the reporter the best bottle of wine the restaurant could produce. That reporter was none other than the poet Eugene Field whose verses for children would later make him famous and rich.

Field was a drinker who made no bones about his cultivated vice: "I just have to get drunk occasionally." But Lawson and Stone somehow understood Field's necessity to relieve himself of writing pressures by tackling old Demon Rum. "I sometimes take a drink," the author of "Little Boy Blue" once confessed to a Missouri publisher, "but Mel Stone, he just fires me and takes me back the next day."

More than alcohol, the need to perform outlandish pranks obsessed Field. It was no secret to Lawson that his star writer had been expelled from three colleges because of his escapades in wild humor. Yet that very humor had readers flocking to read the News. In covering the opening of the World's Columbian Exposition of 1893, Field lampooned those finely dressed hordes of high society matrons in attendance: "The trails of the dresses worn by the ladies would, if spread out to their capacity, cover space exceeding eleven square miles, and the feminine pectoral display would cover whole acres."

Unfortunately for the abiding Mr. Lawson, Field did not confine his zaniness to copy. It was part of Lawson's open policy to allow visiting publishers and editors from out of town to tour his rambling *Daily News* building. On one such tour being conducted by a cub reporter, a group of foreign publishers were being led up the creaking main stairs of the building to the fourth-floor editorial offices. They stopped at the top landing in shock and dismay to see a bald, scarecrow-thin man, obviously in great need of nutrition, feebly shaking ashes out of a coal stove; the poor soul wore a convict's suit of black-and-white stripes.

Before any of the shocked visitors could utter a word, the cub reporter quickly explained in painful whispers, "He's a trusty from the state pen, up for murder, you know. Well, our editor, Mr. Stone, is very economy minded, always thinking of the paper's expenses. He used his influence with certain politicians to get this fellow to work for the *News*. A free janitor, get it? Doesn't cost us a dime."

On other occasions, the same man in the same convict's suit, only wearing a ball and chain, sat riveted to an editorial desk where he was pointed out by the same cub reporter to be a trusty writing editorials for Mr. Lawson, at no cost, of course, to the paper.

Such horrific scenes caused many an out-of-town publisher to return to his paper and immediately launch blistering editorial attacks against Stone and Lawson for employing slave labor on the *News*. Of course such practices did not exist. The convict was none other than Eugene Field bringing a little something extra to his $50-a-week reporter's job. (Field insisted he be the highest paid reporter on the *News* staff. Most reporters received $50-a-week salaries; Field insisted upon and got $50 *plus* 50¢ a week.)

For all of his impossible hoaxes and pranks, Eugene Field remained close to the heart of Victor Lawson. Both newsmen, as a testament to their gentle natures, died peacefully in their sleep, Field in 1895 and Lawson, his financial backer and mentor, thirty years later in 1925. One of Lawson's most devoted reporters, the erstwhile journalistic dervish Ben Hecht said of him, "He had the fairest mind American journalism has produced."

Sculptor Lorado Taft left his epitaph for Lawson carved in granite, a towering crusader of heroic proportions, armor-clad, shield and sword at the ready, a statue that guards the graves of Lawson and his wife Jessie to this day in Chicago's elegant Graceland Cemetery.

By the time Lawson died, he had seen his world of journalism and its wonderful naiveté and innocent blustering shattered in the onslaught of blatant power brokers who bulldozed the news to mountainous sensationalism where a newsboy's shout became an earsplitting screech and papers came wrapped around guns.

2

"It's a Wonderful World"

Two men started it all—William Randolph Hearst and Medill McCormick. Wealth and power clashed in Chicago in October 1910 over grubby little newsstands. From these pernicious podiums of Chicago's press, Hearst's *Chicago American* and McCormick's *Chicago Tribune* vied mortally for the blinking eyes of the city's morning readership. Hearst was the real culprit who spent millions to inaugurate a Wild West system of gang warfare and racketeering which would eventually cost the city and the country untold billions of dollars and the lives of thousands of citizens. There would be no peace for twenty years while the newspaper war raged. And inside of those two decades—an odd, unpredictable pocket of time—the heyday of what has come to be known as Chicago Journalism erupted, crammed to all corners of the era with impish, devious editors who stopped at absolutely nothing for their scoops and their liquor-gulping reporter broods whose tarnished triumphs over tradition became legend and literature for the price of pennies.

A penny was at the root of the Hearst-McCormick feud. Both publishing czars, at the suggestions of their lawyers, ignored the bloodshed resulting from their circulation battles; they were not responsible for what their minions did while attempting to enlarge readership was the excuse. When the *Tribune* dropped its price to 1¢, all hell broke loose as both publishers looked the other way.

Death at the Newsstands

Hearst's Chicago appointee publisher "Long Green" Andy Lawrence had early employed two plug-uglies to run the *American's* circulation—Max and Moe Annenberg, German-Jewish immigrants whose specialty was breaking heads for the greater glory of newsstand sales. The *Tribune* lured the Annen-

27

The mighty William Randolph Hearst at the time he and Medill McCormick began the Chicago newspaper war.

Moses Annenberg, shown in later years as a wealthy publisher, began his brawling career as a slugger for the *Tribune*.

berg brothers and their gunsels from the employ of Hearst, paying Max $20,000 a year on a guarantee to increase its circulation. Hearst was not to take the desertion of his circulation thugs lightly; he sued Annenberg stating that he was under exclusive contract to the *American*. In the zany tradition of Chicago's jurisprudence, the court declared the Annenberg contract invalid in that it was a contract to commit illegal acts.

When the Annenbergs departed for the greener *Tribune* pastures, they took with them their own army of strong-armers—some of the toughest apprentice hoodlums in Chicago—such as Maurice "Mossy" Enright, Red Connors, and Walter Stevens—about thirty hired killers in all. These ham-fisted circulation boosters had been employed by the *American* to persuade news dealers to push the Hearst paper. Now they were just as enthusiastically beating up the same newsys to sell more copies of the *Tribune*.

Lawrence of the *American* immediately countered by hiring his own new army of thugs, led by the murderous-eyed Gentleman brothers, Gus, Dutch, and Pete, and including Jack Nolan, Chicago Jack Daly, Edward Barrett, Vincent Altman, Frank McErlane (who would later be the first man to employ the submachine gun during the bootleg wars of the 1920s as a Capone subchief), and future bootleg kingpin Charles Dion "Deanie" O'Bannion.

Things got serious when Annenberg handed out revolvers to his sluggers and ordered them to tour the city's newsstands in an enormous truck. Medill McCormick, editor of the *Tribune* (and later a U.S. senator from Illinois), appropriated $1 million for its circulation war; Hearst matched it and changed the name of the *American* to the *Examiner*. His musclemen also were issued weapons. The battle was on and the carnage ensued. The *Tribune* brutes would wait in ambush for the *Examiner* slugs to show up at strategic newsstands all over the city. According to Ferdinand Lundberg, author of *Imperial Hearst*, "when they appeared they were greeted with fusillades of shots that brought police and ambulances to the scene. The Hearst forces then resorted to counter-ambushes, with a delivery truck as a decoy. Newsboys, some of them crippled and unable to scamper to safety, were shot. Passing women were clipped by bullets."

The war raged on. In 1911, the *Daily Socialist* compelled a Cook County grand jury to study the wholesale slaughter but nothing was done. Everyone knew that State's Attorney Charles Wayman as well as his successor Maclay Hoyne were owned by the *Tribune*. It was also common knowledge that Chief of Police John McWeeney was in Hearst's wallet pocket.

Typical of Annenberg's daily operations were the activities of Bob Holbrook, a *Tribune* slammer. On August 22, 1911, Charles Gallantry, a newsboy at the corner of Chicago Avenue and Robey Street, told Holbrook he would not take an additional thirty copies of the *Trib*. "I can't sell them," he whimpered.

"You can't, huh?" Holbrook smashed the boy in the face and knocked him

Chicago's first machine-gunner, Frank McErlane (seated, center), an apprentice gangster in the newspaper wars.

down. The boy rose. Holbrook knocked him down again. The boy kept getting up, wiping away the blood from his face and determinedly shaking his head. Holbrook kept knocking him down. Horrified passersby were prevented from interfering by several of Holbrook's fellow thugs. Holbrook then tried to drag the boy into an alley "to finish this punk," but the stubborn newsy held onto a weighing machine, screaming. Holbrook finally settled the matter by kicking the boy unconscious.

Max Annenberg did not scorn his own dirty work. He once jumped from a truck and dealt with a truculent newsboy by knocking him into the street and kicking him repeatedly while two detectives looked the other way. The boy, C. D. Ray, swore out a warrant for Annenberg's arrest but the *Tribune* enforcer was set free with apologies.

The enterprising Mr. Annenberg brooked no excuses from his underlings. One of Annenberg's sluggers got fed up with the boy beatings and told him so. He was not only fired by Annenberg, but, according to testimony given by *Tribune* editor James "God" Keeley (later that paper's publisher) during a senatorial investigation upon a different matter, was shown the errors of false pride. The man "was beaten up, thrown down an elevator shaft [in the *Tribune* building] and shot. He was on the mail-room floor, and he was thrown to the press-room floor. He had been beaten and knocked unconscious on the mailing-room floor before he was thrown down the elevator shaft. Some of the press-room men or stereotypers picked up the man and took him over to a big washbasin and started to wash the blood off him, and then the fellow who was after him came down after him with a gun and shot at him."

Any of the other newspapers who dared criticize the thuggery practiced by Hearst and McCormick goons risked mayhem upon their own personnel. On May 6, 1912, Annenberg and a squad of goons appeared in front of the elevated station at Wilson and Evanston avenues. A news driver for the *Chicago World*, which had condemned the circulation war with considerable vitriol, one Alexander Hickey, was beaten up when he arrived to deliver his papers and was then kidnapped at the point of a gun under the pretext of taking him to the hospital. During the beating, Annenberg threatened crowds of citizens with a gun, roaring that he would just as soon shoot anyone who read any paper other than the *Tribune*. The wild man was described by the *Daily Socialist* thusly: "Annenberg was dressed as a typical tenderloin representative. He wore a flaming red sweater and over his low brow was pulled a soft cap. With a malicious leer upon his countenance, he swaggered around the elevated station . . . using foul language in the presence of women. . . . Carrying in his pocket a commission as a deputy sheriff, he kept raging around the elevated station . . . flourishing and brandishing his revolver like a maniac."

The height of lunacy was scaled one evening in 1912 when a Hearst gunman, enraged at newspaper readers riding a trolley car for not having the *Examiner* in their hands, went berserk. He emptied his revolver in the streetcar's ceiling as a warning. Other Hearst goons, Edward and Charles Barrett along with Louis "The Farmer" Friedman, imitated that same mad act on June 17, 1912, by leaping onto a streetcar at Wells and Washington streets. They shot the conductor, Frank Witt, and two other men who were carrying *Tribune* papers. All three men died. Their assailants received minimal sentences.

Annenberg knew himself to be above the law and flaunted it. He actually fought a pistol duel with Harold C. Whipple at State and Madison streets, Chicago's Times Square, on July 13, 1912. Whipple, who had been thinking of going over to the Hearst forces, made the mistake of telling Annenberg to drop dead. Max Annenberg pulled a pistol as did Whipple. While hundreds of shoppers raced pell-mell from the scene, the two men battled it out, firing ten shots in all at each other. Moe Annenberg then crept up behind Whipple and put a pistol to his head. "Put down the piece or I'll let you have it," Moe yelled. Whipple dropped his weapon and nearby policemen, who had witnessed the entire shooting from cover, walked over and arrested Whipple. "Annenberg," reported the *Chicago World*, "was saluted by the arresting officers but waved his hand deprecatingly, a grin on his face."

The beatings changed to homicide. Newsstands were torched. Delivery trucks were blown up. Thousands of copies of newspapers coated the surface of the Chicago River's already brown waters. Then the gangs began shooting at each other and dozens died. By then the newspaper gunmen had branched out into more lucrative enterprises, chiefly the operation of brothels and union terrorism.

One of the first of the top sluggers to fall was Vincent Altman who was relaxing at the bar of the Briggs House at Wells and Randolph streets. A troop of *Tribune* boosters sauntered into the bar and emptied their pistols into the Hearst slugger. Altman fell to the floor quite dead. Two detectives present in the bar did nothing but wink knowingly at the killers who walked calmly to the street and disappeared.

Next came Dutch Gentleman, one of Hearst's top goons. Dutch was telling one and all in a State Street bar that he was the best shot in Chicago when the Tribune's Mossy Enright appeared. Enright, his gang covering the exits with drawn guns, walked up to Gentleman, spun him about and jammed a revolver into his stomach firing all six bullets into the bragging gunman. Stated one report: "As Dutch backed away, his entrails, which until then had been enjoying food and drink at the expense of William Randolph Hearst, came spilling out on the sawdust floor." Mossy Enright, although he confessed the murder to the police, was eventually freed.

When nervous peace came, twenty-seven newsstand dealers had been killed and dozens more injured and crippled. It was the beginning of the gangster era in Chicago. By then the battle had moved to another front. Both newspapers, never printing one item about the violence they had spawned, went mad for headlines and the zany, treacherous men who could create them. Nothing was too preposterous, nothing too bizarre.

Hearst had lost the street battle. The *Tribune*'s circulation rose while the *Examiner*'s declined. William Randolph Hearst opened his swollen purse. If the *Examiner* couldn't bully its way over the *Tribune*'s head, it would simply buy up all the writing talent.

While Hearst and McCormick were at each other's throats, the fates were kind to Chicago's eleven other dailies. Chicago's late-blooming immigration thrust had caused the great variety of publications, each catering to the editorial appetites of various political and ethnic groups.

Victor Lawson's *Daily News* came up a prominent third behind the *Tribune* and *Examiner*. The civic-minded, crusading Lawson fielded about for an editor to emulate his stellar brand of journalism and discovered the mild, poetry-reading Henry Justin Smith. While Hearst and McCormick journalists aligned themselves with gangsters and zanies, Smith cultivated an elite core of literary talents who elevated the news style of the *News* far beyond the scope of the average reader but kept faith with the purple idioms of Edwardian prose. Smith commanded the *News* from a rolltop desk in the city room

The greatest newsman ever to tickle Chicago's ribs, Ben Hecht.

while such competitors as Walter Howey, city editor of the *Tribune*, issued his orders to fledgling writers from poolrooms and bars.

Conscientiously laboring under Smith's gentle dictums were such high-minded editors as George Wharton and Brooks Beitler. It was Smith who snared a young writer named Ben Hecht away from the *Evening Jounal*.

The Dark Watcher

Hecht was the kind of literary phenomenon that would have caused Horatio Alger to exercise countless entrechats of glee. Born in 1891, Bennie Hecht had run away from his middle-class home in Racine, Wisconsin, at nineteen. An uncle walking down Wabash Avenue in 1911 recognized his errant nephew, collared him, and led him to the *Evening Journal* where he promptly convinced the paper's editor Martin J. Hutchens to hire the young rascal as a picture-chaser. It became Hecht's duty—as it was with many others in the days before sophisticated news photography—to enter people's homes and steal the photographs of loved ones involved in some local scandal that had slammed onto the front page.

At the *News*, following the patient teachings of Sherman Reilly Duffy at the *Journal*, Hecht became a full-fledged reporter. His assignments were the old pressrooms in the County Building and sheriff's office just north of the

river which would later form the setting of his play, *The Front Page*, delight-
edly written with fellow Chicago reporter Charles MacArthur. There he
came to know the reckless writers of the other dailies: Wallace Smith, who
was to ride with Pancho Villa south of the border years later; E. H. "Ned"
Griffith, with whom Hecht shared a cheap room above a bordello; bibliophile
Vincent Starrett; Keith Preston; and future critic Burton Rascoe.

The pressroom in the sheriff's building served as a center for drinking
bouts, poetry readings, and occult contact with departed souls. The windows
were painted black and clocks were banned. From this frazzled nerve center,
Hecht and associates made the rounds of the prisoner's cells below interview-
ing those condemned to hang for murder. Those reluctant to talk to reporters
were conned into confessions. Hecht once cajoled a condemned prisoner, a
Dr. Hugo by name, into confessing after he smuggled a woman's makeup kit
into his cell. It had been the burly murderer's last secret request and he went
to his death on the gallows as a screaming, painted hussy while Hecht scurried
back to the *News* with a signed confession in his pocket. Though high
literature was in his heart, crime was his beat and no story was too lowly to
escape the humanity of the *News* and Mr. Hecht.

The gloom of death permeated Hecht's life. He became almost insensitive
to the bodies falling like heavy rocks through the gallows traps. Killers and
lunatics, sex fiends and terrorists peopled his world, a sphere of events that
made the eccentric normal, the macabre usual. He wrote about bandit Teddy
Webb, who was turned in by his sweetheart because he was sleeping with
another woman. When the police broke into Webb's Cottage Grove Avenue
hideout, one officer dropped dead of a heart attack. To save the face of the
force, Chief of Police Scheuttler fired a bullet into the armpit of the dead cop
so that it would appear he had died in the line of duty.

Police closed in on a maniac who was standing naked in front of the
Congress Hotel screaming out his lungs that the world was about to end. As
officers grabbed the man, he fell dead of a heart attack and Hecht was there
to record it. Then there was the assistant keeper of Cook County Morgue
who suddenly died of poison; Hecht discovered that the man had been eating
the leg of one of the embalmed bodies in his care.

Nothing was strange along Bennie's beat. A pastor trysting in the basement
of his church with the prettiest of his flock accidentally kicked a gas jet open
and died while having sex. Hechtian prose captioned the tragicomedy,
"Preoccupied by love, he had smelled no fumes than those of Paradise and
given up the ghost while still glued to his parishioner." And Hecht was present
with a bevy of hooting newsmen snapping photos of the wife of another
minister as she crawled on her hands and knees four blocks around her
husband's church to collapse in the arms of her clerical spouse; it was her
penance for sleeping with the lead singer of the choir.

It was a beat of city streets the Chicago press almost exclusively covered, and headlines were carved from the local lampposts, editors disdaining news from an outside world that had no relevance to America's greatest inland city. In print, the murderers came first. There was the frustrated swain who rented a room in the Morrison Hotel and there tied his lover to the bedposts, whipping her to death for "not loving him enough" before jumping fifteen floors to his death in the middle of the noon rush hour. There was the machinist who slew his wife and then himself after scribbling, "No one else shall have her." The machinist, pop-eyed pathologists later learned, was a woman.

Those who killed their way out of everyday boredom and frustration finished less than spectacular lives inside black, running print. One such was the car salesman who grew disgusted with a procrastinating purchaser and took a baseball bat to his head, bashing in his brains, and who later swaggered up the gallows stairs. Another was Blackie Weed whose momentary act of madness became the secret envy of many a Chicagoan. An official from the gas company, accompanied by a policeman, arrived at Weed's home one day to demand payment for a bill Weed insisted he had already paid. An argument exploded and Weed shot and killed both men. At his trial, Weed offered as his defense a receipted bill but it did not save him from the rope. Before lunging through the trap, a priest offered Blackie a cross to kiss. The avenging gas company customer was in no mood for reconciliation and spat upon the crucifix.

Of all the Hechtian memorabilia of that violent, innocent time (which Ben rattled nonstop to the author almost two decades ago), the most startling was a courtroom occurrence in which Hecht, perhaps for the first and only time in his life, was held inert and spellbound. A man had been tried for murder, an immigrant who had slaughtered his family, a towering giant who stood solemn and stoic before the judge. Hecht was sitting in a jam-packed reporter's gallery watching the proceedings. The judge calmly sentenced the killer to be hanged. The giant came to life with the judge's sentence of death and yelled, "Hang me, will you!" With that he produced—in testimony to the cavalier security precautions of the day—a long butcher's knife which he immediately plunged into the judge's heart. The jurist fell forward on his high desk gasping out his life. Stunned silence gripped the courtroom. Everyone, including the agile Hecht, was frozen by the amazing scene—everyone except a reporter from the *Inter-Ocean* who, Hecht noted out of the corner of his eye, was writing furiously, the only reporter out of thirty responsive enough to cover the ghastly incident. "Copyboy!" yelled the reporter and a youth ran by, grabbed the reporter's penciled sheets, and scurried off to his newspaper with the scoop.

"None of us in the courtroom had the presence of mind to write a single word, paralyzed as we were by the attack," Hecht later recalled. "Yet here was this guy from the *Inter-Ocean*, who had nerves of steel, who had never paused in doing his job. I just had to find out what he had written." Hecht ran after the copyboy and caught him by the arm, grabbing the yellow paper bearing the scoop. Upon it, written over and over again in a nervous handwriting, were the words, "The judge has been stabbed, the judge has been stabbed, the judge has been stabbed . . ."

"Here's a Pretty Good Story"

One day in 1914, fateful upon the brink of world war, Bennie Hecht was busy in the pressroom at the sheriff's office when Jack Malloy entered with an odd-looking stranger in tow. Vincent Starrett, Hecht, and Ronald Millar (who would become editor of *Liberty Magazine*) looked up from their rummy game.

"I want you to meet my friend," Malloy waxed, "who is a great genius and too fine a man for these precincts. Kindly arise!"

No one moved.

"Just what I expected," Malloy said disgustedly. "Forgive these parasites. They are the untutored scum of letters and unable on a clear day to distinguish their asses from their elbows!"

Malloy's friend appeared shy as he fidgeted with a high celluloid collar

Carl Sandburg, Chicago's unforgettable poet, when he was less than a star reporter.

that did not fit and brushed back a falling halo of stiff hair that slanted into his eyes. "My name is Carl Sandburg," the stranger announced meekly. "I'm a reporter on the *Day Book*. Malloy said I could use one of your telephones."

"Help yourself," said Starrett.

Sandburg placed a call to his office, prattling off some innocuous story. Hecht smiled. It was the usual fare for the *Day Book*, one of America's oddest looking daily newspapers—the *Day Book* was about the size of a railroad timetable and could be placed in a breast pocket without folding. After Sandburg completed his call, Malloy told him, "I would like these gentlemen to hear your poetry." The poet was at first reluctant and sat somberly staring at the the card game.

Another reporter, Ernie Pratt, plunked a soft roll to "Won't You Come Home Bill Bailey" on his banjo. Summer rain beat on the window. Slowly, Sandburg took some battered sheets of paper from his pocket and, in that peculiar singsongy voice, said, "It begins like this:

Hog Butcher for the World,
Tool Maker, Stacker of Wheat,
Player with Railroads and the Nation's Freight Handler,
Stormy, Husky, Brawling,
City of the Big Shoulders . . ."

Hecht, Starrett, Millar, and the rest put down their cards. Here were men who had virtually waded through gore and death, oceans of bad liquor and bizarre love affairs—cynical, embittered reporters whose jobs were manifested by a professional disbelief in everything—listening bug-eyed to poetry, unconscious of the lazy lull it created between their scandal and suicide.

Sandburg stopped. "I will call it 'Chicago' when it's finished."

That night in Mangler's Saloon, the entire crew got drunk and Ronnie Millar railed against Sandburg's poetry. "Rhymeless, witless, pompous Choctaw!" Millar roared. "If those stuttering syllables uttered by that ignoramus in the celluloid collar are poetry, then I am the nabob of Pasoda!"

"Better poetry than Browning or Swinburne," Malloy shot back, "and any man doesn't think so has an asshole for a brain." The two men were then on their feet landing solid blows on each other's flushed temples. Hecht sat amused. Days later, after learning that Sandburg had lost his job at the *Day Book*, Hecht went to his editor Henry Justin Smith. He convinced Smith that Sandburg was a genius who could contribute mightily to the *News*'s editorial columns. The aesthetic Smith, who took in almost any writer down on his luck and whose work hinted artistic promise, agreed to take Sandburg on staff.

Carl Sandburg's presence in the city room seemed to encourage almost every reporter to become a novelist or poet. The style of the copy changed to high-minded prose. Subeditor Brooks Beitler complained to editor Smith.

"They'll calm down," Smith placated.

Superlative editor Henry Justin Smith was a friend to all writers.

"Yeah?" Beitler said sarcastically. "Well, listen to today's big scoop." He picked up the first edition of the afternoon, fresh from the printing press, and pointed to page one. " 'Outside, the pizzicato of the rain . . .' "

Sandburg became Beitler's unconscious nemesis. The poet would shuffle to his desk each day and remain seated reading old newspaper clippings. He took no part in the city room's antics, refusing even to join the Anti-Gonorrhea Club, the members of which "had to perform a violent five-minute jig each morning before settling down to work."

Beitler would glower the day long at Sandburg who was bent intently reading his old newspaper clippings which were stuffed into all of his pockets and retrieved meticulously on the hour for review. One day Beitler exploded at Smith.

"That guy Sandburg. We never get any stories out of him."

"What do you mean?" Smith inquired, hurt at the mere suggestion that one of his scribes was unworthy of his employ.

"Watch this," Beitler said. "Sandburg," he called out sweetly, "oh, Mr. Sandburg."

Sandburg looked up from his reading, surprised. Beitler beckoned him over to Smith's rolltop desk with a motioning finger. The poet got up slowly and shuffled up to Smith and Beitler.

"Got any scoops for us today, Mr. Sandburg?" Beitler asked in a mock-kindly voice.

"What?" the poet asked.

"Stories, Mr. Sandburg—for the newspaper."

Sandburg dug into his pocket and yanked forth a clipping that was easily ten years old. It concerned a statue that had been erected in North Dakota. "Here's a pretty good story, Mr. Beitler," he said. "Those people in Fargo really have something." Then Sandburg walked triumphantly back to his desk.

"See what I mean," Beitler said, pointing to the yellow clipping. "Hmmmmmm," Henry Justin Smith hummed and walked silently back to his desk. Smith himself was not a fugitive from eccentricity. He would become the model for the hero of Ben Hecht's first and finest novel *Erik Dorn*.

Beitler persisted. "I hear this fellow's a genius," he said to Jack Malloy. "You got any idea of what a genius can do?"

Malloy thought. "The A.F. of L. convention is opening in Minneapolis tomorrow. Carl's an expert on labor affairs. Why don't you send him up to cover it?"

Beitler agreed and Sandburg took the night train to Minneapolis.

The next morning editor Smith found Beitler muttering to himself. "What's up, Beit?"

"That fella Sandburg."

"What about him?"

"Sent him up to Minneapolis to do a labor story."

"Good idea."

"Not my idea. Malloy's. Personally, I wouldn't send him across the street. Poetry!"

Hours later Smith checked with Beitler. "How much space you giving the Sandburg story?"

Beitler scowled. "No space. No story."

The *News* used the Associated Press story that day. Two days passed without word from Sandburg. "He's probably gathering a lot of material," Smith assured Beitler.

"If he's there. Who knows."

The following day brought wild news from Minneapolis, not from Carl Sandburg but via the AP wire. A disgruntled labor delegate had pulled a gun during the morning session and begun banging away at one of the orators wounding him severely. Other delegates had pulled guns and several giants of labor were in the hospital struggling for their lives. Smith waited until the last moment before deadline. Still nothing came from Sandburg. The *News* was forced to use the wire story.

"Any orders for our staff correspondent?" Beitler asked Smith.

"Yes. Tell him to come home."

Beitler fired off a wire to Sandburg instructing him to return to Chicago. Within an hour, Beitler received a reply. He walked dumbfounded to Smith's desk. The tolerant editor was red-faced as he read the wire: "Dear Boss. Can't leave now. Everything too important and exciting. Sandburg."

J. God Talking

Probably the shrewdest newsman in Chicago was the redoubtable James Keeley who became city editor of the *Tribune* in 1895. By the turn of the century the cigar-chomping Keeley was made managing editor and for the next three decades regularly jumped the opposition with sensational scoops. Keeley, who was called J. God by those who grudgingly admired him and worse by those who hated him (and the latter were legion), thought of news as the private property of the *Tribune*. "News is a commodity," he would roar around his cigar, "and for sale like any other commodity."

Brought up in the slums of London, Keeley was a tyrannical boss who expected his staffers to work his own endless hours until he and they dropped. His work ethic went unaltered until 1932 when Keeley "dropped" forever at age sixty-four. He had in his bulldog fashion a proverbial nose for news and possessed an army of informants and tipsters who gleaned untold fortunes

James Keeley, the brilliant and conniving city editor of the *Tribune*.

from the *Tribune*'s coffers for their "inside" information. Astounded reporters would report to Keeley to be told to see Joe Blank at a certain address around midnight. He would have a scoop for the *Tribune*. On one occasion Keeley sent a reporter to cover a shooting *before* it happened; how he came to know in advance of this impending homicide baffled newsmen but made him all the more sacrosanct as a sniffer of news.

Although the *Chicago Post* once aptly wrote of Keeley, "Nobody ever spoke of him as a good fellow," Keeley was respected as well as feared. His integrity was boundless and he would suffer no dictates from advertisers. A *Tribune* reporter named John Kelley heard of a terrible accident in one of the larger Loop stores but when he arrived to cover the story of the injured employees, he was told, "We're one of the *Tribune*'s best advertisers, and the manager told me that if any reporter came here to give 'em nothing—forget about it." Kelley reported the stall to Keeley who roared, "John, you sit down and write that story just the way it happened. Don't forget to put in all he said about being a big advertiser. This paper isn't taking orders from anybody!"

Matching Keeley's news acumen with an uncanny memory for detail was the world's most famous copyboy Jimmy Durkin who was Keeley's right-hand runner and sidekick. Uneducated, a product of the Chicago slums, Durkin was as tireless as Keeley. He more or less lived inside the *Tribune* building, and, next to Keeley and his zany city editor Walter Howey, Durkin more or less bossed the entire staff about. As a source of miscellaneous information, Durkin was unequaled. A fire-alarm buzzer would sound. Durkin would yell out, "There's a three-alarm over at Wells and South Water, lots of shacks and granaries there. Get going, Harry, take them dogs off the desk and move it! You ain't doin' nothin'." A rewrite man in a quandary would croak to the aging copyboy, "Hey, Durk, who's the mayor of Hammond?"

Durkin, moving swiftly about the desks in the city room on his chores would pipe back, "John D. Smith. D for Daniel. He ran for Congress two years ago but he was licked."

Another would yell, "Durk, what number did that guy call, the one who shot his wife last week?"

"Yard 2149" would come the perfunctory answer.

To amuse himself, Keeley once sent Durkin as the World's Most Famous Office Boy (with cards imprinted to that effect) to London as social ambassador of the *Tribune* to attend the coronation of King George V. Reportedly, Durkin was introduced to the new monarch and put out his hand, snapping, "Hi'yah, George. How's the king business?"

For thirty-three years, until his death in 1928, Jimmy Durkin was the cock-of-the-walk at the *Tribune*. In the words of Burton Rascoe, writing in *Before I Forget*: "Impish, bland, alert, obscene, he was afraid of no one, deferred to no one, talked back to anybody. He gave out assignments to rewrite men without instructions from the city editor whenever a story came in over the phone and he called 'Thirty!' to reporters, dismissing them for the night."

Keeley's appreciation for Durkin was an admiration of facts. Attention to detail was Keeley's hallmark which he proved during the 1904 holocaust that gutted the Iroquois Theater in which more than 600 persons, mostly children, burned to death. When all of the other Chicago papers were churning out vivid, sob-sister stories on the fire, Keeley, the ever-clearheaded newsman, printed nothing on the story except to run on the first few pages of the *Tribune* an entire, accurate list of the dead and injured. Keeley knew that thousands would be seeking loved ones in the morgues and hospitals. Circulation soared.

Roughneck Keeley tolerated orders from no one, including his nominal boss Joseph Medill Patterson, a young scion of the Medill-Patterson ownership of the *Tribune*, who was slated to someday take over the paper. Patterson, a mild-mannered, intelligent, eager-to-learn young man took much abuse from Keeley and from the staff in general. On more than one occasion, to prove that having wealth and power did not make of him an effeminate creature, Patterson would saunter into Hinky Dink Kenna's notorious red-light saloon and pick fights with the toughest bozos at the bar, acts which resulted in his being punched silly and bounced almost unconscious onto the sidewalk outside. Yet, such bravado did earn him the respect of many, but never J. God Keeley who would dismiss any of Patterson's editorial suggestions, no matter how worthy, as though he were dealing with a rich cretin.

Tyrant Keeley, however, had already proven his amazing ability to organize and run The World's Greatest Newspaper (as the *Tribune*'s masthead later boasted). At his suggestion, Bert Taylor began the first newspaper column in America in the *Tribune*, "A Line-o-Type or Two." Keeley was also responsible for hiring some of the finest writers in the country; James O'Donnell Bennett; Edgar Sisson; John T. McCutcheon; Harvey Woodruff; and the capricious, high-talented Ring Lardner. Of all his literary minions, J. God Keeley especially doted upon Chicago's roaringest reporter Charles MacArthur whose entry into Chicago in 1912 was more than auspicious.

Thousands of excited citizens lined the sidewalks to await the return of an Illinois regiment which had accompanied General John "Black Jack" Pershing on his punitive expedition into Mexico against Pancho Villa. The parade was to be led by Colonel Milton Foreman.

The crowds swelled to more than 100,000 along the parade route. Suddenly whoops in the crowd signaled the start of the parade. Hundreds of policemen strained to hold back the jubilant mobs. But no troops appeared. Ironically, Ben Hecht was on hand to report on the event. "We saw a single battered automobile moving oddly down the empty street. It zigzagged from curb to curb. A uniformed soldier sat at the wheel, steering with one

Ring Lardner, a shining star in Keeley's *Tribune* heaven.

hand and waving a top-heavy American flag with the other. He was Private Charles MacArthur. Never a good driver, in this hour of triumph, MacArthur careened from sidewalk to sidewalk, waving his flag and shouting strange battle cries: 'Down with Colonel Foreman! Down with Tin-pants Milton!' "

The crowds cheered. Scant minutes later, with banners waving and drums beating, a red-faced Colonel Milton Foreman arrived leading his regiment on horseback. MacArthur was promptly arrested.

The errant private was ordered to clean up the Fort Sheridan premises with a stick and a bag. A day later, Colonel Foreman gave a lawn party at the fortress and an elderly woman looked up from her tea, startled. "Milton, what is that general doing?"

Foreman incredulously looked out across the lawn to see Charles MacArthur dressed as a general in the army. He had made epaulets on his prisoner's uniform with gold radiator paint and added a chestful of decorations. With precise military bearing, MacArthur approached bits of paper on the lawn, saluted each, and then impaled them on a glittering sword before depositing each in his bag.

That night Colonel Foreman dismissed MacArthur from the army with the prophecy, "I don't know what the hell's going to become of you. But I'm sure of one thing. You're never going to make a soldier."

Colonel Milton Foreman was right. MacArthur's future wars, except for a stint in the army during World War I, would be fought from the hard end of a typewriter. J. God Keeley had heard that MacArthur had dropped the terror of the local barrooms Lionel Moisse in a five-minute slugfest at Mangler's Saloon.

Moisse (who was credited with teaching young Ernest Hemingway the ins and outs of reporting while on the *Kansas City Star*) had bullied and beaten his way through the journalistic ranks of Chicago. He had worked as a reporter for Keeley, who had hated his lack of discipline. After leaving the *Tribune*, Moisse went to work for the *Chicago Evening Post* where, after throwing that paper's city editor and two copyreaders down a flight of stairs, he was made the assistant city editor out of sheer fright on the part of the bosses.

When Keeley learned MacArthur had drubbed Moisse, he adopted him as one of his own. This meant that MacArthur would have to do his drinking and poker playing with Keeley and his cohorts or forfeit his job. MacArthur, however, had heard how Keeley, endowed with a fat bankroll, would play "freeze-out" poker with his reporters who could not afford to take on his high-stake hands and inevitably lost their week's pay. On top of that, reporters had to listen to Keeley's lectures on how to play poker after he had cleaned them out.

MacArthur invented dozens of excuses—he was a master of evasion—to escape the poker massacres with Keeley. The editor then insisted that MacArthur accompany him on the town as a social companion. Keeley's idea of socializing meant dropping into his favorite assignation house.

MacArthur recalled one bordello visit. "Madam Farrington greeted Keeley as if he were King Solomon. She ordered up three bottles of wine and said two of her fairest would be on deck in a few minutes. Keeley sat down and started banging a piano and moaning out a song. It was about a toy tin soldier that belonged to a little boy [after the Eugene Field poem]. One night the little boy stood the tin soldier in the corner of his nursery and never woke up. After the little boy was buried, the tin soldier remained standing, loyally, in the nursery corner—waiting."

Suddenly, a door leading to the parlor was flung open and a naked girl stood there with her hair down, screaming, "Stop that song! For Christ's sake, don't sing that song!"

J. God Keeley ignored her. He continued singing "Little Boy Blue" louder than ever. Moments later, one of the paying guests burst from the same room to announce to one and all that the girl—named Vera—had swallowed a bottleful of Lysol. She was rushed to Passavant Hospital and died an hour later. Madam Farrington explained to a horrified MacArthur and an angry Keeley that Vera's three-year-old son had died the previous summer.

Keeley's brutal newspaper instincts flared that night as he rushed back to

The incredible Walter Howey, editor of the *Examiner*, was the stuff of the front page.

the *Tribune* and wrote a story of a poor trollop who had ended her life after listening tearfully to *an organ grinder* crank out "Little Boy Blue" beneath her window, pitifully reminded of the little child she had deserted!

Howey, by Jehovah!

J. God wasn't the only inventor of news in Chicago. His aide-de-camp and city editor Walter Howey was a master at creating news where none existed. Howey was the kind of journalistic light that began to fade after World War I; he was of an editorial genre that insisted that all stories be written in a dramatic, a colorful, or a humorous fashion. News stories had to be, in Howey's estimation, readable and entertaining first and newsy second, a policy that, perhaps, if followed to this day, might have prevented the collapse in recent times of so many major daily newspapers.

As city editor of the *Tribune*, Howey's words of admonition to all young reporters were the same: "Don't ever fake a story or anything in a story—that is, never let me catch you at it." Howey haunted the underworld and through his knowledge of ward-heeling politicians, crooks, and assorted maniacs was more than familiar with sources leading to great news coverage on murder, racketeers and their molls, and, especially, political corruption. It was after he had written a series of exposes for the *Inter-Ocean* on Mayor Fred Busse,

The great film director D.W. Griffith, promoted by Walter Howey of the *Tribune*. (UPI)

Chicago's own silent film star Colleen Moore; she caused her uncle, Walter Howey, to lose his job. (UPI)

which drove the mayor from office, that Howey arrived at the *Tribune*. As a city editor, Howey cautioned all reporters, in his typically cynical, embittered fashion, to steer clear of romantic ties with women. "The bitches will ruin you—they have nothing to do with serious newspaper work!" On many occasions the intrepid Walter yelled that he would fire any reporter who even planned on marriage. (Howey would later become the prototype for Walter Burns the managing editor in Hecht and MacArthur's classic play *The Front Page*.) A schemer and a dreamer, Howey was nevertheless loved mightily by his writing fools; no scribbler in Chicago who ever worked for him could forget his stunts, his pranks, his magnetic journalism.

Hearst's move to buy up the writing talent in Chicago included the unpredictable Mr. Howey, whom Hearst offered $35,000 a year to leave his $8,000-a-year position with the *Tribune*. Howey refused. The *Tribune*, he boomed, was a better paper than the *Examiner*, the most powerful medium in the Midwest.

Shortly thereafter, Walter Howey met D. W. Griffith, whose *Birth of a Nation* had established him as the genius of motion pictures. Howey, whose niece was Coleen Moore, a budding actress, thought it prudent to write up his meeting in Chicago with Griffith. (It was through this contact that Miss Moore established herself as a Hollywood star.) The Griffith article aroused the ire of Patterson who chastised Howey for writing press-agent puffery. Patterson went one humiliating step further and apologized for the piece in an editorial. Howey exploded and walked out of the *Tribune* building and over to Hearst's *Examiner* where he took the news king's $35,000 salary and slid grumpily into the managing editor's chair. (He would remain a Hearst man for the remainder of his days, named as one of the eight executives to administer Hearst's 125-page will which disposed of $59,500,000 after the chief's death in 1951 at age 88.) Much of Howey's direct services for Hearst had to do with the Fountain of Youth. According to Hearst's meticulous biographer W. A. Swanberg writing in *Citizen Hearst*, the chief "had Walter Howey . . . check carefully on all news stories about scientific advancements in the prolongation of life, and send him reports. He was much interested on the monkey-gland transplantations performed by Dr. Serge Voronoff for rejuvenating the elderly. When a Chicago millionaire had such a transplantation, Hearst inquired occasionally to find if it did him any good."

Howey never forgot the sting of Patterson's labeling him an advocate of press-agentry. At every opportunity, Howey would try to embarrass the *Tribune*. All editors of Chicago's press read the first editions of the opposition each day (which Howey knew), and the *Tribune* was particularly alert for any undeveloped stories which it might exploit more fully in its own pages. One morning, the *Examiner* ran a short piece on a South Bend heiress living in the Blackstone Hotel; she had arrived the innocent in Chicago and was looking for ways to spend her money. The *Examiner* story hinted broadly that the attractive woman might be a fake and press-agentry might be the root of the hotel publicity release.

Tribune editors jumped at the story and interviewed the heiress, emphatically stating that she was genuine, giving it a big play—several columns worth beginning on the front page—spicing the feature with several photographs of the attractive lady-bountiful. The next day, the *Examiner*, while Howey guffawed himself into convulsions, ran a lead story thanking the *Tribune* for press-agenting an upcoming Hearst fiction-movie property to be called the *Ten Million Dollar Heiress*. Howey had hired the actress and installed her in the Blackstone to suck the *Tribune* into his literary scam.

Howey's influence on Chicago-style journalism was immeasurable. He could take credit for expert phone men like Harry Romanoff who could impersonate anyone on the phone—from the governor of Illinois to the chief of police—to obtain a story or a quote; or impish Buddy McHugh who was once overheard in the pressroom of the County Building to inquire on the phone, "Madam, is it true that you were the victim of a Peeping Tom?"

Under Howey's devilish direction, Ring Lardner and Charles MacArthur, when at the *Tribune*, made their reputations—newspaper reputations that established them as contenders for the crown of the world's leading zanies. Lardner and MacArthur became almost as inventive in their chores as their leader Howey. Once, when attending an important football game in Indiana, Lardner and MacArthur were turned away at the gate for neglecting to bring along their press credentials. The two reporters went to a local bar to brood. Upon inspecting the WC, the reporters discovered that the toilets flushed when one thumbed a button labeled Press. Dismantling two of the toilets, Lardner and MacArthur attached the Press buttons to their coats, rushed to the football game and were admitted to the stadium when they flashed these "credentials."

City editor Howey was to them an odd-looking man who constantly cooed, murmured, and hummed. His smile was wide and wicked. Unlike his rumpled reporters, he was always well tailored, his stiffly pressed suit accented by a polka-dot bow tie. Walter Howey shot a deadly game of pool even with a disabled left eye. One reporter claimed Howey "had fallen into a drunken stupor while sitting at his desk and impaled the eye on a copy spike."

The strange power Howey wielded over public officials when he was seeking inside information was explained when a reporter learned that this mercurial editor possessed, locked away in his desk, the signed resignation of a high state official (some even whispered the governor's name) whom Howey had caught with both hands in the till. The resignation was blackmailed out of the official and henceforth he became a Howey stooge.

Howey's convivial conniving extended to his chosen ones. He attempted to steal Ring Lardner for the *Examiner*, but the great sports writer was too

Tribune newsman Frank Carson, who was shanghaied by Walter Howey to the *Examiner*.

clever and managed to elude his former editor by changing his apartment, bars, and friendships, remaining with the *Tribune* to write his down-home prose and "You Know Me Al" series. Frank Carson wasn't so lucky.

Carson had been Howey's protégé and succeeded him as city editor of the *Tribune*. One of Howey's first acts as the new managing editor of the *Examiner* was to throw a huge fete for Carson, in honor of his promotion, at a favorite Chicago watering hole, Schlogl's Restaurant. After belting down several boilermakers graciously supplied by Howey, a piece of paper mysteriously appeared under Carson's drink-clutching hand. Howey asked for his good friend's autograph and Carson scribbled it out with alacrity.

On the following day, Howey called Carson at the *Tribune*. "Where the hell are you, Frank?"

"What do you mean, Walter? I'm at work."

"Yeah, but at the wrong office. You signed a contract last night to work for me at the *Examiner*. Now get those bones over here." Frank Carson had been shanghaied but he didn't complain. His new wages were enormous and working for Walter Howey was about the most exciting thing that could happen to a newsman in 1920.

It was planned excitement to some extent as Howey went furiously about making the *Tribune* appear ridiculous in missing the scoops of the day. In

1921, during the days of snaillike communication, Carson schemed up the idea of using a mail plane to deliver photos to the *Examiner* of the upcoming Dempsey-Carpentier battle from Jersey City. The post office, which employed the only long-distance fliers at that time, refused Carson's request.

He schemed on. Then Carson remembered a declaration of newspaper principles published years before by the owner of the *Marion Star* in Ohio. The owner had been Warren G. Harding. Carson unearthed the set of publishing dictums, then had them boldly lettered and hammered to the wall of the *Examiner*'s editorial office. Carson and his staff were photographed mawkishly admiring Harding's newspaper credo.

Then Carson was off to Washington with the photo. After conning an appointment with the President, Howey's enterprising city editor displayed his rigged photo to Harding, lavishing praise upon the former small-town newspaperman and informing him that the *Examiner* was always guided by his sterling principles.

Almost moved to tears, Harding heard of Carson's plight to obtain a mail plane. The President immediately called the postmaster general. Carson had his plane. The *Examiner* offered the first photos of the Dempsey battle with Carpentier. The *Tribune* was again out in the cold. Throughout the 1920s, the giant battle for scoops between the *Examiner* and the *Tribune* raged on. Nothing seemed too absurd.

Many downstate Illinois cities were all but wiped out by a tornado. Howey and Carson sent their reporters ferreting into the area to cover the disaster. Moreover, they organized a supply train loaded with food, medical supplies, and clothing to be sent to the stricken area. Immense banners reading *Examiner* Relief Train were plastered on the train's cars.

A photographer working for the *Tribune* ambled down to the freight yard where the train was getting up steam. He photographed the iron horse, banners and all. When the *Trib*'s early edition arrived in the *Examiner*'s city room, Carson was not surprised to discover that the *Tribune*'s art department had gone to work on these banners which now read, Chicago Mercy Train.

Scribbling the words *must correct* on the *Trib*'s picture page, along with some editorial jottings, Carson tore it from the edition and handed it to a copyboy. The *Examiner*'s copyboy had once worked for the opposition and, at Howey's direction, he took Carson's corrected photo section to the *Tribune* composing room where he was recognized. Automatically, the change was made and the *Tribune* printed 25,000 copies of their late edition with the revised banner reading *Examiner* Mercy Train before the presses were stopped.

All work was suspended in the *Examiner*'s city room when the copy of the *Tribune* arrived. The entire staff began to hum "The Merry Widow" as Howey and Carson joined arms and waltzed wildly about the desks of their admiring reporters.

The extraordinary Charles MacArthur, Howey's one-man staff.

Gangster Charles Dion O'Bannion, good friend to newsman Charles MacArthur. (UPI)

The Roaring Boy

Another one of Howey's steals from the *Tribune* was Charles MacArthur. Nothing MacArthur could do warranted Howey's criticism, except his association with the North Side gangster, Deanie O'Bannion. This Howey prejudice was both ironic and perplexing since Howey personally hired O'Bannion (along with squads of other street hooligans) as a strong-arm man for the *Examiner*. The Irish hoodlum was colorful copy for MacArthur and he appealed to the reporter's wild streak. O'Bannion, like MacArthur, was a creation of the Chicago newspaper war, but on the other side of the law. One wag, however, stated, "it's hard to tell the difference between the gangsters and the reporters in this town."

Though O'Bannion, who was on salary at the *Examiner* from 1919 to 1922, was used primarily as a circulation thug-booster, he had other chores that proved his dexterous talents. Edward Dean Sullivan, one of Howey's devil-dog reporters on the *Examiner*, received the impossible assignment of entering the black ghetto—a charred area where incendiaries had torched $2-million worth of buildings—during the 1919 race riots in which 38 people were killed and 543 wounded. No taxi would enter the devastated precincts, so Howey rented motorcycles to putter his reporters through the police lines.

Sullivan later described his harrowing assignment in his *Rattling the Cup on Chicago Crime*. He hopped into a sidecar of one of the motorcycles idling outside the *Examiner* building and shouted to the goggle-wearing motorcycle driver, "How about it? Shall we go in there?"

"Sure." The driver, a burly, wild-looking specimen, stuck a banner with the *Examiner's* name on it across his windshield. "This will get us by. The paper's been giving the jigaboos [Negroes] all the best of it. They won't pop off at us."

Sullivan and his driver roared into the bullet-whanging district. Suddenly, the reporter was almost deafened by a shot fired by his driver at a Negro on a rooftop who was struggling to free a rifle from the grasp of a giant Negress dressed all in white—the man was trying to turn the rifle on Sullivan and his driver.

"One side's enough to worry about," yelled the driver and moved the cycle down the street, steering the vehicle with one hand while banging away at rooftop snipers with an automatic which he wielded with his free hand. The motorcyclist was none other than Deanie O'Bannion, who later set himself up as the boss of the North Side (he controlled the voting blocks in the 42nd and 43rd wards becoming a millionaire before he was thirty through bootlegging and racketeering), and was murdered in his flower shop by Al Capone's machine gunners in 1924, a slaying which caused the bootleg wars to grind into high gear. But in those early days of his crime career, before notching twenty-five lives on the stock of his "tommy," O'Bannion found great delight in hanging around newsmen and poets; he thought of himself as quite the artistic gentleman, attending opera with his gun-toting boys and writing little bits of doggerel which he sent to the newspapers to enhance their literary sections. MacArthur was his favorite press crony.

The mobster would arrive in full-dress tuxedo at dawn, having come from a formal social affair, and would march into such MacArthur-Howey hangouts as Stillson's or Quincy Number 9 Saloon. Howey would spot the smiling, apple-cheeked gangster and growl at his ace reporter, "You're not going with that low, dirty, murdering bastard. You're going home and go to bed!"

MacArthur would grin. "I'll sleep better if I relax first. Deanie is my sandman."

Mobster and reporter would then leave arm and arm and climb into O'Bannion's fast flivver. Deanie would run his large touring car onto the wide sidewalks of Michigan Avenue, and, with a drowsy MacArthur at his side, go through what he termed his daily "bullfight." His car was the bull and the few pedestrians and policemen up at that hour were the matadors. All stepped (or leaped) aside, knowing it was O'Bannion. No one was ever injured. When asked about it, a police sergeant shrugged. "Aww, that's just Deanie's way of having some fun." Chicago was always a tolerant as well as a toddlin' town.

MacArthur, for all of his vaunted escapades, was not as free as some of his contemporaries to roam the city's streets for stories. He was essentially at the mercy of his managing editor Walter Howey. The crafty editor called his favorite scribe into his office one evening and told him that a little girl had wandered into a five-foot safe in the Moline, Illinois, train station. "The stationmaster closed it without noticing the child had stepped inside. I've just been talking with him on the phone. He's in bed with hysterics."

"What? Was he sober?"

"Soberest man I ever talked to. There's just enough air in that safe to allow the little girl to stay alive till midnight."

MacArthur was leery. "If that mug of a stationmaster is so sober, why doesn't he open the damned safe?"

"It's a beautiful story," Howey crooned. "It's an old safe and hasn't been used for ten years. It's been kept open until tonight. Now that it's locked, there's nobody who knows the combination. Dynamiting is out of the question. It would only blow the little one to hell and gone. Our object is to get her out of that safe alive."

Then began one of the roaringest stories of Chicago's Roaring Twenties. Howey explained that he had learned the exact dimensions of the safe and had consulted doctors. From them he had learned how long a child could last with that many feet of cubic air available. "Twelve o'clock is the deadline for the little girl and also for our home edition." Howey then told MacArthur that he had made arrangements for a special train to take him to Joilet to pick up the best safecrackers in the state prison and rush them to Moline to save the little girl.

MacArthur dashed off to his waiting train which made Joliet in record time. "Every goddamn yegg [safecracker] and footpad [mugger] in the place claimed to be another Jimmy Valentine," MacArthur later recalled. "They were all bragging to the warden of the big jobs they had pulled off that the police knew nothing about." Two experts were finally selected and sent along with MacArthur.

Howey had found the president of the railroad in a Springfield hospital where he was recovering from pneumonia and convinced him to put on a fast flyer from Joliet to Moline to accomplish the *Examiner*'s humanitarian mission. The editor had already rushed several of Chicago's top physicians and nurses to Moline. They were standing by the old safe.

Walter Howey was on the phone to Joliet screaming for MacArthur to move more quickly. "And remember, above all else, we've got to keep the story locked up till that little baby is restored to her mother's arms. I've got the mother and several other members of the family under close watch and photographers standing by waiting for that steel door of doom to open. So move fast, Charlie!"

Charlie moved. The fast flyer raced to Moline. Hundreds of people were milling about the depot. Doctors and nurses were everywhere. Two vice-presidents of the line stood by to do what they could. "All pulled out of their beds by Howey," stated MacArthur. "A cheer went up as my safecrackers appeared, still in their prison suits. Everybody wanted to wring their hands. You never saw two such giddy heroes. I had already promised them a governor's pardon, knowing that Howey would expect it of me."

There was little more than thirty minutes to get the safe open before the child died. At ten minutes to midnight, with dozens of anxious, sweating faces leaning and looking above the safecrackers' kneeling forms, the prisoners turned and proudly announced to their warden, "The door is open, Chief!"

Cameras clicked as the vice-presidents slowly opened the safe. "I was half ready for the denouement," MacArthur said. "There was no little girl with golden curls in the safe. Only battered suitcases and ancient ledgers. Everybody was sore as hell, including the two yeggs who started howling for their governor's pardon and had to be taken back to Joliet at rifle-point."

MacArthur was sore as hell too. He got Howey on the phone and told him that no little girl was in the safe, and that he had embarrassed half the state of Illinois, plus his own newspaper. Then he told him that the little girl who had been missing was found in the attic of her home "where she had hidden because she was miffed with her grandmother for getting drunk in front of her schoolmates."

Howey never paused for breath. "It's a great story—I'll get you a rewrite man. Give him all the details. Everything all those wonderful people said. How everybody from the lowest to the highest rode to the rescue of that little girl."

"I told you!" MacArthur screamed at his editor, thinking Howey's mind had turned the final corner. "There *wasn't* any little girl!"

Walter Howey paused and then cooed to his Pythias, "I knew that all along. It's not a story about a little girl. It's a story about humanity, the goodness in people's hearts—the safeblowers, vice-presidents, doctors, nurses, and the warden, the governor, the fellow with pneumonia, and everybody who answered a cry of human distress."

"I got you, Walter," MacArthur said and began to dictate his story.

In the morning, the *Examiner's* seven-column 104 wood-block head bannered the words "IT'S A WONDERFUL WORLD."

It was, it was.

But there were many worlds in Chicago, one darker and more sinister than the city's press imagined. It began with a man who lived in a literal underworld, accelerated with the murder of a newsman (one of MacArthur's own friends), and continues to this day spewing murder in its orbit as it grinds interminably on its evil axis.

3

Underworld, 1858

Some twenty years after Chicago boomed into a bustling major midwestern city (a city where the average citizen went armed at all times and made fortunes in trade, real estate, and outright chicanery), the town's first crime czar emerged, literally from below the surface of Chicago's boggy earth. In the late 1850s, civic leaders realized that the city had been planned with the scheme of a mad hatter; the entire metropolitan area was situated on marshlands leading from the river and Lake Michigan so that citizens were caught in engulfing mire. Mud was everywhere, trapping carriages and pedestrians alike. To combat the quagmires, it was decided to actually raise the entire city, building by building (some as high as ten feet), and resurface the face of Chicago with solid earth and stone. In the decade-long process of elevating Chicago, miles of underground passages, streets, and enormous earthen rooms were created. Inside this dark, abandoned netherworld, Roger Plant built a criminal empire, truly giving birth and significance to the word *underworld*.

Roger the Respectable

Plant was a dimunitive immigrant from Yorkshire, England, who stood no more than 5-foot-1-inch in high boots and seldom weighed more than 100 pounds. His wife tipped the scales at more than 250 pounds, a giant harlot who was the only person in the city who did not fear Roger. When irked at his antics, the Gargantuan wife would collar her strutting husband, hold him one-handed at arm's length as he squirmed in the air, and spank him liberally with her free hand, striking him so hard that tears would course down the face of the terror of Chicago crime.

Most had good reason to fear the indefatigable Mr. Plant. His fame as a fighter was wide; wiry and fast, Roger could not only deliver knockout blows to

This painting by Edward Mendel shows the city of Chicago being raised six feet above the marshlands in 1857, a Herculean project that created Roger Plant's underworld.

all opponents but used his feet—encased in boots with specially made iron tips—to lay low any adversary. He was particularly adept at biting, his teeth being employed as a major weapon. In addition to his physical prowess, Plant was a walking arsenal. At all times, even when sleeping, at least two giant knives, two pistols, and a huge bludgeon were on his person or in his hand.

Plant's headquarters were located at Wells and Monroe streets, "the very core of corruption" according to one early day journalist. The clapboard, ramshackle structure was a two-story affair that spread for half a block with Roger adding rookeries and wings every few years. Roger's Barracks the police called the place, and gave it a wide berth. Plant was more sentimental and dubbed the sprawling hangout Under the Willow after a diseased willow tree that thinly arched over a corner of the building. (Roger's method of sustaining this lone tree was to fill a large bucket with whiskey and water, then get roaring drunk and urinate upon the tree's trunk while scores of his thug-cronies cheered him on.)

Inside the barracks, those free and easy enough with money and with courage enough to enter the dive could find a vast assortment of perversities, from the three groggeries around-the-clock to the many gambling dens which also never closed. The second floor was reserved for sex, Roger's wife supplying as many as 200 prostitutes for interested customers. Upon the blue window shades covering the second-story rooms of these hollering trollops

Mrs. Plant had ordered gilt lettering to be placed that read, "Why not?" The question later became a nationwide catch phrase.

The police not only ignored the army of crooks and killers inhabiting Roger's establishment but refused to believe the crime fortress even existed. Plant paid several high-ranking police officers princely sums each month "so I never have to see a dirty copper." When pressed to close up Plant's operation by a social group, one police captain moaned, "Trying to raid those barracks would be like trying to arrest an elephant!"

Said Frederic Francis Cook in *Bygone Days in Chicago:* "Plant's emporium was one of the most talked about if not actually one of the wickedest places on the continent," and it was "a refuge for the very nethermost strata of the underworld—the refuse of the Bridewell." These denizens—hundreds of pickpockets, jackrollers, highwaymen, and killers for hire, the most fearsome collection of hoodlums anywhere in the U.S. at the time—could be found in the maze of tunnels, underground streets, and enormous cavelike areas which stretched from Wells Street to the south branch of the Chicago River.

At least sixty underground rooms were always occupied by these preying creatures. In addition to underground saloons and brothels, there were, according to Herbert Asbury, "rooms for assignation, procuresses, dens where young girls were raped by half a dozen men and then sold to the bordellos, cubicles which were rented to streetwalkers and male degenerates, and hidden rooms used as hideaways by every species of crook."

One of the more spectacular criminal residents of Under the Willow was Speckled Jimmy Calwell, a master safecracker and burglar who is credited as being the first to use plaster and tape to gag and bind his victims. Chicago's first homemade bomb was manufactured by the inventive Calwell. The device was discovered only minutes before it was set to go off on the Blue Island horsecar line; Calwell had attempted to extort money from the line owners under the threat of destroying their tracks.

Mary Hodges, queen of Chicago shoplifters, made her home in the earthen hovels beneath Under the Willow. Several times a week Mary boldly drove a large cart to the shopping districts, filled it with her plunder, and slowly drove back to Plant's place to sell off the goods. Police looked the other way every time Mary's cart ambled by, knowing that she was under terrible Roger's protection.

Also shielded by Plant was an ancient harridan, Mary Brennan, whom the press labeled "an audacious old sinner." The crotchety Mrs. Brennan was Chicago's first Fagin, running a pickpocket school for little girls. Her own two daughters were not only prize students but later became teachers in the artful-dodger game. The little girl students were required each day to not only pick a minimum of five pockets but grab purses and swipe what loot they could from department-store counters. For their efforts, Mary Brennan cracked a broken-toothed smile and gave them a few pennies for candy.

Plant's residents paid him huge rentals for their hideouts and underworld operations. This, in turn, went toward police payoffs and to finance Roger's various interests which, during the Civil War, included staggering shipments of contraband, the sale of weaponry, and the wholesale fleecing of the thousands of soldiers who swarmed the streets of Chicago. One of Plant's operations during the war was the drugging of young men, usually those foolish enough to enter his bordellos, and the selling of these unfortunate souls to the U.S. Army which was desperate for recruits and paid from $300 to $500 in bounties for enlistees. Many a scion from a good family came to his senses wearing a baggy blue uniform and on his way in a rattling boxcar to the blood-soaked battlefields of the East to die "as a cannon fodder" thanks to Roger Plant.

With millions bulging his coffers, Plant, in 1868, decided to reform. He closed his infamous resort and purchased a splendid mansion in the suburbs. Although Plant "became a patron of the turf and otherwise blossomed into a pattern of respectability," Roger's childern carried on in their father's nefarious tradition. Roger Plant, Jr., became a notorious bandit and, later, according to reformer William T. Stead's blacklist of city property used for immoral purposes in 1894, owned no less than three blood-bathed saloons and two whorehouses. His sisters Daisy and Kitty Plant were keepers of Clark Street bordellos until the turn of the century.

"There's a Sucker Born Every Minute"

Following the retirement of the colorful Roger Plant, Chicago came under the sway of a gentleman crook who ruled the city as a boss of bosses for more than forty years—perhaps the most powerful criminal in American history— the omnipotent Michael Cassius "Mike" McDonald. No man, from mayor to governor, stood in McDonald's way; he was a law unto himself and his pronouncements were treated as royal decrees, his thousands of payrollers, from gambler to cop, obedient in quickstep to his word.

He sweated mightily, struggling to learn the work of his gambling trade at the beginning. Born near Chicago in 1839, McDonald was, at sixteen, a swindling news butcher working the trains between Niagara Falls and Detroit selling phony jewelry and faked prize packages to gullible passengers but chiefly earning his way by inveigling for train gamblers who rewarded him with a few dollars fleeced from suckers.

At eighteen, McDonald plied his trade on the Mississippi side-wheelers, learning subtle card-sharping from such wizards as George DeVol and Canada Bill Jones. He eventually discarded the loud plaid suits he had thought fashionable in Chicago for the more refined garb of the successful gambler solid black with pure white linen, his shirt and tie festooned with diamond studs, cuff links, and stickpin. He vowed not only to be the greatest gambler in the world but to maintain a code of ethics. "Stick to your friends," he once declared, "and keep your word once given." Though devoted to a world of crime, he could shun the more repulsive aspects of that world, along with all other rackets, if he desired. One gambler explained that "a crook has to be decent to work with Mike."

McDonald was ostensibly decent in his dealing with Union army officials during the Civil War. He organized a gang of bounty jumpers who would enlist for the bounty of $500 and then desert after boot camp, only to enlist again and again after returning to Chicago. McDonald took 50 percent of the take. With his swag, Mike backed several faro games which proved so successful that he and another sharper, Dan Oaks, opened their own gambling den in 1867, a swanky two-story operation at 89 Dearborn Street.

The Dearborn operation was crooked and every game was fixed, which allowed McDonald and Oaks to prosper until 1869 when Mike swindled an assistant cashier of the Chicago Dock Company for $30,000. The irate cashier filed a complaint and McDonald was arrested. Unable to furnish the $60,000 bond, McDonald languished in jail for three months. At his trial, the gambler was acquitted, a score of bribed witnesses swearing that the cashier had begged McDonald with tears streaming over his cheeks to be allowed to gamble. The jailing and fines, however, about broke McDonald and he barely managed to pay off the police, falling behind more and more each week. "They're persecuting me," he grumbled, and his hatred for policemen went to his marrow.

So intense was McDonald's loathing for officers of the law that one of his utterances about them became legend. A man appeared at McDonald's establishment one day and asked for a donation.

"We're raising a little money, Mike," the samaritan explained. "We'd like to put you on the list for two dollars."

"What for?"

"Well, we're burying a policeman."

"Good! Here's ten dollars. Bury five of 'em!"

Mike McDonald did not become King of the Gamblers until the ashes of the great Chicago Fire of 1871 were swept away. He turned his considerable energies to politics, organizing the People's party which lobbied mightily against the Sunday closing laws for saloons. A hefty campaign fund was given to McDonald's good friend and high roller Harvey D. Colvin who was then running for mayor. When Colvin won in 1873, he all but turned the city over to Big Mike. Except for a few reform mayors, McDonald was to reign supreme in the city well into the twentieth century. Writer Richard Henry Little said of him in those days, "He never held office, but he ruled the city with an iron hand. He named the men who were to be candidates for election, he elected them, and after they were in office they were merely his puppets. He ran saloons and gambling houses, protected bunko steerers and confidence men and brace games of all kinds without let or hindrance."

The man who was to be portrayed as the gambling czar in Edna Ferber's *Show Boat*, formed a partnership with sharpers Harry Lawrence and Morris Martin and opened a giant gambling den named The Store the day after Colvin was elected. Situated on the northwest corner of Clark and Monroe streets, The Store boasted four floors with gambling of all sorts on the first two floors, and a deluxe boarding house on the third and fourth floors.

Harry Lawrence, however, was nervous. When he spotted the many faro and roulette tables being installed, he panicked. "There's too many, Mike," he carped to McDonald. "We'll never get enough players to fill up the games."

It was at that moment Mike McDonald (not P. T. Barnum) coined his shrewdest aphorism: "Don't worry about that, Harry. There's a sucker born every minute."

The Store, after Lawrence and Martin were bought out, became the gambling center of Chicago. Every criminal politician and money man of note made it his headquarters with Big Mike presiding over all important decisions. "See Mike" became the common suggestion to anyone who wanted anything important in the city. Through the Colvin era and the four consecutive terms of Carter Harrison, Sr., Mike McDonald ran things as he saw fit from his second-floor office at The Store. He backed the play of dozens of confidence gangs and bunko men. At least 1,000 professional crooks were on his permanent payroll. Scores of scammers became millionaires under his patronage and Mike became the richest of the lot. Twice a year, to appease the clamor of reformers, Mike arranged to have The Store raided by the police who were also on his payroll. On such auspicious occasions, squads of cops would amble into The Store, chop up a few old roulette wheels which had been exhibited for that purpose, and arrest a half-dozen dealers who received small fines and were released.

Ever mindful of the sneering press, Big Mike made sure that all of the city's reporters were on hand to relay the triumph of good over evil. In his attempt to gain the sterling image of respectability, McDonald even founded a daily newspaper, The *Chicago Globe*, for which Theodore Dreiser once worked as a lowly reporter. The paper failed after two years. McDonald went back to his lofty fleecing.

The most celebrated confidence men in American history worked for McDonald, including such inventive crooks as Charley and Fred Gondorf, Charley Drucker, Red Jimmy Fitzgerald, Snitzer the Kid, Tom and John Wallace, Lou Ludlum, Johnny Norton, and George W. Post. The take, which was enormous, was always split up the same way—the police got 20 percent, 40 went to the con man, and the remaining 40 was dumped into Big Mike's yawning pockets. In return for his share, McDonald provided the best in protection, supplying bail bonds, hiring lawyers and witnesses, fixing juries, and paying off city officials. Those who attempted to operate con games without Big Mike's approval were quickly arrested and held for a few weeks in jail before being kicked out of town by McDonald's obliging friends, the police.

Friendship between McDonald and the law momentarily ceased when reform-mayor Monroe Heath was swept into office. Raids against The Store became flagrant in Big Mike's eyes and for the first time, on November 23, 1878, police marched beyond their normal search area invading McDonald's private quarters on the third floor. There they found his wife, Mary Noonan, in her kitchen. Mrs. McDonald despised the police almost as much as her kingpin husband. To prove it, she grabbed a revolver and fired off a shot at one of the snooping officers, wounding Patrolman Florence Donohue in the arm. (He later died of the wound.) Mrs. McDonald was promptly arrested but was free in a matter of hours thanks to her husband's influence.

At the end of Harrison's last term, McDonald realized a new reform mayor would soon be plaguing his Store with more raids. He turned the operation over to Parson Davies and severed all direct contact with his army of bunko men but kept an open line to all operations. McDonald then spent millions of dollars investing in legitimate businesses, money which was returned to him tenfold as he became the city's chief supplier of gravel and stone, along with controlling Chicago's first elevated railroad, the Lake Street line.

The call of the gambling wild, however, beckoned with the unprecedented fifth term of Carter Harrison when he was landslided back into the mayor's office in 1892. McDonald's still intact organization went wild as Chicago caught its severest case of gambling jitters. With the opening of the World's Fair in Chicago the following year, the entire city seemed to go berserk. In the words of Hugh S. Fullerton, a magazine scribe of the day, "America has never seen a gambling orgy on such a scale. Tens of thousands of dollars an hour poured over the tables." A disgruntled office seeker ended the mad spree by assassinating Carter Harrison Sr. on the night of October 9, 1893; the reformers massed their forces and soon closed up the gambling. McDonald went back into retirement.

Although he had more money than he could ever spend in his lifetime, and his influence was still supreme, Big Mike's domestic life was a shambles. He, more than any of his breed, found the old adage lucky at cards, unlucky at love to be terribly true. As with generations of other husbands too busy with their illustrious careers to pay attention to pining spouses, McDonald's wives were not content to wait for his morsels of devotion. They proved not only errant in their wifely duties but downright flamboyant in dark trysting that made headlines and dragged Big Mike into running print with them.

After Mike's first wife Mary Noonan, the mother of his two children, shot and killed the policeman who intruded into her apartment at The Store, the gambling czar built a resplendent mansion on Ashland Avenue and installed Mary inside its luxurious confines.

Mary met a traveling minstrel singer who had come to Chicago with the

Emerson Troupe, one Billy Arlington. She ran off with the gigolo to San Francisco. An enraged Big Mike tracked the pair to the Palace Hotel where, gun in hand, he intended to shoot them. As Singing Billy blubbered his excuses, McDonald's wife leaped between her avenging husband and her high-bouncing love. Screamed Mary, "Mike, for God's sake! Don't shoot! Take me back! For the love of God!" Always soft on such sentimental pleas, McDonald pocketed his pistol, embraced his wife, and took her home to Chicago. To insure her fidelity, McDonald had a special altar erected in his mansion. In this private shrine, Mary Noonan was to pray for her tarnished soul. Big Mike arranged for a Catholic priest, Father Joseph Moysant, the assistant rector of the Catholic Church of Notre Dame, to visit Mary several times each week to hear her confession. In 1889, Mary again flew McDonald's lavish nest, this time with none other than Father Moysant. The couple lived in Paris for a dozen years before the priest entered a monastery and Mary returned to Chicago and opened a boarding house.

In disgust, McDonald vowed never to wed again. He doted upon his son and daughter and spent his waking hours with his criminal empire. On occasion he would visit the local burlesque houses and in one song and dance palace he spotted a luscious, buxom blonde cavorting on stage who looked familiar. She was Dora Feldman, a young woman who had been a playmate of his own children.

Dora was married to the ballplayer Sam Barclay but their marriage was shaky. McDonald reportedly called Barclay into his office one day and threw a wad of money at him.

"What's this?" asked the ballplayer.

"Money. What's it look like?"

"What's it for?"

"It's for a divorce, yours and Dora's."

"How much is there?"

"Thirty thousand dollars. Want to count it?"

Barclay picked up the money. "Your word is good with me, Big Mike. And the divorce is OK too."

At the insistence of the twenty-three-year-old Jewess, Big Mike renounced the Catholic faith, converted to Judaism, and obtained a divorce. He next married Dora whom the press described as "an 18-kilowatt blonde," and built for her a three-story limestone mansion on Drexel Boulevard. Dora was no more the loyal spouse than was Mary Noonan. Married to a man thirty-five years her senior, whom she coquettishly called Daddy, dabbling Dora, in kind, turned her attentions to a youth still in high school, a teenager named Webster Guerin who remained Mrs. McDonald's secret lover throughout the twelve years Mike and Dora stayed married. Guerin became a commercial artist and continued to see Dora almost every night. The youth's mother discovered the liaison and visited the vivacious Mrs. McDonald, imploring her to leave her son alone. Dora exploded and chased Mrs. Guerin from her home.

Guerin prospered with Dora's help. His lover provided him with funds to open his own commercial-artist offices, Suite 703 in the Omaha Building at the corner of Van Buren and LaSalle streets. In repayment, Guerin provided Dora, whose sexual appetite was insatiable, with copious coition. The youth, however, met another lady, one of his own age, and began a double sex life, seeing both Dora and the girl of his dreams. Guerin then ran away with his new lover, but Dora, wild with resentment and anger, followed and pressured the youth into returning with her to Chicago. Webster still met with his new lover, however, and when Dora discovered this fact, she marched to a showdown in Guerin's office on the morning of February 21, 1906.

An explosive argument could be heard out in the hall. Then came two loud pistol shots. Breaking down the door, office workers found Webster Guerin dead on the floor; he had been shot through the neck and heart. Kneeling beside the corpse, a smoking pistol still clutched in her small white hand, Dora McDonald wept great tears. "I loved him so much!" she wailed before being dragged off to police headquarters. Dora never flinched from her guilt in her conversations with authorities. Yes, she had shot and killed Webster Guerin. She did not hestitate to add that she had confronted the young man with his infidelities before ordering him at gunpoint to sit in a chair and face her. "I told him I knew where his heart was and I would not miss by an inch."

The news came as a sledgehammer blow to Big Mike. Having no suspicions about his ostensibly devoted wife, this second betrayal in his life overcame his sturdy constitution and, at age sixty-six, he took to his bed, wanting to die. Chicago's kingpin of crime lingered on for months. Dora, released on a $50,000 bond, prayed at his deathbed, and to make the scene all the more bizarre, Mike's first wife Mary arrived and prayed there too.

Big Mike was finally removed to a hospital where he again embraced the Catholic faith and announced to the world that Mary Noonon McDonald was his one and only wife in the sight of God. Paradoxically, he left Mary nothing in his will; most of his vast fortune was directed to his son and daughter, the executors of his estate given strict instructions that the unfaithful Mary was never to receive a penny. Big Mike's last thoughts were of Dora; he willed her one-third of his millions and took pains to establish a special $40,000 cash legal fund for her defense. With that, Big Mike McDonald, on August 9, 1906, turned his face to a drab hospital wall and perished. The *Police Gazette* gave him his best epitaph: "As Mike McDonald might have expressed it himself—a sucker has to die every minute to make room for the one that is born."

With Mike's millions bolstering her case, Dora proudly faced her jurors in 1908. Her lawyers were the finest McDonald's fortune could hire, the shrewd Asa Trude and James Hilton Lewis who had recently been elected a U.S.

Madam Ada Everleigh, the brains behind the bordello trust, and Minna Everleigh, who provided the wit and humor inside the Everleigh Club.

senator from Illinois. Dora's defense came down to a final dramatic witness-
stand appeal, a tear-blotched saga of being driven momentarily insane by a
young ungrateful rake who sneered at her love. The jury was out six and
one-half hours before reaching the verdict: not guilty. Big Mike McDonald's
power still held sway, even from the grave.

The Scarlet Sisters

What Mike McDonald scorned in his lucrative world of vice, prostitution,
left staggering fortunes to be scooped up by the opportunist. Chicago, from
its inception, patronized its trollops with enthusiasm during the nineteenth
century with literally hundreds of brothels, from the grubby to high swank,
operating around-the-clock. With the coming of the Civil War, thousands of
professional harlots invaded Chicago to service the divisions of soldiers
gathering for battle. Prostitution became, during that period and during the
half decade following the Great Chicago Fire of 1871, the most profitable
business in the underworld.

Hundreds of cheap cribs and assignation houses with quaintly misleading
names mushroomed in desperate areas—Shinbone Alley, Conley's Patch, the
Chicago Patch. But the professional man and the rich playboy could find

pleasure in more elegant surroundings such as The Mansion on Monroe Street run by Madam Lou Harper. Kate Anderson's Senate and the houses run by Annie Stafford, Rose Lovejoy, and Mollie Trussell attempted to glean the profits of the upper class but The Mansion remained *the* bordello until the arrival of Carrie Watson. Carrie worked briefly as an inmate of The Mansion before her solid man, Al Smith, a saloon-owner and gambler, backed her in her own establishment at 441 South Clark Street, an establishment once occupied by Annie Stewart. Carrie spent a small fortune on decorating and refurbishing her bordello and then opened her doors strictly to the carriage trade. Hers was one of the few bagnios not damaged by the Fire of 1871. Carrie held top honors in her scarlet field until almost the turn of the century when two sisters, both virgins in the trade, arrived to wow Chicago for a decade.

Lizzie Allen's brothel at 2131–3 S. Dearborn was in the hub of the Levee District—developed since the late 1880s as the boomingest red-light district in Chicago—which centered at about South 22nd and Dearborn streets. Madam Allen took great pains to compete with the likes of Carrie Watson and Lou Harper, pumping $125,000 of her hard-earned money into the three-story, fifty-room double mansion. Lizzie more than made her fortune from the rich patrons she sought. When she died in 1894, the operation went

H. G. Maratta's painting of the notorious Levee at night, 1898.

to Madam Effie Hankins. Then two charming, well-educated sisters, Minna and Ada Everleigh, appeared. Hearing that Effie wanted to try her luck in New York, the sisters bought up her lease and all fixtures. With this purchase, prostitution in Chicago soared into unimagined luxury and genteel legend.

The Everleigh sisters were born in Kentucky, Ada on February 15, 1876, and Minna on July 13, 1878. Both girls were taught the ways of refined young ladies while in their teens, attending a smart finishing school; their father, a wealthy lawyer, could well afford their education. Their real name was never actually determined, but Minna, who was the more aggressive and the leader of the pair, always signed her business and legal papers as Minna Lester, no doubt the true family name. Friends of the sisters were later informed by the super madams that they used the name Everleigh in honor of their departed grandmother, who signed her letters in the southern belle tradition: Everly Yours.

It was the ambition of their father that the sisters become actresses, and to that end he spent lavishly upon their elocution lessons. Ada and Minna married young, but both found their husbands (brothers whose names have been lost to posterity) intolerable brutes. They departed together and joined a Washington-based theatrical group, touring the country until the show was cancelled in Omaha, Nebraska, in 1898. The sisters had in savings and settlements from their dead father's estate more than $35,000, an astronomical sum in that era. They fielded about for an investment opportunity.

One of their actress friends had once remarked, "My mother would be angry if she knew I was on the stage. She thinks I'm in a den of iniquity." The joke sparked an idea. Why not open a fancy resort? Men, the vengeance-seeking sisters concluded, were all monsters anyway. Make them pay! There was plenty of trade available since the Trans-Mississippi Exposition was in progress in Omaha. The girls opened a luxurious bagnio, charging customers $10 a girl and $12 for a bottle of wine. When the Exposition crowds vanished, business dwindled; the local swains of Omaha refused to pay exorbitant prices for their pleasure. Ada and Minna closed up shop after hearing one cheap sport carp, "I'll buy a bottle of beer but I won't go upstairs."

They took their earnings, which had doubled their pot to $70,000, and traveled to New Orleans, then to New York, Washington, and Boston. None of the cities appealed to the Everleighs. Then they heard that Effie Hankins in Chicago wanted to retire.

Arriving in Chicago in the winter of 1899, the sisters quickly purchased the Hankins emporium for $55,000 ($20,000 down and $35,000 to be paid within six months). Redecorating the house from cellar to attic—along with firing most of Effie's girls and replacing them with those of more refined manners— the Everleighs put the southern accent on their club. White help was replaced by black maids and butlers. The cuisine was decidedly Southern. The prices were aimed at the moon. The Everleigh Club opened on February 1, 1900.

The Mannered Brothel

Before the doors were flung wide to the expected carriage trade, Minna Everleigh gathered her sylphs—now dressed in evening gowns, not the traditional corsets and garter belts—and delivered a speech that has gone down in the history of prostitution as a marvel of insight and business acumen.

"Be polite and patient and forget what you are here for," she told her startled girls. "Gentlemen are only gentlemen when properly introduced. We shall see that each girl is properly presented to each guest. No lining up for selection as in other houses. There shall be no cry, 'In the parlor, girls,' when visitors arrive. Be patient is all I ask. And remember that the Everleigh Club has no time for the rough element, the clerk on a holiday or a man without a checkbook.

"It's going to be difficult at first I know. It means, briefly, that your language will have to be ladylike and that you will forego the entreaties you have used in the past. You have the whole night before you and one $50 client is more desirable than five $10 ones. Less wear and tear. You will thank me for this advice in later years. Your youth and beauty are all you have. Preserve it. Stay respectable by all means.

"We know men better than you do. Don't rush them or roll them. We will permit no monkeyshines, no knockout drops, no robberies, no crimes of any description. We'll supply the clients; you amuse them in a way they've never been amused before. Give, but give interestingly and with mystery. I want you girls to be proud that you are in the Everleigh Club. That is all. Now spruce up and look your best."

Looking their best was not enough for the Everleigh girls. The sisters installed a huge library of morocco-bound books and insisted their beauteous courtesans become avid readers to improve their minds as well as their grammar. As the sisters prospered (the girls cost $100 for a few hours; the average take for a night was about $3,000), they also spent their brothel fortunes on the club itself. Everywhere luxury startled the high-paying customers; even millionaires were astonished at the lavish surroundings—thick imported carpets, enormous divans and easy chairs upholstered in silk damask, solid mahogany tables covered with slabs of marble, inlaid beds, gold spittoons, exquisite paintings, statues, tapestries.

Customers ate epicurean meals worthy of Babylon on solid-silver dinner service. They could dance to the strains of three complete orchestras playing in the twin mansions. The ballroom was enormous, and overhead twinkled crystal chandeliers. The dining rooms boasted hardwood floors inlaid with rare woods in mosaic patterns and walnut paneling on the walls. There was the so-called Pullman Buffet which served fifty guests around the clock, an elegant reproduction in mahogany of a section of a railroad dining car.

The ballroom in the Everleigh Club. (UPI)

Twelve sumptuous private parlors were also located on the first floors of the twin mansions: the Moorish, Copper, Gold, Silver, Blue, Rose, Green, Red, Oriental, Chinese, Japanese, and Egyptian rooms.

The entire brothel was festooned with rare plants, Irish linen, Spanish drawnwork, ornamental incense burners, and majestic fountains that regularly spewed forth jets of imported perfume. There were a half dozen pianos, all of them gilded, one sheathed in gold leaf at a cost of $15,000. Inside, the lulls of the orchestras and the piano players (restricted to light classics) were filled by canaries which sang and chirped, dozens of them in gold cages scattered everywhere in the club. So splendorous was the Everleigh Club that the *Chicago Tribune* was moved to awe, blurting, "No house of courtesans in the world was so richly furnished, so well advertised and so continuously patronized by men of wealth and slight morals."

And flock to the Everleigh pleasures the wealthy males of Chicago did, not all of them members of society's elite. On any given night, a regular who's who was present on the man floors watching the spectacular musicals the sisters presented for their clientele. One might see Clarence Clay, a safecracker who fancied himself a gentleman. Clay would slip away from the club for a few hours, crack a safe, and return to spend his stolen money on the Everleigh harlots. Reporters, critics, and social lions such as John W. "Bet-a-Million" Gates and his son Charlie or Courtney Burr could be seen at ringside during showtime.

The Everleigh Club's gilded music room. (UPI)

One eccentric, doddering millionaire went through a peculiar routine in the Music Room every time he visited the Everleigh Club. The ancient roué would sit beneath a baby spotlight as several girls brought him tall glasses of sarsaparilla mixed with a half-pint of vanilla ice cream. Gulping this down, the codger would croak, "Goody, goody," as the girls sipped their wine beneath arched eyebrows. Then his ritual, which had something to do with his snowy youth in the north country, would begin. As related by Charles Washburn in *Come Into My Parlor*, "He would order two buckets of chopped ice, demanding that the pieces be not over two inches square. The ice was promptly deposited in front of the big chair in which he was seated. Two girls, one for each foot, were requested to remove his shoes and stockings. During the undressing interlude one of the sylphs would gently play 'Jingle Bells' on the piano, while the other girls stood at attention, draped around the side of the room like chorus girls taking a bow after a fast-stepping routine.

"A maid would approach with jingle bells, which were placed in his left hand, and a male servant brought a miniature hair mattress, placing it conveniently on a tabouret to the right. [He] then plunged his bare tootsies into the buckets of ice, grasped the bells in his left hand, rattling them gleefully, and putting his right hand into a torn niche in the mattress, would shout: 'There's nothing to equal an old-fashioned sleigh ride!' "

Such bizarre displays were tolerated at a cost of about $3,000 a trip. Ada would shrug at the old gentleman's ritual and comment, "A nut, but how can you get angry with him?"

Then there was the son of a wealthy man who was learning his trade as a bank clerk. He became very tipsy one night after drinking down three bottles of wine. He weepily confessed to Minna that he was battling with the bank's vice-president. "I'm going to have one more bottle, you know, for a little courage, and then I'm going to that bastard's home and have it out with him."

"Why go to his home?" cooed Minna. "You've been leaning against him for half an hour."

When touring the U.S. in 1902, Prince Henry of Prussia, the Kaiser's brother, asked, when in Chicago, to see the Everleigh Club, so celebrated had it become in a period of two years. The party the sisters threw for the prince was unrivaled in bordello history. Minna Everleigh, who was obsessed with mythological revelry, put on a Dionysian orgy that caused the prince's monocle to pop into a champagne bucket.

Thirty of her courtesans were skimpily attired in fawnskins. Their long hair purposely disheveled, the nymphs danced about the main ballroom by flickering candlelight "as they worked themselves up to a state of mad excitement, swinging the tryrsus and clanging the cymbal." As a finale to the rites of old in which eating raw meat was mandatory, "servitors entered with large silver platters of uncooked sirloins" into which the thirty frenzied harlots sank their teeth with the vigor of cannibals. Then ensued a drinking bout with a girl dancing upon the main dining table. The girl tripped and her slipper flew into Prince Henry's lap, the story goes. He noticed that some champagne had been spilled into the shoe. Cavalierly, he lifted the slipper, toasted the gyrating trollop, and drank the bubbly from the shoe, commenting, as best interpretations have it, "The darling mustn't get her feet wet," and thus created a new tradition.

Wealthy men, like a certain notoriously lavish banker, thought nothing of spending thousands of dollars for a night's frolic with the accommodating sisters and their girls. Even the son of one of Chicago's mayors gave a huge fete in the Everleigh chambers. When the bill for $5,000 came, the son begged off, stating he did not have the cash on hand and had forgotten his checkbook. He signed an IOU and staggered drunkenly to his carriage. Upon awakening with an earth-rocking hangover, the politician's son remembered his debt but was skittish about redeeming the note in person. He called a friend and asked him to deliver the money to Minna and Ada. The friend arrived at the club that afternboon but the sisters merely shook their heads politely. "We have no knowledge of such an IOU." The friend returned to the mayor's son who himself nervously went to the club. The sisters smiled, walked him three floors upward to the attic to their hidden safe, and exchanged the note for the money. Such was the precaution the Everleighs took to protect the reputation of their clientele.

One of those who received the special, elegant brochure the sisters used in advertising their palace was Nathaniel Ford Moore, the twenty-six-year-old son of the railroad magnate James Hobart Moore. He visited the club on the night of January 8, 1910. He left the bagnio at dawn, quite drunk. He was found dead some hours later, murdered it was said, in a low brothel in the red-light district. In truth, Moore had died of heart disease. This, however, along with a mounting crusade to rid Chicago of the teeming Levee Disrict by reformers, helped to spur the end of the Everleigh era. The Moore incident recalled another death on November 22, 1905, that of Marshall Field, Jr., the thirty-seven-year-old son of Chicago's merchant prince.

Although every newsman and police officer in the city swore that Field had accidentally killed himself in his Prairie Avenue home while cleaning a weapon ("the accidental discharge of an automatic revolver which he had been testing in his dressing room [of all places]," according to the *Tribune*), rumors never died that Field had been murdered in a terrific battle inside the Everleigh Elysium. Some claimed that Minna herself had shot Field; others insisted that "Mr. Field had been pierced by a paper knife" wielded in anger by one of the sisters' most beautiful harlots over not being offered the permanent position of mistress. Arthur Meeker, a respected author and journalist in later years, who lived at 1815 Prairie Avenue (the Field home- stead was at 1905 Prairie), insisted that Field did not die at home. In his *Chicago, With Love*, Meeker stated, "There was, to go no further, young Field's mysterious end. My sister Mary and I were, it appears, almost the last persons to see him alive. We were playing in the yard in front of 1815 [Prairie] when he stopped to speak to our nurse before going off to get himself shot at the Everleigh Club—if it *was* the Everleigh Club? It's impossible to say now what happened; all we can be sure of is that the version the family gave out, and forced the papers to print—that the accident occurred while he was cleaning a gun at home in preparation for a hunting trip—had no truth in it. That, again, is something that couldn't be put over today; the power of the press would prevent it."

Though the charge was never substantiated, the rumor was more than enough to taint the Everleighs. The reformers, especially the fire and brim- stone Gipsy Smith, gathered their forces and the known brothels and hell- holes in the Levee began to close down one by one under police pressure. The Everleigh Club was never listed on a police blotter in Chicago from 1900 to its closing in 1911. The sisters paid more than $100,000 to Bathhouse John Couglin, alderman of the First Ward, via Big Jim Colosimo, crime boss of the district, for protection which they certainly received. It took a special order of Mayor Carter Harrison, under riotous pressure, to order the sisters to close shop on October 24, 1911.

The Everleighs didn't complain. They gave a last party that night and Minna told a reporter from the *Chicago American*, "You get everything in a lifetime. I'll walk out with a smile on my face. If the ship sinks, we're going down with a cheer and a good drink under our belts anyway." Ada and Minna walked out with considerably more than a smile, taking a cool $1 million in cash from their decade-long enterprise, not to mention priceless jewelry and furniture. Their girls had made great fortunes. Many of them had married millionaires and settled down into prestigious, respectable lives. (One was an exception—Belle Schreiber, who became one of the white sweethearts of heavyweight champion Jack Johnson. In 1912, Belle had caused Johnson to be indicted for white slavery after the federal government charged Johnson with transporting her from Pittsburgh to Chicago for immoral purposes—long after she had left the sisters' employ.)

Ada and Minna departed for New York where they lived quietly as spinsters, husbanding their fortune under assumed names. Minna died on September 16, 1948, and was buried near Roanoke, Virginia, close to her family's long-lost estate. Ada sold off most of her belongings and moved to Virginia, taking a cottage near her sister's grave where she lived in seclusion until her death on January 3, 1960, at the age of ninety-four. She was buried next to Minna. Inseparable in life, the sisters were united in death.

Before leaving Chicago, the sisters, glittering with diamonds, chatted briefly with scores of admirers at Union Station. They could recall only a few of the more than 600 courtesans who had worked for them during their eleven-year dynasty of super sin. "But we loved our butterflies, everyone of them," said Minna. "Where would we have been without them?"

"From bawd to worse," quipped Ada.

4

King Crime

As the newspaper war between Hearst and McCormick gave birth to Chicago's street gangs, the successful sin of the Everleigh sisters implanted the city's whoremasters as overlords of crime. Onetime street cleaner James "Big Jim" Colosimo was the first of these front-running skin-kings.

Born in Consenza, Italy, Colosimo migrated to Chicago with his father in 1887, working in the Levee as a bootblack and newsboy. Except for a few years of odd-jobbing, Big Jim never left the red-light district. While working as a street cleaner for the Sanitation Department, Colosimo ingratiated himself to the powerful political sachems of the area—John Joseph "Bathhouse John" Coughlin and the venal alderman Michael "Hinky-Dink" Kenna—by steering freshly arrived immigrants into the Democratic camp, paying for each vote (with Kenna's money) with a shiny half dollar.

On the side, the burly, six-foot, dark-mustachioed Colosimo (thought to be handsome by the belles of the Levee) had six whores on the string, all hooking for him at 50 percent profit. Such was Big Jim's success at vote-getting that Kenna and Coughlin made Colosimo a precinct captain. From this nonworking, paying position, Big Jim served as the bagman for Kenna and Coughlin, carrying the kickbacks from the red-light madams to the politicos. When making his whorehouse rounds in 1900, Big Jim met Victoria Moresco, an overweight madam who ran a bagnio on Amour Avenue. The amorous Victoria was smitten with Colosimo and proposed marriage, offering the handsome profits of her brothel as a dowery. The two wedded and Colosimo, by 1902, went into the prostitution business in a big way; he was soon the proprietor of several houses, including the swanky Saratoga Club and the Victoria, which Big Jim, as was his swarthy sentiment, named after his wife. Scores of cheap cribs belonged to his domain and from these the whoremaster took $1.20 from each $2.00 trick. Taking a cue from the early-day crime czar Roger Plant, Colosimo established saloons next to his houses and pro-

Chicago's first crime czar, Big Jim Colosimo, shown with his paramour, singer Dale Winter.

vided escape tunnels from bagnio to bar for customers avoiding police raids.

Nothing profitable in the world of crime escaped Big Jim's roving eye. He, along with Dago Mike Carrozzo, organized the city's street cleaners into a powerful union from which the overlords took half of the dues. Big Jim's labor racketeering proved him a pioneer in the field and he was soon moving into all manner of union scams. White slavery added to his profits. Colosimo organized a massive white-slavery ring with Maurice Van Bever in the early 1900s.

Naive girls from farms and small towns throughout the Midwest drifted into Chicago looking for work. They were seized on the street by Colosimo's goons, taken to special assignation houses where professional rapists prepared them for a life of prostitution, and then sold for $10 each to bordello keepers.

Crude and flashy, Big Jim Colosimo found himself a millionaire many times over by 1910. His response to wealth was to spend it as fast as possible, building enormous mansions for his father and himself and buying up hundreds of diamonds from every thief and crook in the Levee. Colosimo acquired diamonds as many men collect rare coins and books of limited editions. He covered his hulking form with snow-white linen and checkered suits. Everywhere he adorned himself with diamonds, a glittering diamond ring on every finger, diamond cuff links, diamond studs, diamond belt and suspender buckles, and a blinding diamond horseshoe affixed to his bulging vest. Moreover, Big Jim carried on his person at all times a large black velvet bag containing handfuls of diamonds. Most of his time not spent in counting his illegal profits was devoted to playing with his diamonds. He would sit at home or in the expensively furnished parlors of his brothels sipping wine and pouring diamonds from one hand to the other or making mounds of diamonds on a black cloth spread before him. But none of his enormous wealth altered his whoremaster personality. As historian Herbert Asbury pointed out, "His morals were those of the gutter and he was without honor or decency, but the police and politicians fawned upon him; to them went a sizeable portion of his unholy gains."

Much of Big Jim's fortune was pumped into his elegant nightclub Colosimo's Cafe which became Chicago's most popular nightspot, a two-room affair that fairly reeked of wealth—mahogany and glass bars, green velvet walls, sky blue ceilings, ornate paintings and tapestries, and a dance floor that was raised and lowered by a hydraulic lift. The cafe, located at 2126 S. Wabash, became the nest of the social and artistic elite. The great opera singers of the day (Big Jim was partial to Verdi and Puccini) from Amelita Galli-Curci to Enrico Caruso, could be seen dining in Big Jim's place, along with a who's who of politicians, journalists, and high society rankers of all stripes. Also jammed into the tables were the worst lot of criminals west of the Alleghenies, most of whom worked for Colosimo one way or another.

Regulars of the underworld included the new gambling kingpin Mont Tennes who had inherited Big Mike McDonald's mantle, murderers for hire Issy the Rat Buchalsky, Julius "Lovin' Putty" Annixter, and Vincenzo "Sunny Jim" Cosmano, who had once been in a Black Hand partnership with Colosimo until he took to extorting money from Big Jim himself. There were union thugs such as Mike Merlo and Joey D'Andrea, but those of Big Jim's own ilk, the whoremasters, received special treatment in the cafe—odious creatures such as Dennis "Duke" Cooney, Charlie Genker, and Mike de Pike Heitler. Certain tables were, of course, held in reserve for the powerhouse political bosses Coughlin and Kenna and for the mysterious Ike Bloom who could fix anything in City Hall for a price.

All was not well, however, since Big Jim's rise brought with it an army of gun-blasting enemies, chiefly the Mafia and a horde of ruthless Blackhanders who threatened to poison the food in his cafe, blow up his patrons, and more or less create havoc with his life if huge extortion money was not forthcoming. At first, Colosimo attempted to handle the Blackhanders alone. It is known that he met with three of them and killed all, two of them strangled with his own ham-hock hands. But such gruesome chores were not for a man of his prestige. Colosimo hired a sharp-shooting army of his own, handpicking each gun-toter and approving of the likes of Jim "Duffy the Goat"

A publicity still of the alluring Miss Winter who gave up her career for Big Jim. (UPI)

Franche; Mac Fitzpatrick (alias W. E. Frazier), imported from San Francisco; Joseph "Jew Kid" Grabiner; Chicken Harry Gullet; and Billy Leathers. Heading this motley crew was Johnny Torrio, a small-statured killer imported from the Five Points Gang in New York and a cousin of Colosimo's wife. Torrio's right-hand killer was his own cousin Roxy Vanilla (alias Vanneli).

At first Torrio's troop of killers merely protected Big Jim and his whorehouses. Then they were employed as strong-arm squads to round up teenage girls for Colosimo's white slavers. As they jack-rolled drunks in the Levee and ran killing in the streets, the First Ward police cooperated fully, smiled, turned away, and did nothing.

For a decade Colosimo's power held sway in the realm of Chicago crime but it was all undone when Beauty met the Beast in early 1920. Dale Winter, a nineteen-year-old singer with a cherubic face and curvacious body, was stranded in Chicago when the comic operetta in which she was appearing folded. She took a job in Colosimo's cafe but hated being called a cabaret singer. Miss Winter intended to quit the job when something better came along and, in her eyes, Big Jim was that opportunity.

Oddly, Dale Winter was a genuine talent, a highbred Ohio girl who had always led a respectable life. Her appearance in the cafe sparked interest on the part of visiting opera stars who gave her lessons at Big Jim's urging. Soon show business tycoons such as Morris Gest and Florenz Ziegfeld appeared at the cafe offering contracts. By then it was too late. Dale Winter had fallen in love with Colosimo and he with her.

Big Jim asked Victoria for a divorce in March of 1920. He gave her $50,000 in complete settlement for any marital claims. The aging madam bowed out with the unhappy comment, "I raised one husband for another woman and there is nothing in it."

Colosimo gave all his moments to Dale after their marriage in Crown Point, Indiana, ensconcing her in his lavish Vernon Avenue mansion. She would never again have to pit her lovely voice, Big Jim told his bride, against the clamor of his cafe. "You don't have to earn a living now," she recalled Big Jim saying. "You can rest and study, rest and sing, and rest and perform roles in the Auditorium. That was the thing we were silliest about—my being a great singer some day."

While Big Jim sponsored his wife's career, Torrio went about organizing Colosimo's spreading empire. His own cut from profits has been estimated as high as $1 million a year. The fact that he took all the chances (Torrio had murdered at least five Blackhanders while protecting Colosimo's interest) and did all the work, coupled with his cousin's mortifying divorce, no doubt convinced the dapper little crime lieutenant to get rid of Big Jim. The final straw that broke the camel's back fell when Colosimo refused to enter the mushrooming bootlegging business at the advent of Prohibition, content to remain with prostitution and labor racketeering. Torrio had vision enough to foresee the millions to be made with bootleg booze. He ordered Big Jim murdered. The man who performed the deed was on hand, imported from Brooklyn a year earlier by Torrio.

Big Jim received a call from the enterprising Torrio on the morning of May 11, 1920, less than a week after Colosimo and Dale had settled into their mansion. Torrio told the vice czar that a shipment of special whiskey would arrive at his cafe promptly at 4:00 P.M. The bootlegger would accept payment from no one but the big boss himself, Torrio explained to his employer. Big Jim sighed and agreed to be on hand. Dale wanted to go along but Colosimo told her no, it was a business appointment, something he had to handle personally. "We'll meet for dinner," boomed Big Jim, affixing his lucky diamond horseshoe to his vest.

Shortly before 4:00 P.M., Colosimo arrived outside his cafe in his chauffeur-driven limousine. He entered and went directly to his office in the rear of the south room, where he conferred with his secretary Frank Camilla. He then went over the day's extravagant menu with his head chef Antonio Caesarino. Suddenly, he stood up. "I'm expecting a visitor," Big Jim announced. "He's late." He strode through the south hall and into the lobby. Moments later Camilla and Caesarino heard two shots; both men rushed out to find Colosimo sprawled on the tile floor of the cafe's vestibule, his shirt ripped open, Big Jim's massive hairy chest bared, his diamonds torn away from shirt and

Big Jim's successor, Al "Scarface" Capone.

suit, his wallet (allegedly containing as much as a half-million in big bills) gone from the inside of his suit coat.

There was a bullet in Big Jim's head which had entered behind the right ear. The second shot had smashed into a wall. The killer had obviously hidden in a phone booth and fired through the glass wall of the booth. There was nothing either the secretary or chef could do for their boss; Big Jim Colosimo was quite dead. Some feet in front of his lifeless body, the doors to his elegant cafe still moved slightly in the wake of his murderer's hasty departure. Camilla jumped to the street to see a heavyset man scurrying down the block, shirtless, panting, his heavy cheeks puffed up, scars on the left side of the face livid. He was Al Capone.

Scarface and Company

New York terrorist and gunman Frankie Yale (Uale) was first identified as Big Jim's killer, but underworld figures in the know could have pointed to Capone, known in his obscure Chicago days as Scarface Al Brown. (Capone claimed to have received the scars while fighting with the Seventy-seventh Division in France; in reality, Capone had been slashed in an argument with a Brooklyn barber.) Although Capone had fast become Torrio's right arm as well as the manager of his worst dive, the Four Deuces at 2222 South Wabash, he was just another thug among thousands in Chicago. As late as August 1922, Capone was mistakenly known to the press as Alfred Caponi after being involved in a traffic accident.

When Capone went to work for Torrio in 1919, he made $75 a week for beating up madams reluctant to hand over their shares of the operation, strong-arming recalcitrant union leaders, and guarding Johnny Papa, as Capone liked to call his benefactor. Within a year, Scarface was making $2,000 a week, and after dispatching Big Jim, Capone's share of Colosimo's empire amounted to 25 percent, with Torrio getting the balance. Beyond the enormous profit that fell to Torrio and Capone was the incredible political influence that went with Big Jim's domain. This was proved sacrosanct beyond doubt when Capone walked into a saloon owned by Heinie Jacobs on South Wabash on the night of May 8, 1924, and approached an independent bootlegger named Ragtime Joe Howard. The drunken Howard had been bragging about his ability to handle weapons and during the course of his diatribe, had slapped about a harmless bookkeeper who worked for the Torrio-Capone combine, Jake "Greasy Thumb" Guzik, the mob's mathematical wizard. Guzik had taken no action other than to complain minutes later to Scarface.

Capone stood nose to nose staring at Howard, bellowing, "Why did you kick Jake around?" He grabbed Howard's lapels and shook him. "Why?"

"Aww," Howard pushed away, "go back to your girls, you dago pimp!"

Capone drew a pistol, put it to Howard's head and, as the bootlegger smiled, thinking it all a joke, pulled the trigger six times. Howard fell to the floor dead as witnesses in the saloon gasped. Capone then quietly ambled from the place.

In the morning, Chicago's papers ran photos of Capone labeling him a killer. Scarface was nowhere to be found. A month later, he strolled into a police station and, with a puzzled look on his broad face, inquired, "I hear the police have been looking for me? What for?"

He was arrested but denied everything. He not only claimed to have been out of town the day Howard was killed, but that he was a "respectable businessman. I'm a secondhand furniture dealer. I'm no gangster. I don't know this fellow Torrio, and I have nothing to do with the Four Deuces. Anyway, you had better do your talking to my lawyer."

During his month-long absence, Capone's men, of course, had reached the witnesses to the shooting. By the time Scarface came to trial, none of them could remember anything about the incident, not even Ragtime Joe Howard's name. Capone went free.

It would remain so all through the 1920s, Capone methodically eliminating rival gangsters—Dion O'Bannion, Earl Hymie Weiss, the O'Donnell brothers, the seven human targets of George "Bugs" Moran's mob on St. Valentine's Day in 1929—without ever being tried for murder. In each instance, Capone

The curious gather in 1924 outside of Dion O'Bannion's flower shop at 738 N. State Street, only minutes after the gangster had been shot by Capone killers.

Police removing O'Bannion's body; his murder was the beginning of the bootleg war between the Italians on the South Side and the Irish on the North.

wailed long and loud to the press that the man he had just ordered murdered by his 500-man army of killers had been his "dear friend," and sent along an expensive floral wreath to his funeral. The ribbon attached always read From Al.

By 1930, Al Capone, then only thirty-one years old, was the supreme overlord of crime in Chicago, his personal income estimated to be about $50 million a year. He owned a luxurious Palm Island, Florida, home; vast real estate in Chicago; and the finest pair of armored McFariand cars available, at a cost of $12,500 each. Whenever a malcontent gangster on his payroll or a reform-minded politicial or law officer attempted change, Capone snapped his thick fingers and death eliminated the annoyance. No one in the city seemed to care; it was mob business. Then Capone snapped his fingers in the direction of a corrupt journalist, but the heat that was generated by that killing caused Scarface's pot to boil over, bringing so much pressure to bear against the crime king that IRS agents moved in to stamp out Scarface where all others had only flinched and cringed.

"I Fix the Price of Beer"

Alfred "Jake" Lingle was nobody's fool. At times, to his fellow reporters at the *Chicago Tribune*, Lingle, a $65-a-week legman, seemed juvenile and naive. Yet he was as crafty and cunning a man as ever stepped into a pressroom. Lingle was an oddity, a reporter who never wrote a word for his newspaper throughout his eighteen years with the *Tribune* where he had begun his journalistic chores as a copyboy at age twenty. He was strictly a street reporter, an expert on crime and hoodlums, high and low, calling in his stories from his pavement beats. A high percentage of his stories turned into scoops over the other papers and created a phenomenal record, one which accorded him the sobriquet Chicago's gangologist. The gangs of Chicago, however, knew the ubiquitous Mr. Lingle as something else, as the city's unofficial chief of police, a title Lingle once wryly conferred upon himself.

Born on the West Side of Chicago to parents of little money, Jake's first job was that of a stock boy and messenger for a surgical supply firm. In 1910 he befriended a cop named William Russell who walked a beat in his neighborhood. Through Russell, Lingle became street-wise about the world of the gambler, the thug, the thief, the crooked politician. He loved visiting the local precinct headquarters and listening for hours to the cop stories of Chicago crime, becoming a walking encyclopedia of who was who in the underworld. For this reason, Lingle joined the *Tribune* in 1912. His sources of information seemed inexplicable and extraordinary, but, unknown to his fellow scribes, all of Lingle's inside tips stemmed from one man—William Russell—who remained the reporter's best friend. The reporter and the cop went everywhere together—golfing, the racetrack, the theater. When Lingle married his

Alfred "Jake" Lingle, *Tribune* reporter who went over to the gangs.

childhood sweetheart, Helen Sullivan, in 1922, the couple joined Russell and his wife regularly each week in social meetings. Russell rose through the ranks from beat cop to sergeant, then lieutenant and captain, until he was the police commissioner. Jake's star rose with Russell.

Jake became the cock-of-the-walk in newsdom. He strolled the city's streets waving hello to hundreds who beamed at his sad-eyed face, chomping on cigars that cost him $3.50 per and talking from the side of his mouth in bantering phrases. Seeming always at ease, nothing escaped Lingle's drooping eyes. He knew his underworld better than any man in the city as one experience amply displayed. One evening he and his wife climbed aboard a crowded streetcar on their way home from the theater. Jostled by the crowd, Lingle's hand suddenly darted to his hip pocket where he carried his wallet. It was missing. He scanned the crowd and spotted a face familiar to his memory but said nothing. He escorted his wife home and then raced to a bar and poolroom on West Madison Street where he knew the pickpocket would be.

"Hand it over," demanded Lingle.

"What's up Jake?" smiled the lift artist.

"You know what's up. My stash. You got. Fork over."

The pickpocket handed Lingle his wallet and the reporter walked from the saloon without another murmur.

Such was Jake's acumen in the world of crime that he could rattle off a definitive physical description of almost any active hoodlum in town, giving his Bertillon measurements. He could recount statistics and labyrinthine details of almost any noteworthy crime, from bank robbery to confidence game. For all his worldly activities, Jake Lingle was, paradoxically, a family man, doting upon his two children and wife. They lacked for little, especially after Jake met Al Capone in 1920 when Lingle was following up Colosimo's killing. That he found out Capone was Big Jim's killer is uncertain. Yet Lingle became a friend and confidant of Capone's from that period on, a juncture in the reporter's life that suddenly found him opulent enough to take a luxury trip to Cuba, returning with a treasure trove of gifts.

The reporter's manner of living altered drastically. He was suddenly wealthy, buying a West Side home; buying an $18,000-a-year summer place in Long Beach, Indiana; and renting an expensive suite of rooms at the Stevens Hotel. His appearance changed from drab to resplendant which made him stand out in the city room when talking to other *Tribune* reporters. His friend Fred Pasley remembered: "He was conspicuous amongst them by reason of his sartorial ensemble; always newly tailored, manicured, barbered, shined, and polished. He was vaguely embarrassed about the newness of his clothes; never entirely at ease in them; he seemed to be expecting his

Detective checking the baggage of New York gangsters in Union Station, looking for the murder weapon that killed Lingle.

Jake Lingle's funeral in 1930 drew thousands; weeks later Lingle was revealed to be a Capone ally.

shoes to squeak. He was Midwest—Chicago. No cane for him; no spats; no yellow chamois or doeskin gloves; none of that rose in the buttonhole stuff his friend Capone affected. And he never packed a heater, as do many Chicago police reporters. He was abstemious. A glass of beer was his limit."

Bootleg beer was much on Jake Lingle's mind. One night when traveling home in a taxi with another reporter, Lingle startled his companion with the remark, "You know, I fix the price of beer in this town." His cryptic comment would later be traced to his liaisons with Russell and Capone.

When reporters inquired about Jake's newly acquired wealth, the legman shrugged and stated that his father had left him property worth $50,000 upon his death. (Following Lingle's death, it was learned that his father's estate amounted to no more than $500, but Jake had at least one bank account bulging with $65,000, an incredible sum for a $65-a-week legman to accumulate.)

Lingle was, of course, power-brokering his influence. He sold his friendship with Police Commissioner Russell to cops on the beat, high-ranking politicians, and chiefly, Capone. One example was a recorded phone conversation between Lingle and former state senator, John J. "Boss" McLaughlin, who opened a gambling place in Capone territory at 606 W. Madison. When the police raided the den, McLaughlin phoned Lingle at the Stevens

Hotel asking him to intercede for him with his friends Russell and State's Attorney John A. Swanson. McLaughlin insisted that Swanson had given him approval to open the gaming resort.

'I don't believe it," said Lingle," but if it is true, you get Swanson to write a letter to Russell notifying him it is all right for you to run."

"Do you think Swanson's crazy?" screamed McLaughlin. "He wouldn't write such a letter."

"Well," replied Jake, his voice with an edge on it, as if he was peeved at not being consulted about the operation before it opened, "Russell can't let you run then. That's final." Jake Lingle's word was final for many a man.

During the last six months of his life, Jake took to living exclusively at the Stevens Hotel, seldom seeing his family. His room, number 2706, was off limits to one and all; his name was in the private register. He kept late hours, sleeping until 10:00 or 11:00 A.M. before checking in at the *Tribune*, a not unorthodox routine for a reporter working for a morning paper. The house detective at the Stevens blatantly confirmed the power Lingle wielded when a reporter tracked him down following Lingle's death.

"Sure he was on the private register," piped the house cop. "How could he get any sleep if he wasn't? His telephone would be going all night. He would get in around two or three and wanted rest."

"Who would be telephoning him at that hour?" asked a reporter.

The house detective was amazed at such a question. "Why policemen calling up to have Jake get them transferred or promoted, or politicians wanting the fix put in for somebody. Jake could do it. He had a lot of power. I've known him twenty years. He was up there among the big boys and had a lot of responsibilities. A big man like that needs rest."

The "big man" would soon get all the rest he would ever need. In addition to the stomach ulcer he had developed by 1930, Lingle was in deep trouble over his one vice—gambling. The horses were his nemesis and he could be seen almost every day at the racetrack where his average would be $1,000. Moreover, he not only lost consistently at the track but was in debt to his friend Al Capone to the tune of a reported $100,000, all lost in Capone's gaming rooms. Scarface, Lingle reasoned, by virtue of his power contacts, would sit still for the debt. They were friends. Why, Capone had even given him a diamond-studded belt buckle, a token of esteem Scarface reserved only for his close associates. Lingle had often been a guest at Capone's Palm Island, Florida, estate where he frolicked in the enormous pool; sipped tall, cool drinks; and enjoyed the various pleasures of crime's Xanadu. Lingle had access to Capone night or day, calling him with instructions on how to fix anything from bootlegging to murder. Ironically, the trouble was that Lingle, to pay off his debt to Capone, attempted to extort money from members of Scarface's own gang, as well as the gang of George "Bugs" Moran, employing his influence with Commissioner Russell to barter liquor and gambling licenses. When Capone learned of Lingle's double-cross, he exploded, then snapped his fingers.

The late morning of June 9, 1930, was bright with sunshine and blue sky. Toward noon, Jake Lingle, attired in a $300 suit, walked onto Michigan Avenue from the Stevens Hotel. His chauffeur drove up in his limousine. Lingle looked around at the fair day and told his driver he would walk the mile and a half north to the Tribune Tower.

Once at the Tower, Lingle had a small conference with the city editor about another impending gang war. He then left and walked southward to the Illinois Central Railroad station at Michigan Avenue and Randolph Street, heading for Homewood and the track. Lingle checked his watch, and seeing he had an hour to kill, he sauntered to the Sherman House for a sandwich and a cup of coffee. As he entered the coffee shop, Lingle spotted police Sergeant Tom Alcock. As Alcock passed him, Lingle said in a low voice, "I'm being tailed." He did not explain the cryptic remark. Minutes later, Lingle walked along Randolph Street and stopped in front of the public library where he purchased the *Daily Racing Form* at a newsstand. He looked up to see a man smiling at him from a roadster parked at curbside.

"Play Hy Schneider in the third, Jake," tipped the driver of the car.

Lingle waved a grateful acknowledgment. "I've got him." Peering again at the paper, Lingle began to descend into the tunnel that led to the train station. As he walked along, his smoking cigar clenched between his teeth, Lingle paid no attention to the thin, blonde-haired young priest moving through the dense crowds after him. Just as Jake reached the east ramp of the tunnel, the priest caught up to him, pulled an automatic from beneath his black suit coat, and shot once, the bullet smashing through Lingle's brain. The legman fell while dozens of witnesses to the crime screamed alarm. The young priest raced through the crowds and began climbing the stairs three at a time.

"Isn't anyone going to stop him?" yelled one woman. Several men gave pursuit but the priest outdistanced them and vanished on Michigan Avenue.

Ironically, Dr. Joseph Springer, an old friend of Lingle's, was only a few feet away from Jake when he was shot. He rushed forward, felt Lingle's pulse, and pronounced him dead.

At the news of Lingle's murder, the press exploded in righteous wrath. Thinking its legman to be consistent with the ethics of its profession, the all-powerful *Tribune* thundered, "The meaning of the murder is plain. It was committed in reprisal and in an attempt at intimidation. Mr. Lingle was a police reporter and an exceptionally well-informed one. His personal friendships included the highest police officials and the contacts of his work made him familiar to most of the big and little fellows of gangland. What made him valuable to his newspaper marked him as dangerous to the killers. . . . [Murder] has become the accepted course of crime in its natural stride, but to the list of Colosimo, O'Bannion, the Gennas, Murphy, Weiss, Lombardo,

Lingle's close friend and pipeline, Police Commissioner William F. Russell, who resigned in disgrace after it was learned that he had pulled strings for Lingle and Capone. (Wide World)

Esposito, the seven who were killed in the St. Valentine's Day massacre, the name is added of a man whose business was to expose the work of the killers.

"The *Tribune* accepts this challenge. It is war. There will be casualties, but that is to be expected, it being war. . . . Justice will make a fight of it or will abdicate."

The *Tribune* then offered a $25,000 reward for the killer of Jake Lingle. Feeling the entire corps of newsmen in Chicago jeopardized by gangsters, other papers followed suit; the *Herald-Examiner* offered $25,000, the *Evening Post*, $5,000, with assorted civic groups adding another $725—a total of $55,725.

Then Lingle's dark and sordid past began to ooze into the light, dragged there by reporters from out-of-town newspapers, especially the *St. Louis Post-Dispatch*. When Colonel Robert R. McCormick, head of the *Tribune*, learned that the *St. Louis Post-Dispatch* was about to expose Lingle's background, he became incensed, exploding every which way in shock and embarrassment. Learning the details of Jake's unholy alliances with Commissioner Russell (who resigned his position a short time later) and Capone, the Colonel ordered the *Tribune* to do an about-face. It did, admitting in print that "Alfred Lingle now takes on a different character, one in which he was unknown to the management of the *Tribune* when he was alive. . . . The reasonable appearance against Lingle now is that he was accepted in the world of politics and crime for something undreamed of in his office and that he used this in undertakings which made him money and brought him to his death."

The hunt for Lingle's killer still went on. A St. Louis gangster and professional killer for hire, Leo Vincent Brothers, who had often been used by Capone and other gang chieftains as an imported killer to deal with VIP victims, was indicted for the murder. Four witnesses said they saw Brothers, while dressed as a priest (he specialized in disguises), shoot Lingle. He was convicted on April 2, 1931, after the jury argued for twenty-seven hours. His sentence reflected the influence of Scarface in Chicago's courts. Brothers received fourteen years in prison (he was paroled eight years later). Not once did Brothers admit his guilt, never mentioning Capone. He swaggered off to prison while mouthing the cliche, "I can do that [sentence] standing on my head."

Capone lamented the death of Jake Lingle in print. Harry T. Brundige of the *St. Louis Star* traveled to Palm Island to interview the crime king as he sat by his pool, a servant fanning him.

"I thought I'd ask you who killed Jake Lingle?" Brundige boldly put forth.

Scarface smiled. "Why ask me? The Chicago police know who killed him."

"Was Jake your friend?"

"Yes, up to the very day he died."

"Did you have a row with him?"

"Absolutely not."

"It is said you fell out with him because he failed to split profits from handbooks."

"Bunk, bunk. The handbook racket hasn't been really organized in Chicago for more than two years."

"How many rackets was Lingle engaged in?"

Capone shrugged, as if to say he didn't know.

"What was the matter with Lingle?"

"The horse races," laughed Capone.

"How many other Lingles are there in Chicago?" probed Brundige.

"In the newspaper racket? Phooey—don't ask."

"How many reporters do you have on your payroll?"

"Plenty—listen, Harry. I like your face. Let me give you a hot top: lay off Chicago and the money-hungry reporters. You're right and because you're right, you're wrong. You can't buck it, not even with the backing of your newspaper, because it's too big a proposition. No one will ever realize just how big it is, so lay off. They'll make a monkey out of you before you get through—"

"I'm going to quote you as saying that."

"If you do, I'll deny it."

Capone's successor, Frank "The Enforcer" Nitti.

Denials or not, the *Star* and the *Chicago Tribune* printed the whole of Brundige's interview. It was the kind of explosive talk that aroused not only the reading public but Chicago civic leaders in high places; one group, the Secret Committee of Six, paid for an extensive investigation of Capone's financial affairs. Information from this probe proved the downfall of Scarface Al Capone when it was turned over to agents of the Internal Revenue Service. Capone was tried and convicted of tax evasion in 1931, given an eleven-year sentence, and fined $80,000. He went into Leavenworth the following year and then was sent on to Alcatraz. He was released in 1939 because the advanced stages of syphilis—a condition brought about by nonstop whoring in his palmy Chicago days—had seized his mind. He died a raving lunatic nine years later at Palm Island.

A doctor, Kenneth Phillips, asked the Capone family for the gang czar's body. He wanted to perform an autopsy "to make possible the study of the brain for medical history."

He was refused.

The Inheritors

The organization established by Capone during the 1920s not only prospered following Capone's departure but, employing the considerable "re-

Capone henchman and new crime kingpin, Paul "The Waiter" Ricca (wearing hat) in a police line-up with Louis "Little New York" Campagna. (UPI)

spectable fronts" Capone had established and linking up with the Luciano-Lansky-Lepke syndicate in New York, overlorded all interstate illegal operations across the country. With the demise of Prohibition, the Chicago syndicate, with Frank "The Enforcer" Nitti at its head—Capone's personal selection while he was in prison—branched out into labor racketeering; gambling, from casinos to slot machines in candy stores; high-level extortion of big business; sleek prostitution which introduced the call girl and the B-girl; the blossoming numbers (policy) game; the control of customer services such as linen supply, dry cleaning, and vending machines; and the growing distribution of narcotics. The millions rolled in.

Sharing the spoils with Nitti were many an erstwhile Capone henchman, including Al's brother Ralph "Bottles" Capone; Scarface's cousins, Charles and Rocco Fischetti, with Charlie heading up the mob's gambling enterprises; Paul "The Waiter" Ricca and Louis "Little New York" Campagna in charge of captive unions, both of whom were later involved in shaking down motion-picture moguls for millions (with George Browne and Willie Bioff and receiving long prison sentences); Jake Guzik, the mob accountant and treasurer; onetime Capone bodyguards Phil D'Andrea and Tony "Joe Batters" Accardo; Sam "Mooney" Giancana, who headed the outfit's strong-arm squad; Murray "The Camel" Humphries; Hymie "Loud-Mouth" Levin, the mob's collector; Eddie Vogel, who was in charge of the slot-machine racket; and Sam "Golf Bag" Hunt, who carried a sawed-off shotgun in a golf bag when he was a gunner for Capone during the Jazz Age and then took over the handbooks of the great South Side.

Following Capone's original plan, the new Chicago syndicate drove all the non-Italian gangs out of business in the 1930s until the Mafia was in complete control of the city's illegal activities, an ironbound cartel that controls Chicago to this day. To enforce its policies, the syndicate relied less on Capone's methods of the "Chicago typewriter" (the submachine gun) and more on leg-breaking persuasion. Yet an occasional murder was still necessary.

In the case of Edward J. O'Hare (whose son Butch would later become a war ace and national hero in the Pacific), the mob felt an execution mandatory. Eddie O'Hare had not only proved to be a reluctant partner in the syndicate's racetrack rackets but one of the chief informers who helped to put away Al Capone.

O'Hare began as a bootlegger in St. Louis during the early 1920s. Moving to Chicago, O'Hare, by then a lawyer, represented many of Capone's interests, specifically overseeing the crime czar's horse- and dog-racing tracks, a position that soon made him a millionaire. As the chief operator of the old Hawthorne Dog Track, wholly financed by Scarface, O'Hare took vast interest and profits from Capone's broad-based gambling empire. He later became the first president of Sportsman's Park.

In 1930, when Secret Service agents for the IRS began assembling evidence against Capone to put him in prison for tax evasion, Agent Frank J. Wilson contacted some of the high-ranking Capone lieutenants, one of whom was Eddie O'Hare. In Wilson's own words: "On the inside of the gang I had one of the best undercover men I have ever known: Eddie O'Hare."

On one occasion, when Wilson was close to clinching the case against Capone, O'Hare rendezvoused with him, telling the agent, "You've got to move out of the Sheridan Plaza, Frank. The big fellow is going to get you. They know where you keep your automobile and what time you get in at night and what time you leave in the morning. The big fellow has brought in four killers from New York to do the job. You've got to get out of there this afternoon."

Wilson got out. O'Hare kept meeting him secretly. Just before Capone's trial was to convene, O'Hare told Wilson that the Capone mob, in particular Phil D'Andrea (who was later arrested in the courtroom for carrying a concealed weapon and sent to prison for six months for contempt), had obtained a list of the jurists in the case; they would either be bribed or killed, Wilson was told. Armed with the list O'Hare handed over, Wilson went to the presiding judge, James H. Wilkerson, who, in turn, switched complete juries with another judge hearing a different case only moments before Capone's

Edward J. O'Hare, President of Sportsman's Racetrack, who worked undercover to help send Al Capone to prison.

The mob's revenge—Edward O'Hare was shot gangland style while driving his car in 1939 because he had worked against Scarface.

Police photos of Joey "Mourning Doves" Aiuppa, present-day syndicate sachem.

trial commenced. It was one of the many shrewd moves by the government that helped to convict Capone.

(Oddly enough, Wilson had also tried to contact Jake Lingle in 1930 to help him with his case against Capone. Wilson later claimed that he went personally to Lingle's supreme boss, Colonel Robert R. McCormick, head of the *Tribune*, and quoted the *Tribune* chief as saying, "I'll get word to Lingle to go all the way with you," a strange remark for McCormick to make in that it obviously proved McCormick knew of Lingle's strong tie to Capone despite his bellowing editorials to the contrary, editorials which portrayed Lingle as a newspaper martyr when he was killed the next day.)

While Capone languished in Alcatraz he heard from newly arrived Chicago gangsters that his good friend O'Hare had double-crossed him. He swore revenge. The Chicago syndicate received word from Capone that he wanted O'Hare dead before he was released. Even though Nitti and company paid lip service only to Capone as the boss, a gesture to the founder of modern-day organized crime was obligatory.

Eleven days before Capone was released, on the afternoon of November 8, 1939, Eddie O'Hare wrapped up his final meeting at Sportsman's Park in Stickney, a southern suburb of Chicago, fixing the controversial racing dates before he departed for Florida where he was to operate another track. Several of Nitti's lieutenants were at the meeting and, suspicious of their remarks and actions, O'Hare suddenly dashed from his office to his coupe roadster and drove at breakneck speeds into the South Side of Chicago. O'Hare must have known he was marked for death. Nitti and Guzik, to defray the mob's own expenses in financing Capone's retirement in Florida, had been shaking down wealthy Chicago businessmen with syndicate links to provide a "welcome home" treasure chest for Scarface. They demanded $50,000 from millionaire O'Hare. He refused.

When only a few minutes from the track, O'Hare drew a .32 caliber automatic pistol and placed it on the seat next to him. He continued to drive wildly through the streets, looking every which way for following cars. (O'Hare had for several weeks lived in fear of being murdered; he had kept a secret North Side apartment and had given up his automobiles to ride the elevated trains in anonymity.)

Suddenly, three long, black cars converged upon O'Hare's speeding coupe. Shotguns stuck from the windows and all seemed to fire simultaneously. More than 200 shotgun pellets plus several bullets from the automobiles struck the racetrack operator. He was long dead when his car careened over the curb and smashed into an electric light pole. It was one more shot for Big Al. (That the syndicate never forgets was demonstrated with devastation on February 12, 1952, when slammers for the Chicago mob traveled to San Mateo, California, crept into the garage of Tom Keen, age sixty-four, and attached a twenty-two-inch strand of copper wire to the ignition of Keen's car. The other end of the wire led to twelve sticks of dynamite. Keen, a manufacturer of tote boards—electrical computers that flash betting odds at dog tracks—stepped into his car, started the engine, and blew himself to pieces. His offense to the Chicago mob? He had once been a partner of Edward J. O'Hare's.)

Gangland killings, however, were kept to a minimum by the syndicate, which acquired polish and poise. Nitti, despite his enforcer image, was gun-shy and preferred to use his considerable intelligence in overseeing mob operations. After serving one sentence for tax evasion and facing another term on the same charge in 1944, Nitti sent a bullet into his head.

From that time on, Paul "The Waiter" Ricca and Tony "Joe Batters" Accardo jointly ran the Chicago syndicate and all was peaceful until, in the early 1950s, Sam "Momo" Giancana, as fierce a thug as his murderous lieutenants Sam DeStefano and Milwaukee Phil Alderisio, fought for the top-dog spot in an outbreak of gang slaughter that brought back the shudders of the Capone era. (Capone's heyday, from 1926 to 1931, saw 418 gangland slayings. Accardo and Ricca bowed out and Giancana took over in 1957, holding the reigns until 1966 when pressures from federal government officials drove him from syndicate leadership.)

Giancana, never more than an oafish, loudmouth, kill-crazy goon, did not give up easily. His was in the old style of Capone and Moran. He shot off his mouth, cozied it up in Las Vegas with singer Phyllis McGuire of the McGuire Sisters, and generally operated with the discretion of an orangutan.

To save the Chicago syndicate embarrassment, he was ordered to keep on the move, and he did, vacationing for long spells in Mexico and Texas. In June 1975, while frying sausages in his fortresslike brick home in Oak Park, Illinois, Giancana, still threatening to take back the leadership of the Chicago mob, was visited by his executioners. That he was passive toward his fate was indicated by his being seated when shot, seven .22 caliber bullets sent crashing into his face and neck at close range.

Today, Chicago's heir apparent to the throne of Mafiadom is a short, overweight ex-prizefighter and Capone gunner, Joey Aiuppa (alias Joey O'Brien), who began as the gambling boss of Cicero and quietly slipped into the syndicate hierarchy. Accardo remains the supreme boss of bosses, an old, ailing man of seventy-one; Aiuppa is only two years his junior. Both men live in luxurious suburban (well-guarded) homes, Accardo in River Forest, Aiuppa in Oak Brook. Beneath Aiuppa's general managership, Jackie "The Lackey" Cerone is the chief underboss; Gus Alex, chief counsel. Vincent Solano runs the North Side; Al Pilotto, the South Side.

The mid-1970s once again saw a rash of killings of mobmen by mobmen, but it was nothing more than cleaning Giancana's cluttered house. There is peace at the top at this writing. Aiuppa, whose criminal career trails back to 1935, has a record for bribery, gambling, and intent to kill. But the main mobman sees himself as a rather pleasant fellow. Peering through his horn-rimmed glasses, he once told a law officer, "The laws are flexible. They are made to bend, just like a big tree standing there—it's made to flex. I agree with this. I am a servant of the law and a citizen."

5

Ball Park Afternoons

That the great American folk monster Al Capone would rather sit through a warm afternoon in a Chicago ball park than run his nefarious rackets there was never any doubt. Scarface could be seen throughout the 1920s in his box seat with his son next to him and an army of bodyguards surrounding him, all suited in the hot day to shield the guns. Capone was no exception. Chicago has, almost from its birth, been a dogged baseball town.

The city was only an infant when Abner Doubleday gave the present form to the game in 1839. By the mid-1850s several teams were playing, the most prominent by 1858 being the Unions and the Excelsiors. On July 21 of that year a convention was held by the Chicago Base Ball Club wherein local teams adopted the rules governing the Association and Congress of Base Ball Clubs of New York. By 1870, Chicago's first big-time manager Tom Foley was putting together the city's professional club the White Stockings' raiding eastern teams and paying as much as $2,500 a season to experienced ball players, twice the salary of the day.

Foley's piracy was legitimate since no players' contracts existed in that era, but his act did incur the wrath of eastern sportswriters who thought Chicago uppity in its bid to establish an organized baseball team. Money, however, talked and such early day stars as super catcher William H. Carver moved to Chicago from the Haymakers of Troy, New York, and second baseman Jimmy Wood deserted another eastern club for the White Stockings. Fred Treacy came from Brooklyn; Charlie Hodes also joined the team. With such stars, Foley couldn't help but have a magnificent organization, one that brought about, in 1870, the biggest score on record for organized teams when the White Stockings beat the Memphis (Tennessee) Bluff Club by a whopping 157–1.

Pitcher Albert G. Spalding—he won 47 games in 1876—one of the chief founders of Chicago baseball.

The Saintly Entrepreneurs

The first king of Chicago sports was Albert Goodwin Spalding, a farm boy who joined the Forest City club of Rockford as a pitcher at age fifteen in 1865. On this club, Spalding set many a record with his straight-arm fastball. (His fellow players were equally innovative; Bob Addy of the same club, not the much-vaunted Mike Kelly of the White Stockings as many believe, was the first, in 1866, to slide into a base.) Few of Spalding's pitching feats survive on paper but Henry Chadwick, baseball editor of the New York *Clipper*, named him the greatest pitcher up to 1908, which was saying a lot since in that era the titans of the mound were Amos Rusie, Cy Young, William Arthur Cummings, and Christy Mathewson.

Spalding saw baseball as a peerless American sport. "It is a man-maker," he was the independent nature of most early-day ball players who insisted upon unrestricted freedom, a philosophy he archly maintained all his days. "Have a was the independent nature of most early day ball players who insisted upon restricted freedom, a philosophy he archly maintained all his days. "Have a lemonade stand with your own name on it, if you have to," he once advised his son Keith, "but never work for anybody else." One habit displayed by Spalding during his boyhood in Byron, Illinois, succinctly portrays his nature.

As a tot Spalding, his mother later related, "had a habit of eating the inside of the bread and hiding the crusts under his plate."

But there was no hiding of Spalding's blazing talent on the mound. While playing for Boston in 1875, Spalding won 56 games and lost 5. Through his efforts, Boston won its fourth consecutive pennant in the National Association, the powerhouse organization that controlled all the big money teams of the East.

One man thought it was too much power, especially since Chicago was excluded from the association. William A. Hulbert, a dynamic Chicago businessman and one of the backers of the White Stockings, was out to break the eastern monopoly of the best players in baseball, all for the greater glory of his hometown. ("I'd rather be a lamp post in Chicago," Hulbert once thundered, "than a millionaire in any other city.") The businessman was convinced that he needed one other man to realize his dreams—Al Spalding.

When Spalding visited Chicago with his Boston club in 1875, Hulburt met privately with the pitcher. He told the hurling ace that Chicago was being shut out of big-league baseball and that he wouldn't stand for such spurious treatment. Wooed the financier, "Spalding, you've no business playing in Boston; you're a western boy, and you belong right here. If you'll come to Chicago, I'll accept the presidency of the club [the White Stockings] and we'll give those eastern fellows a fight for their lives."

The pitcher agreed. Not only would he join the White Stockings, but he would bring along three other Boston stars—Ross Barnes, Cal McVey, and Jim "Deacon" White—all powerhouse sluggers. With the coming of Spalding to the White Stockings as pitcher and manager, the National League was born. Spalding set an amazing pace for the Stockings, pitching 60 out of the season's 66 games and also hurling the first shutout on record in 1876, following this feat a few games later with another shutout, both against Louisville. (George Washington Bradley of St. Louis had, earlier that year on July 15, pitched the first no-hitter against Hartford.) He is credited with winning the championship for the Stockings that year. Spalding, Barnes, White, and McVey (known as the Big Four) were labeled traitors to the Boston team, unscrupulous opportunists who would sell out their loyalty for a buck. When Spalding first appeared in a Chicago uniform in Boston to play his former teammates, small boys who had once worshipped him dogged his footsteps hooting, "Your White Stockings will get soiled!"

Far from presenting a soiled image, Spalding and Hulbert became the shining towers of the game, considered by most as the men who saved baseball. Hulbert, as the newly elected president of the National League, ran headlong into the game's first gambling scandal.

Driven from New York by Bible-toting reformers, scores of gamblers muscled their ways into the embryonic baseball clubs, ordering teams to lose whatever games they chose. The Mutuals and Athletics, in 1876, were riddled with fixed games controlled by gamblers. When the teams failed to finish their schedules, Hulbert expelled them from competition. The following year proved even more disastrous. Considered to be the strongest team of 1877, Louisville inexplicably began to drop its offense and dump games. In a blatant series of errors, Louisville lost seven straight games at the close of the season, throwing the championship to Boston. Found guilty of game-fixing were outfielder George Hall, third baseman Al Nichols, and pitcher Jim Devlin. All were expelled from the sport by Hulbert. Devlin, who had thrown away his career for a paltry $100 payoff, was one of the era's great pitchers and a longtime friend of William A. Hulbert.

Devlin was broken spiritually, as well as financially. In midwinter of that year, he walked penniless all the way from Louisville to Chicago to plead with Hulbert for a second chance. White Stockings manager Spalding was seated at his desk when the forlorn pitcher arrived without an overcoat. "His dust-covered garments," remembered Spalding, "were threadbare and seedy. His shoes were worn through with much tramping, while the red flesh showing in places indicated that if stockings were present they afforded not much protection to the feet." The pitcher staggered past Spalding in the outer office, his eyes fixed on Hulbert seated at his desk in the inner office. Moving to the big man, Devlin dropped on his knees before Hulbert, his body quivering with emotion.

Spalding watched as Devlin began to beg forgiveness: "His lips gave utterance to such a plea for mercy as might have come from one condemned to the gallows." He knelt in abject humiliation, tears running down his cheeks. Hulbert too was in tears as he beheld his friend.

"I beg of you, Mr. Hulbert," Jim Devlin pleaded, "remove the stigma from my name. It's not for me, but for my wife and child." The pitcher confessed throwing the games and asked for mercy. Hulbert's large body was shivering with emotion. Then his hand dipped into his pocket. He withdrew a $50 bill and pressed it into Devlin's palm. "That's what I think of you personally," the president of the National League said softly. Then his voice rose in anger, "But, damn you, Devlin, you are dishonest! You have sold a game, and I can't trust you! Now go, and let me never see your face again. Your act will not be condoned as long as I live."

Spalding and Hulbert, along with their erstwhile adviser Abraham Gilbert Mills, revolutionized baseball. Between them they organized the three leagues—the National League, the American Association, and the Northwestern League. They forced the gamblers out of the game. Spalding and Hulbert spent weeks writing a constitution and bylaws for the National League, a document that has lasted almost intact to this day. Spalding wrote new rules for the playing field in his *Spalding's Official Baseball Guide*— outlawing outs on the first bounce and announcing that all putouts, fair or foul, had to be caught on the fly to count.

Abraham Gilbert Mills, who helped Spalding and William Hulbert revolutionize baseball. (UPI)

In April 1882, the noble-minded Hulbert died. Spalding became president of the White Stockings and A. G. Mills ascended, by unanimous vote, to the position of president of the League. At age thirty-two, Spalding was Chicago's leading sports magnate and the most influential figure in the game across the country. He was not without business sense. When the National League adopted new uniforms with caps with colors designating each team, Spalding's sports firm got the contract.

Spalding's first sports emporium at 118 Randolph Street was a thriving enterprise from its inception. Not only did Spalding own the monopoly on baseball uniforms for all the organized teams, but he issued the first regulation balls and bats used by professional players. (So that no one would ever forget, the pitcher turned tycoon had his portrait and signature on all the balls, bats, and gloves produced by his firm.)

As the Thomas Edison of his field, Spalding's inventiveness never lagged. He instituted box seats in the parks for the first time, was the first to insist on spring training, and developed minor-league teams or farm clubs from which the major-league teams drew their future talent. He authored innumerable rule books for baseball, as well as other sports, even croquet.

With his brother J. W. Spalding, the youthful tycoon advertised his firm as "the largest sporting goods house in America," and he soon proved it, opening up branch stores in fourteen cities, including New York, Portland, and

Denver. Spalding did not hide the fact that he intended to not only head a vast sporting-goods empire but that he would tolerate no competition. "Everything is possible to him who dares" became his motto as his firm expanded into every known sport.

By the 1890s, Spalding was fielding about the world in search of more sporting goods to monopolize; in 1890 he brought back from England the first golf clubs and balls ever put on sale in this country. He branched out, gobbling up firms such as the American Bicycle Company. His magnificent sporting goods exhibit won the Grand Prix at the Paris World's Exposition in 1900. By then, the prestigious *Sporting Life* had taken to labeling Spalding the Big Mogul.

Emperor of the game or not, Spalding's fertile mind kept churning out new devices and new methods for his beloved baseball, such as the catcher's mask he designed to protect the most injured man in the game, or the invention of the baseball glove to soften hand-bruising catches, or the new and simpler system of scoring games advanced in his scorebook.

He could also be a rigid marinet when he thought himself in the right. He never pardoned a contract jumper and with A. G. Mills was the first to establish the exclusive-players' contracts with a reserve rule that allowed owners to sell their players at will (which prompted the press and part of the public to accuse Spalding of acting like a slaver). When Spalding insisted that his players sign a total abstinence pledge for the duration of the season, there was shouting and fuming in the clubhouse. The pledge, if broken, meant stiff fines and perhaps expulsion. Mike "King" Kelly, considered the greatest ball player of the time, was an incorrigible drinker and led the White Stockings in scoffing at Spalding's crusade against Demon Rum. It was perhaps for this reason that Spalding sold Kelly to Boston for $10,000, an enormous amount for that era.

In 1900, Spalding left Chicago for the sunny climes of southern California, building with his fortune an imposing residence called Point Loma on the Yerba Santa cliffs overlooking San Diego Bay. He was married for a second time to one Mrs. Elizabeth Churchill Mayer, onetime secretary to Mrs. Katherine Tingley (who was the successor to Madame Blavatsky and head of the Theosophist colony in San Diego). He halfheartedly ran for a seat in the U.S. Senate and won by popular vote but was repudiated by the California legislature.

By 1915, just before he was sixty-five, Spalding had been reduced to a physical wreck. The once sturdy ball player had, in the words of one of his biographers Arthur Bartlett, "aged rapidly, his hair turning completely white, and the firm flesh shrinking away from the tall form that it had so long rounded out." He suffered two strokes and, on September 9, died in bed.

Praised the *New York Times*: "Al Spalding was the Father of Baseball as it is played professionally." *Sporting Life* applauded the man with a most fitting

Adrian "Cap" Anson in the uniform of the Chicago White Stockings (later White Sox). (UPI)

epitaph: "In the annals of baseball, he will always stand out as the game's chief constructive genius, and its greatest missionary, as long as the noble game shall endure, and that, we hope and believe, will be forever."

A few months before Spalding hung up his worldly uniform, a burly, young pitcher for the Boston Red Sox, Spalding's old alma mater, hit his first major-league home run. His name was George Herman "Babe" Ruth.

Young Powerhouse

When Al Spalding moved to Chicago to play for the White Stockings, he urged Hulbert to sign up Adrian Constantine Anson who was with the Philadelphia Athletics. Anson, a tall, large-boned man who had been born in a log cabin near Marshalltown, Iowa, on April 17, 1851, was a great slugger who had attended the University of Iowa before switching in 1869 to the University of Notre Dame where he organized that institution's first baseball team. Anson had been getting $1,800 a season in Philadelphia. Hulbert offered him $2,000 and Anson agreed, signing a contract. Then Philadelphia offered him $2,500. The slugger balked at the Chicago move.

"You can't afford to break your contract," Spalding told Anson. The reluctant ball player agreed but offered $1,000 to Hulbert for his release, the first such offer ever made by a player. Hulbert refused the deal but confided to Spalding that he should allow Anson an honorable way out. "You have his contract," Spalding said in his usual stoic manner. "He'll play for Chicago."

When spring training began in Chicago in early 1876, Anson did arrive but he looked like anything but a baseball player when he strolled onto the field wearing a Prince Albert coat and striped trousers. Anson stood about for several minutes while all tried to ignore him. Finally, he felt the baseball itch and shouted to Spalding who was on the mound, "Toss me one, Al."

"What? With those togs on? Not any!"

Anson shuffled his feet in embarrassment for a moment, then shed his coat and ran out onto the field. Spalding threw him the ball.

"Now, Anse," chided the great pitcher, "come tomorrow in uniform."

Cap Anson, so named after becoming the captain and player-manager of the team when Spalding retired, would be in uniform for the next twenty-three years, known to the country as the greatest hitter and player-manager of the nineteenth century. The records he set with the old Chicago White Stockings were nothing less than astounding, even when compared with the superstars of today. Anson hit .300 in twenty seasons, won four National League batting championships, won five pennants as a Chicago manager and was the winningest manager in the White Stockings (later the Cubs) history. In addition, Anson was to play a record twenty-seven seasons and the first to make 3,000 safe hits.

A tough but fair manager, Cap refused to nod in the direction of the front office. Spalding appeared on the field one day and was critical of Anson's strategy. The Irish in Anson boiled over; he swore so loudly at Spalding that the boy wonder of baseball turned beet red. Then Anson's outrage compelled him to charge toward Spalding who spun on his heels and was literally chased off the field.

Anson's eye for talent was sharp. He picked up a rookie pitcher named John G. Clarkson who had been throwing for the Lumberjacks of Saginaw, Michigan. When the Lumberjacks collapsed, Anson bought Clarkson for the White Stockings; the price was a one-way railway ticket and a box lunch. Clarkson would later be considered by many as one of baseball's greatest pitchers. Upon visiting his home town of Marshalltown, Iowa, Cap, spotted a youngster running a race at a firemen's carnival. He hired him for the club, the fellow being Billy Sunday who would later become the leading ripsnorting evangelist of the 1920s. Sunday was a good player but a weak hitter. He might take a beer or two with the boys in the off-hours but never touched liquor and avoided the all-night revels. Sunday was lightning fast and was considered a demon base stealer. While sitting in a barroom in 1891 with Mike "King" Kelly, Sunday heard the hymns of an outdoor revival meeting waft inside. Billy followed the music to conversion and revivalism, but he never forgot his days with the Chicago club.

Sunday was fond of telling his rapt throngs decades later of one afternoon in 1886 when Chicago and Detroit were in a desperate championship battle.

Another White Stockings star, Billy Sunday, who would become the greatest evangelist of the 1920s.

"The last half of the ninth inning was being played," Billy would intone to his flock. "Two men were out and Detroit, with Charley Bennett at bat, had one man on second and another on third. He had two strikes on him and three balls called, when he fell on a ball with terrific force. It started for the clubhouse. Benches had been placed in the field for spectators and as I saw the ball sailing through my section of the air I realized that it was going over the crowd and I called, 'Get out of the way.' The crowd opened and as I ran and leaped those benches I said one of the swiftest prayers that was ever offered. It was 'Lord, if You ever helped a mortal man, help me get that ball.'

"I went over the benches as though wings were carrying me up. I threw out my hand while in the air and the ball struck and stuck. The game was ours—I am sure the Lord helped me catch that ball."

By the 1890s, Anson was still at first base. Although he batted .300 at age forty-five, sportswriters were beginning to razz him, calling him Pop Anson or Old Man Anson. Cap took the jibes quietly, as was his quiet nature, but the needle apparently began to nettle him for one day he showed up in his club's dressing room where he opened a bundle containing a snow white wig and a false set of long white whiskers.

"For Pete's sake," said fellow player Fred Pfeffer, staring at the wig and whiskers, "what's that for?"

"Never mind," replied Anson. "Wait and see."

Anson took the field wearing the wig and whiskers. As reported in *Baseball in Old Chicago*: "The crowd was struck dumb. With the long white locks and whiskers floating about his shoulders, Anson played the entire game with his usual effortless skill, and thus turned the guns of ridicule upon his detractors."

Baseball immortal in Chicago that he was, Anson's career ended in 1898 when he fell out with Spalding and the new president of the club James A. Hart. Spalding tried to get Anson, who was a minor stockholder in the club, to resign. He would not. In desperation, Spalding sent Anson a document which appeared to be an option to buy the club for $150,000, an amount Spalding knew Anson did not possess. The great Cap ended his association with the White Stockings. He drifted off into other fields, becoming a chief of umpires and running for and being elected in 1905 to the City Clerk of Chicago post for two years. He then entered vaudeville with his two daughters, Dorothy and Adele.

Ring Lardner and George M. Cohan wrote a monologue for the trio with music to back up their finale when Cap would appear in his old Chicago uniform holding a silver bat given to him by Notre Dame alumni. The daughters would sing, "We're going to take you to the game, / Where dear old daddy won his fame," while tossing dozens of papier-mâché baseballs into the audience. Taking his famous stance, Cap Anson would then hit the balls thrown at him by the audience. In Baltimore, songwriter Jack Norworth came to Anson and asked him to introduce a new ditty he had composed. Anson and his daughters were the first to happily render "Take Me Out to the Ball Game" to the nation.

Anson was as unimpressed with dignitaries as he was with money. He could have been a millionaire many times over. (He was once offered a franchise as well as a managership by the infant American League. Anson's reply was typical: "I would not insult my twenty-two year record by affiliating myself with minor-league ball.") A private audience was arranged for Anson and his daughters with President Warren G. Harding by D. C. Clark Griffith, the owner of the Washington Senators. Mrs. Dorothy Anson Dodge remembered how, "at the last minute, papa decided his new suit needed pressing. The theater was very close to our hotel, so he hurried over to the theater to have the job done. He hadn't returned by the time the chauffeur arrived to drive us to the White House. I hurried over to the theater and there he was, stretched out asleep in his long underwear and derby. I guess he wasn't as thrilled as we were about meeting the president."

Content to spend the rest of his days quietly in Chicago, Anson opened a billiard hall. He died on April 14, 1922. He had a special epitaph in mind for his tombstone, one that went unused: Here lies a man that batted .300.

"Slide, Kelly, Slide!"

More was everything with the White Stockings and there was plenty more beyond Anson, Sunday, and George Washington Bradley (who invented, they say, the curveball). During the team's heyday, Chicago boasted a bevy of unbeatable players: the "stone-wall infield" was composed of Tom Burns at third base, Ed Williamson at shortstop, Fred Pfeffer at second base, and Anson at first base. They ate grounders as one gobbled egg salad and could spear the most vicious line drives as if catching tennis balls. In the outfield, the sluggers George Gore and Abner Dalrymple waited for anything that got beyond the "stone wall," with Billy Sunday, the fastest man in baseball, covering more ground than anyone on the team. The two top pitchers of the team were John Clarkson, whose fast overhand delivery and perplexing drop took its dizzy toil of batting opponents, and the fast-pumping John McCormick, one of the best and most tireless hurlers of the nineteenth century.

But behind the plate, as catcher, was the real draw of the team, the most colorful, ebullient, and cagey player of the time, Michael J. "King" Kelly of legend and song. Kelly, who also doubled as an outfielder, had played two seasons for Cincinnati before Spalding and Hulbert brought him to Chicago in 1880. There was none like him; even Babe Ruth in the next century never approached the national popularity generated by this titan of the diamond, the very man who inspired "Casey at the Bat."

Tall and dark, this handsome, rakish Irishman charmed the entire baseball world in that soft Victorian age with his wit, humor, and great performance. Writer George Creel said of him: "When he swaggered out on the field, his cap at an angle, the crowds searched their souls for new bellows."

The most resounding of cheers, now American folklore, was "Slide, Kelly, Slide!" Though he didn't invent the slide, he was its supreme master. His headlong dives into bases thrilled the throngs and baffled the opponents. The venerable Connie Mack watched Kelly with agony taking his bases against his beloved Athletics. Mack called Kelly the Ty Cobb of his day, admitting that the King had "all of Ty's stuff—the fadeaway, fall-away, hook slides, and a few so distinctly his own that others could not copy them."

King Kelly the show-off was also King Kelly the innovator, a brainy ball player who brought new techniques to the game in his usual unpredictable manner. Lee Allen, in *The National League Story*, credits the King as "the inventor of the hit-and-run play, now an established part of baseball offense and a maneuver that is taken for granted." And his bat was mighty. In 1886, when the Stockings took their second pennant, Kelly led the league with an average of .388. Poet and writer Eugene Field paid homage to Kelly's stroke at the plate by coining a new word to describe his batting. Said Field, others might buffet, knock, swipe, bunt, or pound, but "the only Mike'" *swat*, an Anglo-Saxon word signifying sweat. "Swat on," said Field in his popular column, "most admirable paragon, swat on!"

Brainstorming on the field often found Kelly "inventing" his way out of tight spots, using tricks and outright hoaxes, for the most part, that confused and infuriated opponents. The resourceful, delightfully dishonest King was languishing in the outfield during one game with Boston, a game that went into extra innings. In the top of the twelfth Chicago pushed ahead by one run. But at the bottom of the twelfth, with two outs, Boston managed to fill the bases. It was very dark—these were the days when no park had lights—and Cap Anson could just barely see Kelly and the other outfielders from his first-base perch. Boston put up one of its most powerful sluggers and the batsman slammed a ball, long and deep, in Kelly's direction.

The King knew that the umpire (there was then only one on the field, at home base) could not see the ball from his position any better than he could. Kelly backpedaled in a studied manner, as if taking a sharp fix on the ball as it descended in the darkness. He posed, waited a moment, then leaped into the air with a wild yell of joy, pantomiming a catch. Laughing in victory, Kelly then raced toward the clubhouse as if the game were over, while the umpire, utterly hoodwinked, yelled, "Out!"

Kelly's most outrageous stunt came at the bottom of the ninth in a game with Detroit. The score was 2–2. Kelly came to bat and belted a single. Ed Williamson was then sent to first on balls. Both men then made a mad dash, each stealing a base, but as Kelly dove into third base, he let out a screech of pain and begged for time.

Williamson trotted from second base to check his teammate. "Ed, boyo," moaned Kelly, "it's me arm. Faith, I think it's out of joint. Pull it out for me, will you." As Williamson leaned forward to yank on the King's arm, Kelly whispered, "Say, Ed, as soon as Weidman [the Detroit pitcher] raises his arm, I'm gonna make a break for home. They'll play for me, sure, and forget about you, but when I'm close I'll straddle me legs and you slide under."

A minute later, King Kelly was sprinting for home plate; the Detroit pitcher was so dumbfounded he forgot momentarily to throw the ball. Williamson was right behind Kelly, admitting years later that he cut third base by fifteen feet. Just as the catcher got the ball, Kelly stopped abruptly and spread his legs, while Williamson slid beneath them in a dusty roar, touching the plate without being tagged by the flabbergasted catcher.

When Silver Flint took up the catching chores, Kelly would take to the outfield where he proved to be a master at snaring fly balls, although he did have his off days, particularly after his prodigious appetite for whiskey the night before caused him to be "bowled up," as Cap Anson so quaintly put it. On those occasions, Kelly would sometimes miss a fly ball, but by very little. He would than crack his face into a comical leer and shout to a disapproving Anson, "By Gad, Cap, I made it hit me glove anyhow!"

Kelly's drinking was never in moderation. He loved to party, and off the field, he could be seen in almost any of the better Chicago nightspots, his luxuriant handlebar mustache waxed at the ends, his high hat at a dapper angle, his ascot tie spliced by a diamond stickpin, his patent-leather shoes gleaming beneath the candlelight, every inch the Beau Brummell of his day. Mike's capacity for liquor was unequaled. He could drink several bottles of whiskey until three in the morning and play a superb game of baseball the following day. Said Cap Anson of his superstar, "The man never lived who could drink King Kelly under the table."

Teetotaling Spalding found it impossible to live with Kelly, especially when the affable, popular King suggested a party to his fellow players, who idolized him as much as the fans did and who drank with him until the wee hours, thinking that to be a great ball player was to be exactly like Kelly. Spalding took his star aside one day and cautioned him about Demon Rum and the poor example he was setting for his impressionable teammates.

"What are you running here?" Mike grinned, treating the warning as a joke. "A Sunday school or a baseball club?"

Spalding first thought of suspending the King, but he knew how that move would not only demoralize the team but affect the attendance, which of course meant a loss of great profits. The shrewd Spalding went to his friend William Pinkerton and had the sleuth assign a detective to shadow Kelly and his carousing teammates. The detective dogged the King and six other players for a few nights as they roamed up and down Clark Street and in and out of the most notorious red-light resorts in the Levee District as they nibbled upon the tenderloin. The next day, Spalding called the seven men together and read the detective's detailed report of their adventures to them. All were expectantly shamefaced—all but the King.

"I have to offer only one amendment," he said through a laugh. "In that place where the detective reports me as taking a lemonade at 3:00 A.M., he's off. It was straight whiskey; I never drank a lemonade at that hour in me life."

A few days later the Chicago club lost to Boston; Kelly gave a wry explanation for the defeat to a reporter from the *Herald*: "Too much temperance!" He became extremely paranoid about being shadowed by detectives, believing that Spalding was having the entire team watched around the clock. A week or so later, when about to board a train for Detroit with his team, the King spotted a tall stranger all dressed in green on the platform. As the train began to pull out, Kelly leaped back on the platform, raced up to the innocent fan and shouted "Another Pinkerton, eh? Well, put this in your report!" With that Kelly punched the startled gawker flat, raced after the train, and jumped aboard at the last moment to the cheers of his fellow players.

Spalding had had enough of the King and, in 1887, he sold Kelly to Boston for the then astronomical sum of $10,000, making sure that Kelly got a contract for $5,000 a season, a staggering amount, twice that of the highest paid player at the time. The King took it all good-naturedly and spent like a drunk on a spree.

Cap Anson saw him off on the Boston train, then turned to reporters and said, "The King has but one enemy, that one being himself. Money slips through his fingers as water slips through the meshes of a fisherman's net."

Kelly opened the window of his compartment, smiling, and whooped, "I heard that, Cap! Mike Kelly will never go broke!" Then to his friends, the beaming reporters: "Oh, I'm a beaut—you can bank on that! A regular ten thousand dollar beauty! I come high but they have to have me!"

That year Kelly returned with the Boston club and as he stepped out on to the field at the old Congress Street grounds, a band struck up and the Chicago club taunted their old teammate with the following ditty:

Michael Kelly came to town,
To sing a little chanson,
He said, "I've come with Boston beans
to do up Baby Anson."

"Oh, I come high but Yankee land
With its bright shekels bought me,
And though I didn't like to go,
Ten thousand dollars caught me."

Kelly's response was a wide grin, a bow, and vengeance. That afternoon, the King slammed out a triple and two singles. But there was more to Michael Kelly than selling his ability to the early-day baseball moguls. In 1980 a host of the best players in the National League and the American Association quit en masse and formed what they termed the Brotherhood League, putting up their own eight-club circuit. Leading the revolt was Michael King Kelly. The move spelled ruin for the overlords of the leagues and Spalding attempted to go after the most popular and outstanding figure of the Brotherhood— Kelly—by simply offering a bribe of $10,000.

They met in Chicago. Kelly was full of woes. "What's the matter?" Spalding encouraged, playing the indulgent parent.

"Everything's the matter," the King said in a low voice. "Everybody's disgusted—clubs all losing money. We made a damn foolish blunder when we went into it."

At that point, Spalding placed a check made out to Kelly in the amount of $10,000 on the table before him. He also offered him a three-year contract with Boston, as had been agreed upon by the management of that team. "I'm authorized to let you fill in the amount of salary yourself," tantalized Spalding.

"What does this mean?" the King blanched. "Does it mean that I'm to join the League? Quit the Brotherhood? Go back on the boys?"

"That's just what it means. It means that you go to Boston tonight."

Kelly wanted an hour and a half to think about it. He walked through the familiar streets of Chicago and returned to Spalding at the appointed time.

'Have you decided what you're going to do?" Spalding asked Kelly.

"Yes," the King said without hesitating. "I've decided not to accept."

Charles Comiskey, the iron-willed president of the Chicago White Sox.

"What? You don't want the $10,000?"

"Aw, I want the $10,000 bad enough, but I've thought the matter all over and I can't go back on the boys."

Kelly played in the major leagues until 1893 when his drinking finally dissipated his game. He died in Boston of pneumonia on November 8, 1894, after catching cold during an open-boat ride from New York to Boston; King Kelly had given a destitute passenger his coat to wear on the trip.

Comiskey the Obstinate

King Kelly's devotion to the rebellious Brotherhood League was mirrored by a powerful first baseman named Charles Albert Comiskey, a tough Chicago-born-and-bred baseball fanatic who began his career on the sandlots of the city. He first played ball in Dubuque, Iowa, then went on to the St. Louis Browns where he led that team to four pennant championships and two world championships in the 1880s. It was the large, big-boned Comiskey (whose enormous nose caused him to be dubbed The Old Roman) who led the players revolt in 1890 for which he was banished from Chicago by the powerful National League moguls who refused to hire him when the Brotherhood collapsed. He vowed not only to return but to own his own club.

Bancroft B. "Ban" Johnson, one-time sports writer, who helped Comisky establish the American League. (UPI)

Big Ed Walsh, who pitched for the White Sox from 1904 to 1916.

After managing stints in Cincinnati and St. Paul, Commy, as his friends called him, marched back to Chicago with empire on his mind.

With the organization of the White Sox, Comiskey, borrowing to the hilt, built a magnificent ball park for $1 million at 35th and Wentworth streets, proclaiming to all the world that "Chicago is the greatest of all baseball cities." The Sox, which would rise to greatness, fall in utter shame, and then bounce back and forth in and out of the money up to the present, have always had the most staunchly loyal fans in the history of the game. Boasted Comiskey: "A winner in New York is apt to wear out the turnstiles but the average crowd is not up to the standard with a loser. At home here, my team has played to 12,000 and 15,000 on a weekday with the club in the second division. That is the test of loyalty."

Nothing existed in Comiskey's world except baseball and his White Sox. When offered the mayoralty once, the baseball tycoon heaved his great frame in laughter and chortled, "I already have one game, and that's enough for me." Comiskey devoted all his waking moments to baseball, inventing a score of helpful new rules and methods such as the advanced coach-boxes at first and third bases and a double umpiring system.

He was a born maverick and with his good friend onetime sportswriter Bancroft B. "Ban" Johnson he helped to establish the American League in complete defiance of Spalding and his fellow moguls. Comiskey, like his earlier day counterparts in the National League, along with other American League owners, raided other teams and wound up with most of the best players available. His sacrifice while leading the Brotherhood revolt a decade earlier helped him achieve that end.

Ban Johnson and Comiskey, while their friendship bloomed, played innumerable practical jokes on each other, particularly while on their hunting and fishing expeditions. They also had the habit of sending each other their prize trophies from various hunts. This backfired on Commy when he shipped his greatest catch of one season, an enormous bass, to Johnson. It was delayed in delivery and by the time Johnson received the fish its stench was overwhelming. The baseball czar of the American League took the gesture as an insult and it was the beginning of the long-lasting feud between Ban and Commy.

Soon a millionaire after establishing his White Sox on Chicago's South Side, Comiskey displayed his generosity by often donating 10 percent of the gate receipts to the Red Cross and other worthy charities. He allowed the public almost free use of his famous ball park. When someone criticized the fact that hordes of Sox fans were ruining the grass (which never did grow beyond a brown stubble in the park) by trampling it in their free picnics and carnivals, Comiskey only shrugged and replied, "The fans built the park, didn't they?"

Reporters were gods to Comiskey and he lavished his profits upon the freeloading sports scribes of the era, providing them with feasts before and

Baseball manager John J. McGraw, shown as a player for the Baltimore Orioles, forced Comisky's hand on the race issue in baseball.

after his home games, as well as on the road, and paying for a private Pullman car for their free and exclusive comfortable travel. Naturally, he received the same kind of lavish attention in the sports columns of the city's papers.

Where Comiskey would not stint on the press or his public, he proved to be niggardly tyrant with his ballplayers. When the press gorged itself at Commy's expense, his players had to be content with a three-dollar food allowance while on the road. This proved not only insulting but inequitable since the Sox, in the days of Shoeless Joe Jackson, were the best team in either league yet received a dollar less a day for food than the worst squads in either league. His players were notoriously underpaid, almost all of the star performers receiving about half what the worst rookies on other teams got. To Comiskey, ballplayers were his private chattels to be used as he saw fit.

Of the host of players who battled for Comiskey none were more inventive than the two pitchers Elmer Stricklett and Ed "Iron Man" Walsh who joined the Sox a few years after the team's birth. Stricklett appeared at spring training in 1904 and he startled his fellow teammates by hurling a ball that could not be hit. As G. W. Axelson related in *Commy*: "He handed up a ball in practice that took twists and turns in approaching the plate that were against all the laws of gravity. Everybody took a swing at it. Most of them missed it, sometimes by a foot or more."

Billy Sullivan, who was catching, discovered the ball was slippery and wet. Disgusted, Sullivan approached Stricklett and dropped the dripping sphere into his glove. "What the hell's the idea?"

Stricklett shrugged. "Oh, that's just my way of pitching."

"What do you call it?"

"Don't know. I suppose *spitball* explains it as well as anything."

Spitball it was and Ed Walsh studied Stricklett's methods. The Iron Man soon became the master of the spitball, combining a drop and a curve, both in and out. From 1904 until 1913, when Walsh was released because of a sore arm, he became a titan on the mound with the spitball pitching in 415 games for the Sox.

Comiskey encouraged any new methods that won ball games but he was part of the clique that kept Negro athletes out of the major leagues. John McGraw, when managing the Baltimore team in 1901, yanked Comiskey's hand on the race issue but in a way that was anything but direct. McGraw had discovered a powerful player in one Charlie Grant, a Negro from Cumminsville, Ohio. Though he knew the unwritten law prohibited Negroes from playing the professional game, McGraw offered Grant a job with the majors. "Charlie," intoned the great McGraw, "I've been trying to think of some way to sign you for the Baltimore club, and I think I've got it." McGraw pointed to a large map on the lobby wall of the Eastland Hotel in Baltimore. "On this map, there's a creek called Tokohoma. That's going to be your name from now on, Charlie Tokohoma, and you're a full-blooded Cherokee."

McGraw signed Grant to his team but Comiskey soon heard of the deal and called a press conference, stating, "If McGraw really keeps this Indian, I will get a Chinaman of my acquaintance and put him on third. Somebody said this Cherokee of McGraw's is really Grant, the crack Negro second baseman, fixed up with war paint and a bunch of feathers."

Comiskey's charge proved the end of McGraw's experiment. Grant, who might have been the first Jackie Robinson, was never sent for by the Baltimore club and drifted off into backwater baseball.

The Old Roman's flags began to dip at the time of the First World War. Opening his treasure chest, Comiskey decided to buy the greatest team the world had ever seen. He purchased the finest second baseman anywhere in early 1915 by paying Connie Mack of the Athletics $50,000 for Eddie Collins plus a $15,000 bonus to Collins for his signature on a contract that called for five years of service at $15,000. Next, Comiskey shelled out $31,500 for the great outfielder Shoeless Joe Jackson who came from Cleveland. Oscar "Happy" Felsch, a slugger, was grabbed up from the Milwaukee team. By the beginning of the season, Comiskey realized that the Sox had the best players in either league, a juggernaut that would smash everything in its path. In three years, the Sox rose to an unbeatable position with an iron-man squad: Jackson, Felsch, Arnold "Chick" Gandil, Charles "Swede" Risberg, George

New York gambler Arnold Rothstein, who fixed the 1919 World Series, staining the White Sox to black. (UPI)

The great Sox pitcher Eddie Cicotte, who helped to set up the fix.

Oscar "Happy" Felsch. (UPI)

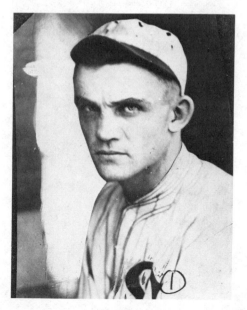

Arnold "Chick" Gandil.

The once great Joseph "Shoeless Joe" Jackson, who wounded the hearts of his fans.

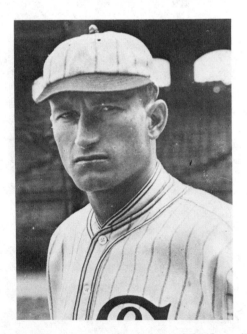

Hard, mean, and unscrupulous Charles "Swede" Risberg. (UPI)

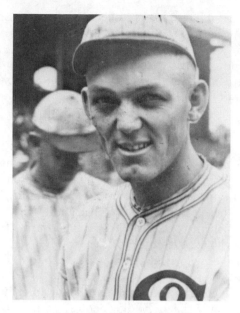

George "Buck" Weaver. (UPI)

Claude "Lefty" Williams. (UPI)

"Buck" Weaver, and the two best pitchers in any park, Eddie Cicotte and Claude "Lefty" Williams. Yet these very men, the pride of 50 million fans across the country, would, for the skimpy payoffs of sleazy gamblers, betray Comiskey, the fans, the game they loved, and their prosperous futures, staining the White Sox to black in the most unforgettable baseball scandal on record, the selling of the 1919 World Series.

"Say It Ain't So, Joe!"

Arnold Rothstein, the "Big Bank Roll," the tricky New York gambler, everyone said (including F. Scott Fitzgerald when presenting him as Wolfsheim in *The Great Gatsby*), was the culprit who fixed the 1919 World Series. And there were other gamblers—Abe "The Little Champ" Attell, Joseph "Sport" Sullivan, William Thomas "Sleepy Bill" Burns, Billy Maharg, Nat "Brown" Evans—who were claimed to have established the big fix, but it was the players themselves who arranged the disaster, and it was Comiskey who served as the goad.

The team had clinched the pennant and the world championship in 1917 with the pitching of the brilliant Eddie Cicotte leading to victory; he won 28 games that year. The following season was equally impressive. By 1919, the Sox scorched the American League. There was nothing to stop them from snaring another world championship, nothing but Comiskey, according to the eight defectors. Though he had promised bonuses to Cicotte and others, Comiskey reneged, paying the team off in bottles of champagne instead of dollars. In 1919, Comiskey was paying Cicotte, the top hurler of both leagues, less than $6,000, even though he was to win 29 games that year. His thinking was standard for baseball czardom. Cicotte was thirty-five years old, almost over the hill as a pitcher. He would soon burn out, great star or not. Why waste money?

It was the same story with the other players. At the beginning of each season, the great ones would show up, face Comiskey's ruthless secretary Harry Grabiner, and try to argue their salaries upward. Grabiner would throw them the usual bone and tell them all, "Take it or leave it." If they didn't like Comiskey's pay they could become hodcarriers. The much hated reserve clause in all their contracts guaranteed that if they did not play for the White Sox, they played for no one. So the stars of the White Sox played, but they were an embittered, loathing lot and manager William "Kid" Gleason had all he could do to keep the team operating, its amazing performances regularly punctured by locker-room revolts. Cicotte was not the only malcontent on the team.

The great Joseph Jefferson Jackson was unhappy with his baseball pay. Jackson was known as Shoeless Joe after appearing barefoot in a game as a youngster with a Greenville, South Carolina, team. His spikes didn't fit him. During the game, a fan, irate at Joe's magnificent play, yelled from the stands,

"You shoeless bastard, you!" An illiterate who could neither read nor write, Shoeless Joe went on to write his name as an immortal in the game with Connie Mack's Athletics. By 1911, his batting average was .408, just behind Ty Cobb. Walter "Big Train" Johnson said of him, "I consider Joe Jackson the greatest natural ballplayer I've ever seen." So did Comiskey when he bought Shoeless Joe in 1915. By 1919, Jackson was hitting .350 and the promise of a baseball future was bright and powerful, yet Joe was a big spender, purchasing businesses that failed and farms that grew nothing. He needed money and Comiskey only patted him on the back instead of reaching for his checkbook.

It was the same story with Risberg, the big shortstop; Buck Weaver, the brilliant third baseman; the pitcher Williams; the speedy outfielder Felsch; and utility infielder Fred McMullin. Most of all, Chick Gandil, the huge first baseman, was so upset with his job on the Sox that he openly lobbied for a fix as early as 1918. Gandil loved nightlife, big money, and was enamored of gamblers. He had been feeding Sport Sullivan tips on games for years, being plied with liquor and gifts in return. Three weeks before the 1919 World Series was to start, Gandil met with Sullivan in his room at Boston's Hotel Buckminster. "I think we can put it in the bag," Gandil told Sullivan. He had already picked out the roster that would deliver the Series into the hands of the gamblers. He asked for $80,000 to fix the 1919 series, $10,000 for each of the eight players involved. The gambler told him to go ahead with his plans and he would raise the payoff money.

Gandil first approached Cicotte, knowing that no game could be fixed without involving the pitcher. At first the great hurler ignored Gandil's pleas. Then one night, as the team rattled toward Boston, Cicotte plumped down in a Pullman seat next to Gandil and said in a whisper, "I'll do it for $10,000. Cash. Before the Series begins."

The avaricious first baseman knew he could tie up all the loose ends with Cicotte's participation. The rest fell into line once they knew their ace pitcher was going to throw the Series. He would pitch at least two games. Claude "Lefty" Williams, also in on the fix, would pitch another two. Those four thrown games would insure the fix.

When Sullivan failed to arrive with the payoff money, Gandil parlayed the deal with Sleepy Bill Burns and Billy Maharg, small-timers from the East. Ironically, both Sullivan and Burns, unknown to each other, had approached the gambling king of Manhattan, Arnold Rothstein, for the front money. Rothstein was his usual detached self, stating that the Series could not be fixed; there were too many variables, too many wagging mouths. He did assign Nat Evans to look into the possibilities, however. Abe Attell, once featherweight boxing champion of the world and a Rothstein crony, was present when Burns approached the Big Bank Roll and decided that if Rothstein would hedge his bets on a Series fix, he would not; he made his own plans to set up the deal.

After much wheeling and dealing, the fix was set only a few days before the

Sox met with the weak Cincinnati Reds in Ohio. By that time, Rothstein had
advanced, through Sullivan and Nat Evans, $40,000 to bribe the players. The
Sox defectors would receive the balance of their payoffs as each game was
thrown. Gandil and others wanted their money immediately, arguing that it
was difficult enough fixing the games since half the squad was ignorant and
innocent of the deal. Men like Eddie Collins, catcher Raymond "Cracker"
Schalk, outfielder John "Shano" Collins, and hotshot rookie pitcher Dickie
Kerr (all of whom received salaries much higher than the eight superstars
involved in the fix) would be playing to win every game. The fix had to be
sneaked past them and they were hard eyes, all. The players grumbled but
waited.

Sullivan gave Gandil only $10,000. The rest of A. R.'s up-front payoff he
withheld, using it to place his own bets. The frustrated first baseman slipped
the entire $10,000 under Cicotte's pillow one night, figuring that, as the key
man who was going to pitch the first game of the Series, he had to receive the
money first. Cicotte found the bribe and hastily sewed it into the lining of his
coat. Cicotte was also informed that Rothstein wanted a sign that he would
go through with the fix; he was to hit the first batter he pitched to in the
opening game.

Though the rest of the players received no money in advance, most of
them agreed in a hotel meeting to throw the games. Gandil borrowed money
to bet against his own team, wiring his wife, "I have bet my shoes."

The first game was a farce. Cicotte played it according to Rothstein's
dictates. The first Cincinnati player, Maurice Rath, came to the plate and,
after throwing a ball, Cicotte struck Rath between the shoulder blades.
Rothstein, getting detailed reports on the action at the Hotel Ansonia in New
York, smiled. Cicotte was going all the way. He immediately placed a half
million dollars in bets with selected plungers like millionaire Harry Sinclair,
the odds all in his favor (Rothstein bet so heavily that he drove the odds down
against the Reds so that his mediocre team was drawing, incredible to most
gamblers, even odds everywhere).

Cicotte's intentionally poor performance was obvious to Schalk and to Kid
Gleason. He did everything wrong, throwing juicy lobs to weak hitters who
got on base. Even the Reds pitcher, punk-hitting Dutch Reuther, got a single.
Though Gleason roared and ranted, nothing improved Cicotte's game. All
the Sox heavy hitters collapsed at the plate. By the fourth inning, the Reds
soared ahead with a 6–1 lead. Gleason marched to the baseline and yelled
furiously to Cicotte, "That's all, goddamnit, that's all!" By then, the Series was
convincingly lost for most, definitely in the minds of the eight Sox players
involved.

The second game was artlessly thrown away by Lefty Williams. Dickie
Kerr, not in on the fix, won the third game for the Sox in the best pitching
performance of his life. Cicotte put the fourth game on ice for the Reds,

deliberately cutting off throws to home plate to allow runners to score. Again the Sox lost, 2–0. Williams threw the fifth game, 3–0. By the end of the Series, the Reds marched into the world championship or were rather pushed there by the bought-off players.

Comiskey was suspicious from the start, going to Ban Johnson, head of the American League, following Cicotte's first loss. He had received dozens of anonymous tips that his players were bribed. Johnson still held his grudge against Comiskey, telling the Comiskey emissary that the Old Roman's fears of a fix were nothing more than "the whelp of a beaten cur!"

Kid Gleason felt the same way but was helpless to prove the fix. Sportswriters Hugh Fullerton and Ring Lardner smelled fix almost from the beginning but could learn nothing. Following the disaster, Comiskey hired private detectives to learn the facts of the fix, but the sleuths turned up nothing.

At the beginning of the 1920 season, Gandil announced that he was through with baseball, that he would open a restaurant. Others in the conspiracy—Jackson, Risberg, Cicotte, Weaver—were reluctant to sign new contracts. The players finally came around and the season opened with the usual Sox gusto, the team appearing to be headed for another Series.

But in July, Ring Lardner overheard Abe Attell telling one and all in Dinty Moore's, a Manhattan bar, that the 1919 Series had been fixed by Arnold Rothstein. It was chalked up to hearsay. "Who would print that," Lardner moaned. Comiskey was relentless to ferret out the culprits. A grand jury was finally convened at his and others' request and the players, one by one, were to be called in. Before the first session, Kid Gleason, knowing Cicotte was about to have a nervous breakdown, brought him to see Comiskey. In the privacy of the Old Roman's office, Cicotte sank pathetically into a chair and began to weep.

"I know what you want to know," he began to sob. "I know, I know—Yeah." Through uncontrollable tears the great pitcher gulped, "We were crooked—we were crooked."

Comiskey barely contained his wrath. "Don't tell me! Tell it to the grand jury!"

Cicotte did. He put it on Gandil and named the names and the way he and the others managed to throw the Series. "It's easy. Just a slight hesitation on the player's part will let a man get to base or make a run—I've lived a thousand years in the last twelve months. I would not have done that thing for a million dollars. Now, I've lost everything—job, reputation—everything. My friends all bet on the Sox. I knew it, but I couldn't tell them. I had to double-cross them. I'm through with baseball. I'm going to lose myself if I can and start life over again." Cicotte said he dumped his life in order to pay off a $4,000 mortgage on his farm.

The rest of the players, after arguments and threats, followed the pitcher. Swede Risberg told Joe Jackson, who was a wreck before he testified, "Just

As a result of the Black Sox scandal, Judge Kenesaw Mountain Landis became the arbiter of honesty in American baseball. (Wide World)

keep your own mouth shut, that's all, Joe. I swear to you, I'll kill you if you squawk."

But Shoeless Joe was undaunted in his guilt. He talked, telling authorities that he received only $5,000 for his part in the fix. Guards were assigned to protect Jackson who said to reporters, "Now Risberg threatens to bump me off if I squawk—old Joe Jackson isn't going to jail. But I'm going to get far from my protectors until this thing blows over. Swede is a hard guy."

Exiting from his nonstop confession with the grand jury some time later, Shoeless Joe stepped from the courtroom to see a knot of tearful boys, who, like millions of other youths, had idolized him.

Reporters took in the unforgettable scene of a tarnished champion facing those who meant the most to him. A small boy clutched the fallen hero's sleeve holding on to it as Jackson tried to break away. "Say it ain't so, Joe," he begged with tears in his eyes, "say it ain't so."

"Yes, kid," Jackson choked. "I'm afraid it is."

Acquitted of criminal action by a jury that carried the eight men out of a courtroom on their shoulders, the guilty players were nevertheless ruined, expelled from the game forever to live out wincing lives, shirking in the shadows of their infamy, dying one by one with the ever-present thought that they had labeled their great team the Black Sox. As a result of the scandal, the stern-minded Judge Kenesaw Mountain Landis was appointed baseball

The man who gave the White Sox a clean, if not crazy, image, Bill Veeck.

commissioner, ruling on the slightest misconduct of players for the next decade.

The gamblers who reaped millions from the fix escaped punishment. Rothstein appeared before the Chicago grand jury, in all his pomposity, with mouthpiece Bill Fallon at his side. He denied everything and was graciously shown the door. Comiskey was the real hero, refusing to suppress a scandal that would wreck his own team.

The Old Roman never forgot how his squad, thought by many experts to be the greatest team ever put together anywhere, had shamed him. He took these memories with him to the grave in 1931 when his son J. Louis Comiskey inherited the Sox dynasty. Commy's son was the nervous type, however, and would go on eating bouts that ballooned his normally corpulent body to inhuman proportions. He died of a heart attack in 1939 brought on by overweight. J. Louis tipped the scales at 375 pounds at death. His wife, Grace, after fighting court battles, inherited the Sox and became the second woman to head a major-league ball club. (Mrs. Schuler P. Britton succeeded her husband to the presidency of the St. Louis Cardinals for a brief period in 1916.)

Under the conscientious but less than driving personage of Grace Reidy Comiskey, the Sox went into a long decline. Upon her death in 1956, the Comiskey dynasty remained intact, with the Old Roman's grandson Charles Comiskey at the Sox helm.

Sox Player Luis Aparicio, loved by the youngest fans. (Wide World)

Pitcher Early Wynn, the great Sox pitcher who helped mightily to win the 1959 pennant—the first in forty years—talking with the elderly Dickie Kerr, one of the few honest players for the Sox during the infamous 1919 World Series. (Wide World)

The Zany Genius

In 1959, Bill Veeck (as in *wreck*), Jr., then forty-five, took over the White Sox. He purchased the bulk of the team's stock and brought to Chicago the kind of showmanship and promotion the team sorely needed. Veeck's career was one of oddball promotions and provocative play. The diamond has always been a circus arena to Veeck which he proved mightily first in Cleveland with the Indians in the late 1940s, then in St. Louis where he ran the Browns with such hoopla as fireworks, flagpole sitters, and auto races. He even sent a midget, Eddie Gaedel, to the plate to bat once for the Browns. Gaedel wore the number ⅛ and got on base by taking four balls. Anything but stodgy and reserved, Veeck has always played to the crowd. "My friends are the fans, not the owners," he is fond of saying. "Dignity isn't my suit of clothes."

In addition to clowns cavorting upon the playing field, Bill Veeck even tried to induce the crowd to arbitrate its home team's playing. Fans flashed Yes and No cards as to the strategy of each game and the moves each player might make. When Veeck, who lost a leg in 1943 during World War II, moved to Chicago, he immediately mixed in the stands with the fans to learn their

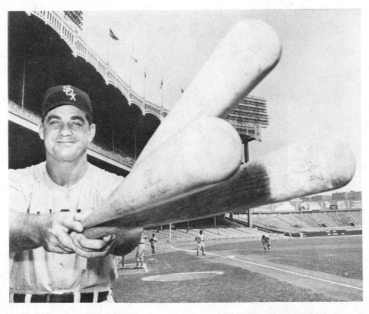

The 1959 pennant could not have been won without the powerful bat of Ted Kluszewski. (Wide World)

gripes and their ambitions for the Sox. One found him at the turnstiles taking tickets and, of course, counting the house.

Veeck's first appearance in Chicago sparked the club to record attendance. With a patchwork team of veterans such as Ted Kluszewski and Early Wynn along with novices like Luis Aparicio and Barry Latman, manager Al Lopez pulled off a miracle for Veeck. The Sox won its first pennant in forty years in 1959 and the hovering images of Shoeless Joe, Eddie Cicotte, and Chick Gandil vanished.

Veeck's early career with the Sox was short-lived. Despite his statement that he was "evicted" from baseball in June 1961 by baseball owners enraged at his Barnumesque conduct, the lively Sox owner simply suffered a vascular ailment that caused his reluctant retirement. Veeck promised to come back: "Sometime, somewhere, there will be a club that no one really wants. And then Ole Will will come wandering back to laugh some more."

Veeck came back with a roaring guffaw in 1975 when he arranged to buy the Sox one more time, a club no one wanted except him. Back was the scoreboard that exploded with $1,000 worth of fireworks when the Sox won a game. Back were the milking contests on the diamond and the mock invasions from outer space that homed in on Comiskey Park. Anything for the fans went under Veeck's colorful direction—Ladies Day, Bat Day, Bartender

An unbeatable combination for the Cubs, Joe Tinker (left), and Johnny Evers, who is about to throw to Frank Chance.

Day, Gourmet Day, Cab Driver Day and Name's-the-Same Day (when everyone with the same name as a player gets in for free).

The Sox are without pennant and power at this writing, undergoing the rigors of new management. When Veeck was at the helm, the big wins were hoped for but not ruthlessly sought. "We are in the entertainment business," once chuckled the Barnum of Baseball. "The important thing is the relationship between the fan and the game."

The Down-home Cubs

Comiskey's hot-headed idea about starting his own Chicago club brought about a talent depletion in the ranks of the National League at the turn of the century. Because of the talent-raiding, the once sacrosant White Stockings found its club gutted of veterans. Younger players, scraped from bush leagues, were recruited for the Stockings. Newspapers ridiculed the effort, calling the new youngsters kid players or cubs. In defiance, the club was renamed the Cubs in 1901 and the team has been known ever since under that Wizard of Oz banner. (Reflecting upon the appeal of the two teams today, the Sox belong to the beer-guzzling adult fans while the Cubs retain that youthful aura of some seventy years ago, a team that basically appeals to kids and is supported by children from eight to eighty.)

Spalding's erstwhile partner James A. Hart sold the Cubs in 1905 to one Charles Webb Murphy, a clotheshorse and former newsman who was backed by banker Charles P. Taft, the president's brother. A troublemaker whose dealings were always shady, to put it kindly, Murphy secretly purchased a piece of the Phillies in 1909 with Taft's money in an attempt to organize syndicate baseball. Moreover, Murphy had little interest in the game except to turn it into profit. In addition to owning a half interest in the LaSalle Opera House in Chicago (the title of which was in Mrs. Taft's name), Murphy fancied himself an author and busied his hours by churning out plays; none of his bad melodramas were ever produced. He treated as cold investments such great Cub players as shortstop Joseph B. Tinker, second baseman John J. Evers (pronounced EE-VERS, not EVV-ERS), and first baseman Frank Chance. When Murphy unceremoniously fired Evers as Cub manager in 1913 for finishing third in the league (he had fired Chance the year before from the same role), the league erupted and pressures were brought against Taft to force Murphy out of basebll; Taft bought up Murphy's stock for more than $500,000. Five years later the Cubs were under the directorship of William Wrigley, Jr., a position from which an odd baseball dynasty would later develop.

In the embryonic days of the Cubs, all the color and glory was supplied by the traumatic trio Tinker, Evers, and Chance, the team's player-manager. (Chance was dubbed The Peerless Leader by baseball scribe Charlie Dryden

in 1906. He earned the sobriquet by hustling the Cubs to four pennants and
two world championships before Murphy fired him after the Cubs lost a
postseason City Series to the Sox, fired him by sending a lackey to the bench
with Chance's release.)

These three Hall of Fame immortals were unbeatable in their heyday,
dominating the diamond on defense as no other combination ever did. They
first played together on September 13, 1902, recording their first double play
two days later. Though they appeared on the playing field for a decade as the
most winning trio in baseball, the three men had little to say to each other in
private life. In the case of Tinker and Evers, they had nothing to say. In fact,
for three years the great shortstop and second baseman uttered not a word to
each other.

The silence dropped between them as a result of a petty argument so
typical of the game. The team had traveled to Bedford, Indiana, on September 13, 1905. The Cubs were preparing to leave their hotel for the ball
park, waiting for hacks to arrive. Evers, a mean little Irishman with a lantern
jaw who weighed only 115 pounds and hailed from Troy, New York,
brushed aside his teammates at the curb and jumped into the only available
hack, riding to the park alone and leaving the other players stranded. Tinker
was furious. That afternoon after an exchange of grunts and growls, Evers
and Tinker staged a slugging match at second base in the middle of the game,
much to the delight of the fans.

A day later Joe sidled up to Johnny and blurted out, "Look, Evers, if you
and I talk to each other, we're only going to be fighting all the time. So don't
talk to me, and I won't talk to you. You play your position, and I'll play mine,
and let it go at that."

"Suits me," snapped Evers.

Never again were they close but they did soften in their dotage and were
happy to see each other elected to the Baseball Hall of Fame.

Evers was a natural costermonger of debate on the playing field. One day
in 1909 he erupted, dumping his lavalike wrath upon the greatest of all
major-league umpires Bill Klem, challenging the honest umpire's decision.
The verbal battle concluded when Evers yelled that he would leave the final
decision to those in the league office.

"Okay," Klem roared back, "I'll see you in the office in the morning!"

Evers snorted, "I'll bet you five dollars you don't even show up!"

"You're on!"

The next morning Evers cooled his heels in the office but Klem did not
appear. In the following days, whenever Klem was an umpire in a Cubs
game, Evers went into his taunt. Each time he came to bat, the feisty second
baseman would demand his five dollars from Klem who ignored him. Johnny
would then draw the figure five in the dirt in front of home plate with his bat.
From his second base slot, Evers would scream at Klem throughout the game

Cubs star Gabby Hartnett signs a baseball for Al Capone, Jr., as Scarface bows before camera while bodyguards sit behind the crime czar; note the bodyguard startled by a vendor and resting his hand on hidden revolver.

Cubs owner William Wrigley, Jr., with his favorite manager, the indefatigable Joe McCarthy. (UPI)

and, getting his eye, would hold up his hand with the fingers and thumb spread into a nagging five.

Klem could bear the pressure no more and, when the Cubs were traveling by train to Pittsburgh, the umpire collapsed in the smoking car under Evers' dogged pestering. He handed Johnny a five-dollar bill. Evers handed back a signed receipt marking the debt paid in full, a receipt he had been carrying for weeks. Klem tore the receipt to bits and dropped it like snow on Evers' head as the triumphant second baseman laughed himself close to convulsions.

It was Franklin P. Adams, later the capricious F. P. A. of the Algonquin Round Table fame who embedded the names of Tinker, Evers, and Chance into the undying memory of baseball fans everywhere when he wrote the following doggeral for the *New York Mail* in July, 1910:

> These are the saddest of possible words—
> Tinker to Evers to Chance.
> Trio of Bear Cubs and fleeter than birds—
> Tinker to Evers to Chance.
> Thoughtlessly pricking our gonfalon bubble,
> Making a Giant hit into a double,
> Words that are weighty with nothing but trouble—
> Tinker to Evers to Chance.

The Cubs (for all of the team's hard-luck history, which could mostly be placed at the door of P. K. Wrigley, William's son and inheritor of the club) would boast over the years some of the game's most memorable players as well as events. On a biting cold May 2, 1914, a game between the Cubs and the Reds went down as the greatest pitching duel of all time with right-hander Fred Toney throwing for the Reds and southpaw Hippo Jim Vaughn hurling for the Cubs. Neither team made a safe hit for nine innings. Though the Reds scored in the tenth, the game was scored as the first double no-hitter (in nine innings) in major-league history.

Charles L. "Gabby" Hartnett, the Cubs backstop (though many may argue the fact), was undoubtedly the greatest catcher the National League has ever seen. Gabby, who was born the son of a streetcar conductor in Worcester, Massachusetts, began as a notable marble player, assembling 55,000 marbles which he kept, as a boy, in three twenty-five-pound sugar sacks. Joining the Cubs in 1922, Hartnett began to roll up records. He was a superb receiver and possessed a deadly accurate and fast throwing-arm when whipping balls to bases. A slugger, Gabby racked up 236 home runs in his twenty-year career. He caught 1793 games from 1922 to 1942. Hartnett, elected to the Baseball Hall of Fame in 1955, was also the subject of one of baseball's most controversial events.

During the late 1920s, Scarface Al Capone waved him over to his box seat. Hartnett obligingly autographed a ball for Capone's son while photographers

Cubs second baseman and slugger Mark Koenig. (UPI)

Cubs immortal Lewis Robert "Hack" Wilson who boomed out fifty-six home runs in one year.

snapped the scene, pictures showing the crime czar's army of goons surrounding him and beaming approval at Hartnett. Charlie Grimm, Cubs
manager at that time, recalled that Hartnett's action "brought about an order
from [Judge] Kenesaw Mountain Landis, the baseball commissioner, excluding players from posing with fans." (The Cubs, strangely enough, not the Sox,
drew all the attention of the Chicago gangsters. In addition to Capone, thug
watchers could spot such underworld figures as Joe Saltis, Frankie Lake,
George "Bugs" Moran, and Murray "The Camel" Humphreys in attendance.
"Once," Grimm stated, "when a search was on for John Dillinger, there was a
report he was out in the bleachers watching the action. But mostly the hoods
had box seats near the Cub dugout.")

One-time Yankee power slugger Mark Koenig joined the Cubs in late 1929
to help the North Siders clinch the pennant, batting .353 in thirty-three games
and driving across 17 runs, which provided the winning margin. In return for
such titanic efforts, Koenig was voted a miserable half share of the World
Series money that year. It was typical clubhouse politics that has marked the
personality of the Cubs to this day as losers in more ways than booting
pennants and World Series.

No other Cub player in the team's history was more controversial, more
colorful and more promising than the amazing slugger Lewis Robert Wilson,
commonly known to thousands of lung-rooting fans as Hack. Wilson, a squat,
barrel-chested player, was called Stouts when he began playing as a catcher
for a Maryland country team in 1920. The name Hack evolved from Wilson's
resemblance to the dumpy German strong man Hackenschmidt. Even
though Hack looked like a fireplug with legs, his bat was to prove the
mightiest ever swung on behalf of the woebegone Cubs. He came to the club
from the Giants in 1926, purchased for a mere $5,000. He was worth every
penny of it, and soon was called the Million Dollar Slugger from the Five-
and-Ten-Cent Store.

Wilson only saw six seasons with the Cubs, from 1925 to 1931, but Chicago
never forgot the Little Round Man who slammed 190 homers in Wrigley
Field (in this order: 21, 30, 31, 39, 56, 13) and pushed across 159 runs in
Chicago's pennant year of 1929. He was a fine center fielder whose throwing
arm was incomparable.

The genial Hack was an exciting by-product of Prohibition; he loved to
party and nipping was his joy. Like the great King Kelly decades before him,
Hack trained on beer and the speakeasy life. Before even being asked if he
wanted a drink, Hack would boom, "I don't mind if I do."

Under the patronage of Joe McCarthy, who thought Hack could do no
wrong as a player, Wilson tripped the life fantastic while the Cubs manager
looked the other way. McCarthy did not necessarily approve of Hack's
life-style or methods of training. He merely chose not to punish his most
valuable player, for Wilson always produced for the Cubs, no matter what

hours he kept. But McCarthy did keep Wilson on guard. He had a habit of asking Hack for a match. He would note the advertisement for a nightclub and then inform Wilson and his fun-loving companion, pitcher Perce Leigh "Pat" Malone, where they had caroused the evening before. Malone, a towering, tough right-hander tipped Hack off to the trick and the next time McCarthy asked for a match, Wilson handed him a packet with no identification. Chuckled the stubby clown to his chagrined manager, "Now tell me where I was last night!"

It surprised few policemen raiding Chicago's countless speaks to find the inimitable Hack Wilson inside, seated at the stage with a retinue of cronies enjoying the drinks and the show at his expense. Usually the easy-going Hack was identified and released, but on one occasion the slugger was arrested with the rest of the patrons for violating the Volstead Act. McCarthy was informed and he, in turn, contacted William Veeck who managed to have Hack released before the newsmen arrived. McCarthy confronted Wilson the next day in the Cubs locker room. "What happened to you last night, Mr. Wilson?"

Hack looked sheepishly at his mentor. "Well, it's like this," Hack said slowly, after much evasion. "Me and the wife take in a movie, see, and I says to her, I says, 'Let's get a couple of sandwiches and a couple of bottles of beer and go home and listen to the radio.' So we go by this speakeasy I heard about. We push the button and all of a sudden there's a million cops behind me, pushing me into the place!"

The story made the rounds. The Cubs met the Phillies some days later in the old Baker Bowl. A gong taken from an old police wagon had been placed in the Phillies dugout which was used to signal the beginning of each game. When Wilson came to the plate for the first time, the Phillies in the dugout began clanging the police gong and shouting, "Hey, Hack, here comes the wagon!"

Wilson's response was to hit the first pitch straight out of the ball park. Seeing the homer, Phillies manager Art Fletcher screamed at his squad members, "Stay away from that gong when Hack goes to bat. You're waking him up!"

Jibes and taunts from the fans caused Hack Wilson to react differently. In June 1929, one spectator so inflamed Wilson with his cursing that the squat powerhouse climbed into the stands and began punching his tormentor. The bruised fan, a milkman named Edward Young, sued the Cubs for $50,000. The club paid a $20,000 out-of-court settlement to Young but let Wilson off with a reprimand. Hack was too valuable a property to suspend, a notion which the little giant supported the following year in 1930 when he belted out 56 home runs to set a National League record that stood for decades.

Yet Hack Wilson's hard living and brawling brought about his end when, in 1931, the new Cubs manager Rogers Hornsby, a stickler for rules and

The unpredictable and unforgettable pitcher Dizzy Dean in a Cubs uniform, 1940.

The venerable Cubs player Hank Sauer.

regulations, traded the Little Round Man to Brooklyn. It was typical Cub foresight. Wilson's year with Brooklyn proved him capable of his old powers; he hit 23 home runs, had a .297 batting average and drove in 123 runs.

Cub dealing and wheeling has a proven history of disaster. P. K. Wrigley, the austere owner of the club who certainly knew more about chewing-gum than baseball, was taken to the cleaners in 1938 when he purchased Jerome Herman "Dizzy" Dean (real name Jay Hanna Dean; born Lucas, Arkansas, January 16, 1911). Dean's torrid fast ball and cross-eye curve led the St. Louis Gas House Gang to a World Series in 1934. Wrigley paid the Cardinals $185,000 for Dean and sent St. Louis his two best pitchers Curt Davis and Clyde Shoun plus outfielder Chuck Stainback. Dizzy, whose arm had been hurt in 1937—a fact the entire baseball world knew, except P. K. Wrigley— went on to win all of sixteen games for the Cubs in the next three years, while Davis alone won forty-two games for the same period.

The Cubs, under the more than able direction of lantern-jawed managers Joe McCarthy, Rogers Hornsby and Charlie Grimm, managed to stay in the first division, but with P. K. Wrigley's appointment of James Gallagher (who was wholly incompetent to manage anything other than perhaps a girls' softball squad), the Cubs promptly got rid of Billy Herman, the finest second baseman in the league, selling him for $12,500 to Brooklyn and receiving Johnny Hudson and Charley Gilbert, neither of whom finished the next season. What successes the Cubs did enjoy were brought about through the years by the team's superb players, not by game acumen on the part of ownership. In the apt words of Stanley Frank, writing in the *Saturday Evening Post*, baseball persons in the know "looked upon Wrigley as a lucky dillettante."

Chicago's spirits were kept alive in the doldrum years by players such as Phil Cavarretta, a hustling outfielder and first baseman, who later managed the Cubs; Hank Sauer, the Big Dutchman who hit 37 homers in 1952 to lift the club into fifth place; slugger Billy Williams; hurler Ferguson Jenkins; and "Mr. Cub," Ernie Banks, the incurable optimist who clubbed 512 home runs out of the park for the Cubs.

Yet at the root of the pennantless Cubs' troubles was always P. K. Wrigley, the chewing-gum millionaire whose quirks and whims certainly pulled the team toward the cellar year after year. Wrigley's father, William, who purchased the Cubs in 1919 and who built the beautiful Wrigley Field for $2,300,000 before retiring to his Xanadu on Catalina Island, had a fair handle on the game and, unlike Comiskey, treated his players fairly and paid them well. (Wrigley spent more than $6 million in an attempt to bring pennants to Chicago before his death on January 26, 1932.)

P. K. Wrigley was, quite simply, an oddball owner. To this day there are no lights in Wrigley Field and night games are forbidden. Wrigley's attitude was that "night baseball wasn't demanded by the fans; it was put in by the owners

Mr. Cub, slugger Ernie Banks hitting his 1,000th run in 1965. (Wide World)

Leo "The Lip" Durocher, the most colorful Cubs manager ever, giving it to the ump in 1967. (Wide World)

who wanted to boost the gate." Yet, when assuming control of the Cubs in 1932, Wrigley told two newsmen that "he knew little about baseball and cared less for it." He changed managers willy-nilly and paid his players what he pleased. In 1943 he all but destroyed the ego of power hitter Lou Novikoff by giving him a measly $500 raise when, at the same time, he was investing $100,000 in a midwestern girls' softball league (ostensibly because of the shortage of available men players during World War II).

To prove he knew nothing of baseball, Wrigley, during the 1930s, hired a university psychologist to study his Cubs and give him an exacting profile of the kind of player who wins pennants. He also hired for $5,000 down and $25,000 to be paid in full if the Cubs won the pennant, a bizarre creature who caused Wrigley to believe he could cast an evil eye on all opponents. The bad whammy never worked in any game. Wrigley groaned, "I really don't see why people think I acted strangely."

The Cubs czar hated to be called P. K. and thought of himself as Mr. Nobody. Wrigley further emphasized his penchant for anonymity by preferring to watch his own team, unrecognized, in the bleachers. "My ambition," he said once with straight face and serious tone, "is to go live in a cave somewhere with no telephones and a big rock over the door."

Eccentric Wrigley had the same turn the back attitude toward his own faltering Cubs. It was not a ball club in his mind, no, that was ridiculous; it was simply "a corporation organized for profit," according to *Sports Illustrated*.

To that end Wrigley improved his ball park to the point where it is undoubtedly the most comfortable in the country. He revamped the box seating when he discovered that the chairs in those sections were too small. Each box contained ten seats. Ironically, when Wrigley ordered the chairs enlarged, he lost two seats per box and considerable revenue.

P. K. Wrigley's devotion to the volatile Leo Durocher was uncanny. He allowed the flashy manager to do as he wished with the club and, although it climbed into the first division under his hortatory urgings, Durocher never delivered a pennant for Chicago, causing strife and dissension among the players along each agonizing step of the way. The Cubs are still no closer, at this writing, to a pennant than when Leo the Lip left hurling epithets over his shoulder. The Cubs haven't won a world championship since 1908 when Tinker, Evers, and Chance were dusting them off. At best, the club's future looks gloomy.

In the history of the game, however, the Cubs will always be known as memorable losers. One of the great Chicago moments in Wrigley Field involved none other than baseball's greatest immortal Babe Ruth.

In the 1932 Series, Ruth's last, the Sultan of Swat came to bat in the third game. The Cubs hounded him relentlessly from the dugout. Charlie Root, on the mound for Chicago, served up two strikes. Then the Babe, enraged by the torments from the Cub bench, stepped out of the batter's box and pointed to center field. A moment later he drilled Root's pitch to the center field bleachers, having called his shot. Chicago was niggardly about the classic home run, most claiming that the Bambino was only indicating that he had one more strike. Yet it was Pat Pieper, the Cubs public-address announcer, who set the record straight. "I was sitting within a few feet of Ruth when he pointed and it wasn't any myth. He was pointing toward the bleachers. You can forget that indicating the count stuff. Ruth called his shot, pure and simple."

And pure and simple is the style of the colorful, unforgettable Chicago Cubs. Anyone unfamiliar with the team's home location can always tell when he is near Wrigley Field at game time. Emitting from the innards of the stadium is a wholly distinctive sound that can be heard nowhere else in baseball. It is known as the Cubs cry. "Yaaaaaa-awwwwwwww!"

6

The Game's the Thing

In sports, Chicago has and still can boast of the most stimulating and exciting personalities to be found in the country, but when it comes to football, the most venerated man of his day or any other was a boy who clawed his way out of poverty in West Orange, New Jersey, to work his way through Yale in the 1880s as a divinity student. He lived in a dollar-a-week unheated room in New Haven while at college and allowed himself a meager twenty cents a day for food—five cents for breakfast, ten cents for dinner, and five cents for supper—which provided a diet of soda crackers, stale bread, and milk. He would die at 102 in 1965 of beriberi as a result of living on soda crackers. He would also be remembered as the greatest figure in football—Amos Alonzo Stagg.

The Days of Double A

Upon graduation from Yale's Divinity School, Stagg received his first and only significant defeat in life. He realized that he was a terrible public speaker and without being able to communicate in the tongues of angels, a religious life was impossible. "I sized myself up," he would later recall, "and decided I wasn't cut out to be a pulpit man. My goal, though, remained the same: to guide and train youth."

Where Stagg did not bring his religious fervor into church, he carried it to the mound when pitching Yale into championships. "I prayed before every pitch. I simply prayed, 'Help me do my best.'"

He did more than pray in one sensational game against Princeton, an exhibition match given in honor of the president's wife, Mrs. Grover Cleveland. The First Lady tactlessly appeared in the stands wearing the black and orange colors of Princeton. The affront was too much for the mild-mannered Yale pitcher, and Stagg, in one of his rare moments of pure anger, hurled his

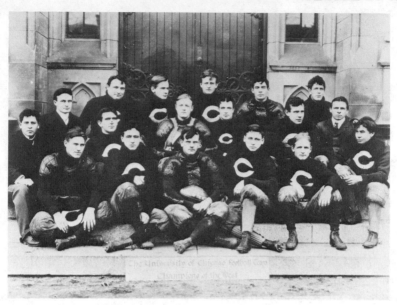

Coach Amos Alonzo Stagg (extreme left, in street clothes) with his first championship team at the University of Chicago in 1899. (Wide World)

Coach Stagg at age 101 in 1963. (Wide World)

arm almost out of its socket, allowing only two hits and striking out twenty men for the victory. His teammates deliriously carried him from the field to a local brewery, but he refused to partake of any spirits, feeling that if he broke down his own rigid rules he would never regain them.

Stagg's college record was so impressive—pitching the Bulldogs to five championships, striking out 241 batters, and allowing 262 hits—that the New York Nationals (later the Giants), upon his graduation, offered him $4,200 to pitch for three months. Lonnie, as Stagg was known to intimates, turned the offer down feeling that he would be used up by age thirty and that, in the words of one biographer Ellis Lucia, "the college educated man, if he desired monetary wealth, should seek it by longer-lasting, more secure means, other than his physical skills."

Those personal physical skills had also established Stagg as Yale's first great end; he stood 5 feet 6 inches tall and weighed no more than 160 pounds yet his feats on the gridiron caused him to be named to Walter Camp's first All-American Team. Stagg's football prowess, however, was also not for sale. He wanted to teach youth the good life in sports.

The abstemious Stagg took a coaching job with the YMCA College in Springfield, Massachusetts, where, for two years, he labored with apprentice baseball and football players. In 1892, William Rainey Harper, one of Stagg's Yale professors, called him to a meeting in New York. At a pancake breakfast at the Murray Hill Hotel, Harper explained that John D. Rockefeller was providing some of his millions for a brand-new university in Chicago, a free-thinking experimental institution unlike anything in the U.S. Harper, knowing of Stagg's devotion to physical fitness and the spiritual emphasis he placed in handling youth as well as Stagg's belief in sports for the building of character and the lofty standards he set in playing games, offered Stagg the head position in the new school's athletic department with a salary of $1,500. Lonnie was stunned speechless.

Harper, thinking Stagg was holding out, drummed his fingers on the tabletop and said, "I'll offer you $2,000 and an assistant professorship."

Still Stagg was silent, purely out of shock.

"All right, all right," Harper intoned. "Then I'll give you $2,500 and an associate professorship which means an appointment for life!"

Before Harper felt compelled to raise the ante, Stagg found his voice and accepted. Then began a forty-one year career that made Amos Alonzo Stagg, "Old Double A," synonymous with the University of Chicago. At that always exciting university Stagg "invented just about everything there is in football today," according to *Time* when reporting his death in 1965. Lonnie was the first to use mattresses in practice and created football's first tackling dummy. In the days of the flying wedge, a bone-crushing movement of the entire team in forward motion, it was Stagg who brainstormed new techniques that made the game simply fun to watch—the huddle, the man in motion, the essential

T-formation, the direct pass from center, the fake pass, the unbalanced line, the onside kick, the sleeper play, the delayed buck, the shift, the Statute of Liberty, the quarterback keeper, the forward pass, and the use of flankers.

In practice, it was the ever-initiating Stagg who was first to hold spring practice (in 1914) and to compel his charges to perform wind sprints. His teams were the first to practice beneath the lights, using a white-painted ball. He developed the charging sled, and, for safety of the players, was the first to order the dangerous goalposts padded. A year after joining the university, Stagg insisted that his players have a field. He simply passed the hat around and collected $866 from his students and faculty. The first collected dollar was sent to Marshall Field as payment for the vacant block of land he had donated just north of the campus proper. First called Marshall Field, the university stadium later became known as Stagg Field. (It was here, beneath the stands in what had been the tennis and squash courts, that Enrico Fermi and other scientists developed the atomic bomb during the early 1940s.)

For all his much-vaunted new ideas for the gridiron, Lonnie Stagg's greatest achievements were his teams and the highborn character he imbued in his players and in the game. "You can't bluff in football," he was fond of saying and that meant living the good life according to Amos Alonzo Stagg. Drinking and gambling were taboo. Swearing was also outlawed on the field. If Stagg even suspected a player of smoking—as early as 1900 he noticed that athletes who smoked were short of breath—he would be benched. "He could smell smoke a mile away," one of his players remembered. Even at Chicago alumni meetings years later, former Staggmen would hastily grind out burning cigarettes and hide the butts in suit pockets when the Old Man appeared.

On one occasion, a former University of Chicago player who had returned from France and the hell of trench warfare in 1919, bummed a cigarette from a sportswriter at Stagg Field. Suddenly, the much wounded soldier dropped the cigarette and quickly ground it out with his shoe.

"What's the matter?" asked the newsman. "Don't you like my brand?"

"Shhhhhh," whispered the bemedaled soldier. "There's Old Man Stagg behind us."

No prouder man on the university campus was one who possessed a varsity letter accorded by Stagg, the first to make such awards. The Order of the C meant much more than performance on the field. When one player, who had an exceptional season with Chicago, asked Stagg why he had not been given his letter, the venerable coach told him quietly, "You did not qualify in manhood."

Those qualifications Lonnie put down in what he called the Ten Commandments for the Football Player which included, "keeping your mind and body clean and alert; being square and honest; using your imagination; helping the other fellow; refusing to complain, whine, knock, or quit; throttling your conceit; never being discouraged by failure; always being a

The great running quarterback for the University of Chicago, Walter Eckersall.

sportsman and a gentleman; developing courage and determination; and saying a prayer each evening."

Stagg's nemesis, he felt in righteous wrath, was the neighborhood saloon. He mustered his religious zeal against speakeasies during Prohibition, thundering that the neighborhood bar was "our substitute for the movies, the theaters, the motor car, the radio, the seashore, reading, and all. In bad luck men drown their sorrows in the bar, in good luck they celebrate it there. When too warm, they drink; when too cold, they drink. In high spirits, they let off steam in the saloon; when bored they buy high spirits from the bartender."

The man who most personified great football and manliness for Stagg was the piston-legged Walter Eckersall, a product of Chicago's Woodlawn district on the South Side. Eckersall, who was highly sought after by Fielding H. Yost, coach of the mighty Michigan team, decided to play for Chicago because he so much admired the high-principled Stagg, a decision which was to enrage Yost and cause a lifelong feud between Yost and Stagg.

The Midway Mite, as Eckersall was called, proved to be Stagg's greatest performer, a 138-pound marvel who became the college game's all-time quarterback. There was nothing Eckersall couldn't do, from passing to kicking. He once kicked five field goals against Wisconsin. In another great clash, the 1904 meet between Michigan and Chicago, Eckersall, who also played all four quarters on defense, missed a tackle on the fast-charging

Willie Heston only to get his man a second later from behind. "Eckie, Eckie, break your neckie!" screamed the encouraging Chicago fans whenever Stagg's team needed the extra points to win. Eckersall invariably provided those points and the winning game.

Stagg was a great one for halftime speeches, Knute Rockne notwithstanding. In one game against archrival Illinois, Stagg looked about at his head-bowed team; Illinois had gained the lead in the first half. "What's wrong out there?" asked Stagg in his usual mild voice. "Can anyone tell me?"

The excuses gushed forth. "The field is muddy. Our cleats won't hold!"

Lonnie raised his hands to stop the jabber. "Conditions are no worse for you than they are for Illinois. If Beethoven had used his troubles as an excuse, we'd never have had his music. If there's a father's son among you who thinks he's done his level best, stand up and say so."

No one stood up. The Maroons then dashed to the field and, stung by Stagg's words, won the game. One of those on that squad was Herbert O. Crisler who received a nickname from Stagg he would wear all his days.

In practice one day Crisler was running a new play. He fumbled the ball three consecutive times. Stagg called him over. "What's your name?" he said to his star back, pretending not to know it.

"Crisler, sir."

"Oh, Crisler," Stagg said in his most sarcastic tone, "are you related to the great artist—the violinist?"

"No sir."

"Well, I'm going to call you Fritz after him. He too had great poise and great hands."

When angry to the boiling point, Stagg's strongest epithet was jackass. If a player particularly enraged him with poor play, the coach would use his strongest blast—double jackass. Such argot caused a rival coach to once state, "By the end of a Chicago workout, there are no men playing, just jackasses grazing."

The coach's sarcasm was spent on all, high and low, even his great drop-kicker Clarence Herschberger, who, in order to get his weight up once against a huge Wisconsin team, downed thirteen eggs for breakfast before the game and was promptly ill by halftime, the Maroons having fallen behind.

"What's the matter?" Stagg asked Hershie.

"Sick, that's all."

By the end of the game Stagg had learned of his star's gluttony and remarked to the entire squad as Herschberger hung his head, "We weren't beaten by eleven Badgers out there today. We were beaten by thirteen eggs!"

No other man in college football ever approached the integrity displayed by the amazing Stagg. Once, in 1909, Stagg watched as one of his speedy Maroons raced for a touchdown. Lonnie stepped onto the field and ordered

Legendary drop-kicker Clarence Herschberger of the U. of C.

startled officials to call the play back. Unnoticed by them, Stagg pointed out, his man had stepped out of bounds. "I would like to be thought of as an honest man," he explained. So honest was the Old Man thought to be that he was asked twice to referee games in which Chicago was playing.

Stagg was never a man to borrow money, living for a half century on his no more than $8,500-a-year salary. The only loan he ever took out was for $2,500; this he used to send five University of Chicago trackmen to Paris for the Olympics of 1900 when the school could not afford to finance the trip.

Samuel Goldwyn of Hollywood called Stagg one day and offered him $300,000 for the rights to his life story. Stagg never hestitated before replying, "I can't do it. All my life I've taught strict amateurism. If I accepted money for this, I might be reneging on my beliefs."

In 1932, University of Chicago officials asked the seventy-year-old Stagg to retire as active coach of the Maroons but offered him a post in public relations at a $10,000-a-year salary. Stagg, who had fielded four unbeaten teams for Chicago as well as having gleaned six Big Ten titles, refused even though the new pay would be $2,000 more than his coaching salary. He said he intended to go on coaching. He did, taking on the head coach position at the College of the Pacific at Stockton, California, where he was to remain for the next fourteen years. He was eighty-five when he moved to Susquehanna University in Pennsylvania to assist his son in the coaching chores there.

Stagg ran into his old backfield star Crisler before going to Susquehanna. "You're pretty old to be signing a ten-year contract, aren't you?" Crisler teased.

"Fritz," replied the indestructible Stagg, "I'm looking forward to being able to renew it!"

At Susquehanna the Old Man made the final moves, not his son. Said Amos Alonzo Stagg, Jr.: "He was my assistant. Practically, he was in charge. To disagree with my father was like breaking with God." Stella Stagg, to whom the Old Man remained married for sixty-nine years, acted as scout for the Susquehanna team. She once passed the following scout report on to her husband: "By the way, Alonzo, you can get a pass receiver behind their left halfback. He's slow." Susquehanna won the game by one touchdown by completing a pass over Dickinson's left halfback.

When Stella fell ill, Stagg moved back to the warmer climate of California where he coached the kicking squad at Stockton College, finally retiring at age 98. He celebrated his 100th year on earth by joking, "I may go on forever, because statistics show that few men die after the age of 100." By the next year, Stella was dead and Stagg was suffering from Parkinson's disease, his once piercing blue eyes clouded with cataracts, his thick shock of hair snow-white. He had outlived college football in Chicago, the University of Chicago having abandoned the game. Within five months of his 103rd birthday, on March 17, 1965, Amos Alonzo Stagg died in a Stockton nursing home.

His friend "Fritz" Crisler liked to remember Stagg as he found him on his 96th birthday, mowing his lawn in Stockton. A neighbor came over and told Stagg that children had been playing on his grass kicking up the dirt. "You'll never raise grass that way," carped the neighbor.

The man who will always be remembered as the great coach of the University of Chicago laughed and retorted, "Thank you, but I'm more interested in raising boys!"

Mr. Football

If the game of college football owes more to Amos Alonzo Stagg than to any other man, its big tough brother professional football owes a similar debt—perhaps the reason for its existence—to a spry human now dancing through his eighties, George Halas, better known as Papa Bear.

The son of immigrant parents from Bohemia, Halas played for Bob Zuppke at Illinois, finishing his college football in 1917. He was also a promising outfielder in baseball, or so Miller Huggins, manager of the New York Yankees, thought and he joined that club in 1919. He proved himself a speedy center fielder and a better than average hitter. One day he slammed a triple off the super Dodger pitcher Rube Marquard, but, as he slid into third base, he hurt his hip. Even though he started the season with the Yankees,

Coach George Halas of the Chicago Bears, 1933.

charley horses in his leg emanating from his hip caused him to sit out many games. Halas went to Huggins and asked that he be sent to Youngstown to see a character named Bonesetter Reese, a phenomenal nonmedical healer of broken bones who had learned every bone and muscle in the human body while resetting the bones of miners injured in Youngstown's steel mills.

Halas hobbled into Reese's office, threw himself on the table, and, in a few moments, as Papa Bear remembered, Reese "dug his powerful fingers down into my side and said, 'Yes, when you slid into third base you twisted your thigh bone.'" Reese took hold of the bone and with one motion twisted it back into place. "That afternoon," Halas laughed, "I was running like wild in the stadium in Cleveland." His cure came too late. By the time Halas reported back to the Yankees he had been replaced by a bruising, paunchy man with spindly legs and a potato face named Babe Ruth.

Undaunted, Halas switched back to football, his greatest love, by playing right end in 1919–20 for the Hammond Pros, one of the few splinter professional football teams operating then. America's greatest athlete, then or now, Jim Thorpe was also making ends meet the same way, playing for the down and out Canton Bulldogs. Halas was getting $100 a game, sometimes less.

Professional football was a myth, a ragtag operation that drew scant crowds and received little press. Halas was determined to lift professional football out of the doldrums. He put together his own team, the Decatur

(Illinois) Staleys, or the Staleys Starchworks, named after Decatur businessman and sponsor A. E. Staley who owned a prosperous corn products firm.
Halas then proposed his dream to Ralph Hay, owner and operator of the
most successful professional football team of the day, the Canton Bulldogs.
Why not form a league of pro teams setting up fixed schedules and obtaining
the best talent available?

Hay and other owners liked the idea and a meeting was called on September 17, 1920, in Hay's automobile agency in Canton. Papa Bear laughs
when he remembers how "that meeting in Hay's showroom must have been
the most informal on record. There were no chairs. We lounged around on
fenders and running boards and talked things over." The owners agreed to
call the new league the American Professional Football Association, the
precursor to the National Football League. Jim Thorpe, the great Sac-and-
Fox Indian whose Olympic feats as well as his baseball diamond and gridiron
feats were legend, was elected the league's first president.

From the outset, the league, which changed its name to the National
Football League (NFL) in 1922 (much to Halas's doing), was a risky business.
Even Jim Thorpe's name failed to bring the anticipated crowds. Of the
original pro teams—the colorfully named Staleys, the Chicago Cardinals, the
Muncie Tigers, the Rock Island Independents, the Hammond Pros, the
Canton Bulldogs, the Rochester All-Stars, the Cleveland Indians, the Akron
Professionals, and the Dayton Triangles—only two survive to this day: Ha-
las's Staleys, now the Chicago Bears, and the Chicago Cardinals, now the St.
Louis Cardinals. Most went broke in the early 1920s. Detroit started and
folded a pro team three times before it caught on.

For Halas and his newly renamed Bears who had moved to Chicago it was
no different. Papa Bear struggled along with a $100-a-game salary and
supplemented his meager income by coaching on the side. Halas moved his
Bears into Wrigley Field in 1921 after arranging to play every Sunday during
the season. (He proved himself an astute businessman by giving Bill Veeck,
Sr., then the boss of the Cubs, 15 percent of the gross receipts and the
concessions, all except the sale of the scorecards which proved to be a
lucrative plum.) The Bears would remain at Wrigley Field for several decades until moving to Soldier Field.

In his first year at Chicago, Halas wound up in the red; his teams, after all
expenses were paid, lost $71.63 at the end of the season even though the title
game between the Bears and Buffalo drew 12,000 fans to Wrigley Field for a
profit of $1,476.92. The following year the Bears edged into the black, and by
1924 Halas and his partner Edward C. "Dutch" Sternaman (whom Halas later
bought out) received an offer of $35,000 if they would sell the Bears franchise.

Publicity from the press was still given niggardly to the Bears. At one point,
Halas, seeing that no Chicago papers had assigned staff writers to cover his
games, hired a press agent at ten dollars per game and handed out the results

Perhaps the greatest back of all time, the immortal Harold "Red" Grange (center), flanked by Dutch Sternaman (left) and George Halas, in 1925. (UPI)

Harold "Red" Grange in action for the University of Illinois when he was known as "The Galloping Ghost"; he carried for more than 4,000 yards in three seasons of college play. (Wide World)

of the action through press releases, little of which was used by the newspapers.

Halas and Sternaman were player-owners. Halas at end, Sternaman at halfback. College men were eagerly sought to fill out the squad and the Bears first roster listed such stalwarts as All-American backs Chick Harley and Pete Stichcomb along with the aggressive guard John L. "Tarzan" Taylor, all from Ohio State's Big Ten championship team. Later, stars such as the big right end Guy Chamberlain, the bruising tackle Ed Healy, guard Hunk Anderson from Notre Dame, fullback Oscar Knop from Illinois, and end Duke Hanny from Indiana joined the team. The Bears still failed to draw the crowds Halas expected. He and the Bears needed not only a superstar but an international attraction. That incredible type of drawing power stepped forth in the form of a man who had produced through his amazing gridiron feats for the University of Illinois the kind of mass hysteria that registered wealth in the box office. He was known as the Galloping Ghost and the Wheaton Iceman. Harold "Red" Grange could do anything with a football and, lured from college before his senior year, he began to do it for the Bears as a magic halfback in 1925.

Grange was the hero of every boy in America. He himself was the all-American boy of clean living and hard play, especially when crunching through any kind of line or running around it or passing over it. As a summer job while attending the University of Illinois, Red delivered ice for a small firm in his home town of Wheaton, a sleepy little place just west of Chicago. When his blinding star began to rise, Grange told one interviewer for *The American Boy* that lugging around blocks of ice "is what every fellow should do. . . . It gives me lots of walking, which hardens up my legs, and it strengthens my arms, shoulders and back with the lifting it entails."

Entering college in 1922, Grange became a super player in his freshman year and the following season he fairly burned up the fields with an incredible display of broken-field sprinting and dodging. Walter Camp selected him as an All-Amerian halfback two years running in 1923 and 1924. In 1924 Grange astounded the world by putting on a one-man exhibition that has never been equaled in the annals of football. He carried the football precisely five times and scored precisely five touchdowns, four of which were runs of from 45 to 95 yards, against powerhouse Michigan, all in the first twelve minutes of the game!

Red owned the press, as Halas knew well, and Papa Bear decided to buy not only the finest football player alive but world publicity to boot. He signed Grange in 1925, making a special deal wherein the Ghost got a percentage of the gate receipts. The Wheaton Iceman first appeared in a Bears uniform on Thanksgiving Day. "His drawing power was just tremendous," Halas still delights in remembering. "We used to sell out tickets at A. G. Spalding Sporting Goods Store. I got a call from Spalding to hurry over, that there was a tremendous demand for tickets and a huge crowd. I walked over. Here I saw a line, four abreast, down State Street, down Monroe, back up Wabash, and around the block. That was the most thrilling sight I had ever seen up to that time."

The sellouts didn't stop. Grange was, like the sport gods of the day (Babe Ruth, Jack Dempsey, Bill Tilden, and Bobby Jones), something inhuman in the minds of fans, a surging charge of power in the high voltage of the Jazz Age. The money poured in all that season as capacity crowds fought to see the football hero of the decade, 77,000 fans cramming into the Polo Grounds toward the end of the season when the Bears met the Giants in New York. The Galloping Ghost, who had decided to turn pro to make his fortune, became rich overnight. In two weeks alone during his first Bears year, working a man-killing schedule, Grange and his managers pocketed $50,000 as his share of the receipts.

During the season the Bears were humiliated only once when the Providence Steam Rollers stopped the Chicago squad in front of 25,000 Boston fans. Grange, with little sleep, had managed to gain only eighteen and a half yards that day, for which the press pilloried him.

Hours after the game, Red's depression was lifted when Babe Ruth strolled into his hotel suite. Noticing the hangdog look on Grange's face, the immortal Bambino boomed, "Don't be too thin-skinned, Red. You've got to expect a lot of knocks in this professional racket, and you've got to take a lot of criticism and a lot of insults that you didn't get before. But keep your head up. And don't be afraid to say no when the pressure gets too rough. Get the dough while the getting is good, but don't break your heart trying to get it."

Halas certainly began major-league pro ball but Red Grange was the man who dragged the American public into the stadium on the long way to pro-football-dominated Sunday afternoons and $20-million franchises. George Halas, always a modest man, was the first to admit his debt to the Wheaton Iceman. "Red Grange had put us on page one of the sports sections in every paper in the country. This was a great day for football."

Ironically, though Halas had wooed Grange away from the University of Illinois before Red completed his schooling, Papa Bear was also the man who initiated a standing pro football rule that a player could not be signed by a pro team until he finished college. To new college graduates arriving in the Bear camp, Halas would, year after year, deliver essentially the same speech. "You are here to play pro football. You are getting pretty good money and you should use it to further your education, to go into business."

Pro ball was rough business back in the 1920s and one of the roughest players Halas ever put onto the field was the enormous center George Trafton who enjoyed the sound of breaking bones. In one game against Rockford, Trafton tackled a Rockford halfback so hard that they both flew into a fence bordering the field, crashing through it. The halfback's leg was broken. Trafton proceeded to knock three other Rockford players out of the game.

George Trafton (right) with Charles Berry, early Chicago Bears. (UPI)

Irate Rockford fans began to threaten Trafton's life from the stands, explicitly calling out what they would do to him at game's end.

"This is getting serious, Halas," Trafton gulped during a time-out.

"Head for the bench when the gun goes off," Halas whispered. "We'll cover you."

The moment the final gun sounded, Trafton darted for the bench where trainer Andy Lotshaw hurriedly handed him a sweat shirt telling the worried player to "put it on—cover up your number." Trafton not only slipped on the sweat shirt but grabbed two empty milk bottles from the water bucket as weapons should he need them. Just as the burly center was to race for an exit, Halas stopped him and handed him a brown envelope. "Stick it in your pants!" Papa Bear shouted after Trafton who was already sprinting for an exit with scores of club-wielding Rockford fans after him.

Outside the park, Trafton jumped into a cab but the fans were almost on him, crashing a fusillade of rocks through the windows. Trafton jumped out the other door and began running. About 300 yards down the road a shiny new Mercer car pulled up and a kindly driver, seeing Trafton's look of utter desperation, asked, "Where you going, kid?"

"Davenport!" gasped Trafton. "In a helluva hurry!"

"Jump in." Trafton leaped into the car which sped off leaving dozens of injury-bent Rockford fans bellowing in the dust. The badly frightened center did not open the envelope until he reached Davenport. Inside he found

$7,000 in cash, the Bears' share of the gate receipts (Halas always collected in cash in those touch and go years).

Entrusting the money to Trafton seemed like a brainstorm to Halas when he recalled the harrowing day. "I know that he'd be running for his life, whereas all I had to run for was the $7,000."

All of Halas's players through the years have performed with equal vigor, albeit some of his rough-and-rowdies were what might be termed strange, like John "Bull" Doehring, a muscular halfback with the most incredible arm ever seen in pro football. Even Papa Bear could not believe Doehring's throwing power when the new recruit showed up for practice in 1932. Reporters hearing of Doehring's unbelievable arm harrassed Halas one day about it. "I don't know how far he can throw," joked Papa Bear. "You don't expect me to be in two places at once, do you? I've seen him start the ball but I've never seen it land!"

Yet getting Doehring into a game was another thing. In his first scheduled game against the Redskins in Boston, Doehring was nowhere to be found. He appeared in the Bears clubhouse following the game and began to undress.

"What are you undressing for now?" asked one of the angry Bears coaches.

"I'm going to take a shower," Doehring replied.

"Where were you during the game?"

"In the stands, watching."

"But you were supposed to play. We planned to use you!"

Doehring appeared sad and disgruntled. "I know, I know, but I got to thinking it over on the way to the park and decided maybe my mother wouldn't want me to play professionally."

Halas finally convinced Doehring to play and the following week he appeared against Portsmouth proving that his amazing throwing arm was anything but a myth. Taking a lateral from quarterback Carl Brumbaugh, Doehring delayed as long as possible before hurling the pigskin. Downfield raced the Bears end Johnson. In the safety position for Portsmouth was Roy "Father" Lumpkin. As Johnson ran past him in his deep position, Lumpkin roared with laughter, "Where in the hell are you going." The laugh changed to curses as Bull Doehring unleashed a sixty-five-yard pass that ended up in Johnson's arms for a touchdown.

The Bull never did throw to his capacity since there was no Bear player who had time to run far enough downfield to snare it. It is a fact that the Bull did send a ball ninety yards in one pass during practice, or so the Bears swear to this day.

Old-timers still talk about Doehring's indifferent attitude toward Halas's lectures and chalk-talks. Papa Bear cornered the evasive halfback one day asking why he had not been present at a lecture.

"George," responded the bored Doehring, "you say the same things over and over. I went to a movie."

The Bears went into high gear with the coming of Bronko (christened

The smashing Bears fullback, Bronko Nagurski (shown with ball) running through the line in 1937. (Wide World)

thusly by his Ukranian parents) Nagurski, a 230-pound, 6-foot-2-inch dynamo that could crunch through any line in the league. Halas scored his shrewdest coup when signing up the Bronk who visited Papa Bear in Chicago where he was offered $5,000 a season. Nagurski wanted a $10,000-a-year contract for two seasons. He boarded his homeward-bound train without an agreement. Halas then sent a wire agreeing to Bronk's terms; this was delivered at a stop along the way and Nagurski dashed off a wire accepting. Upon arriving home, Bronk found, to his disgust, an offer from the New York Giants for $7,500 for a single season's play.

The Bronk was unstoppable for the most part all through his pro career. Only once, in 1933, did he seem to meet his match during a game with the Bears all-time arch rival the sterling Green Bay Packers. In that game, Green Bay's behemoth fullback Clark Hinkle fought an offense to defense duel with Nagurski. Hinkle won. "The two collided head-on like two runaway locomotives," wrote one gridiron scribe, "and with roughly the same result. Hinkle's headgear smacked into Nagurski full in the face, and the indestructible Bronk was led away with a broken nose."

For the most part, Nagurski won almost all his great "bumping" matches on the field. He had a habit of never looking up when running as fullback through the line. During another Bear-Packer meet, Nagurski ran the ball

Chicago Bears center Clyde "Bulldog" Turner.

The best quarterback in Chicago Bears history, Sid Luckman, about to hurl a bomb (it was completed for a touchdown to Jimmie Benton) against the Giants in 1943, one of the seven touchdowns—his all-time record—Luckman threw that November 14 at the Polo Grounds.

The unforgettable Bears back, Gail Sayers.

thirty-five yards into the Packer end zone trampling three would-be tacklers (all of whom were removed from the game on stretchers) and slammed, going full speed, into a brick wall and was temporarily knocked out. Regaining his senses, the great Bronk moaned to Andy Lotshaw, "Who in hell hit me?" In a 1933 game, Nagurski smashed through a Spartan line with such force for a touchdown that he was carried by his own momentum into the dugout at Wrigley Field. Attendants later swore that he created a large hole in the brick wall. Following that Nagurski charge, the dugouts at Wrigley Field were boarded up during football season.

It was Steve Owen, manager of the Giants, who awarded George Halas's greatest fullback his due. "He's the only man I ever saw who ran his own interference!"

Nagurski retired in 1937 to work his farm but returned six years later on September 26, 1943, to replace his old friend George Musso. Following a bruising game with Green Bay, Nagurski was heard to say, "Some of us old-timers are getting a little slow now, and we feel those explosions a little deeper, then a little deeper." Yet on November 28 of that year, Nagurski trotted into a game against the Cardinals telling coach Hunk Anderson, "I guess it's time for old Bronk to go to work." He crunched through the Cardinal line in seven plays to score the winning touchdown. He was thirty-five then and went on to aid the Bears in their title play-off win against the Redskins with a punishing 41–21 score.

"There's only one defense against Nagurski," commented Steve Owen. "Shoot him before he leaves the dressing room!"

Nagurski's Bear record was laurel wreathed after his nine seasons; Bronko carried the ball 4,301 yards (almost three miles) and scored 242 points. He completed 38 out of 80 passes.

Before bowing out of Bears action, Nagurski figured in the worst slaughter of an opposing team on record, the historic drubbing the Bears handed to the Washington Redskins on December 8, 1940. The Bears ran and passed for eleven touchdowns. Nagurski carried for long runs. All the Bears players contributed to the incredible triumph, including center Bulldog Turner who intercepted a pass and scored a touchdown. Sid Luckman, the finest quarterback the team was ever to have, engineered the Bear victory in this championship game which ended 73-0.

Near the close of the game, after the Bears had already scored ten touchdowns and each extra-point ball that sailed into the stands was kept by a fan as a souvenir, one of the officials approached Luckman. "Would you mind awfully," asked the sheepish official, "passing or running for the point after this touchdown? You see, this is our last ball."

Gentleman that he was, Luckman nodded agreement. Following the eleventh and final humiliating touchdown, the great quarterback passed for the extra point. He was to go on throwing bell ringers for a number of happy

Pulitzer Prize winning Chicago cartoonist John Fischetti, who believed in the Bears to the end of his wonderful life.

years with the Bears, Luckman's all-time record achieved on November 14, 1943, when he threw seven touchdown passes in one game at the Polo Grounds.

To be sure, the Bears would later boast of Bobby Layne and Johnny Lujack as wonder-boy quarterbacks, but there would never be another Luckman, whose aim and toss had everyone in pro ball marveling. In the words of his mentor Papa Bear: "He could fake the ball, drop back, and hit an ant in the eye with a thirty-yard heave."

Much of the Bears success was due to the ever-expanding inventiveness of George Halas who initiated the use of the wide-spread, modern T-formation in pro football. He considered traditional wing formations outmoded by the 1940s and came up with puzzling off-balance attacks. He was the first to add a man in motion to his T, and offered each year at least 400 new plays to befuddle the opposition. Halas was also the first man to film his games for detailed study by team members and coaches.

During the 1950s the Bears slumped badly. It was not until 1964 that the Bears won another championship when quarterback Bill Wade teamed up with Bear end Mike Ditka to upset the Giants under Y. A. Tittle in a 14–10 victory. The team played seesaw battles with superstars Gale Sayers, Dick Butkus, and others futilely attempting to regain the Bears former glory and standings. By then George Stanley Halas had turned over the reigns of leadership to other coaches, although Papa Bear is still very much alive and casting a keen eye on the team that will always be known as his.

Other eyes, sadly enough, are not riveted on the bad news Bears, although the fans hang on in a sort of love-hate relationship with the aching team. In the words of the late Pulitzer Prize-winning cartoonist John Fischetti who braved the bitter wind inside Soldier Field to see the team squirm and wriggle: "You go to every game, hoping this one will be the turn. Then they screw up, and your hope turns bitter. By the end of the game you hate every man on the team and Halas, too. It's love going in, hate coming out. But by Wednesday your hopes go up again."

7

The Mad Money Merchants

Chicago's members of the superrich, compared with the conservative tycoons of the East, have always manifested distinctive, often bizarre, traits; they have been tyrants of taste, often bad to abdominable, have, until recent years, flaunted their garish fortunes and built impossible monuments, in the streets and cemeteries, to their own mad egos. These autocrats of Monte Cristo wealth also provided Chicago's generations with laughter and bathos that rivaled any Max Sennett comedy. On the whole, Chicago's wealthy presented the picture of mercantile frontiersmen lacking the manners and ofttimes the high-minded morality the Vanderbilts, Morgans, and Whitneys set down as hallmarks of their class. Self-serving, often crude, the midwestern moguls of business and finance were as public as streetcars and reveled in the gaudy, the crass, the gauche. They saw themselves as little different from the average person, except that they had more money.

From Gum to Barbed Wire

Perhaps the most amazing huckster of his era was the huffing, red-faced William Wrigley, Jr., a roaring Babbitt who made the chewing of gum as American as apple pie. Expelled from school in Philadelphia at age twelve, Wrigley ran away from home to sell newspapers on the wintery streets of New York. He later worked in his father's soap factory for $1.50 a week, then began to sell the soap as a drummer, establishing himself as a premier salesman. A total extrovert, Wrigley decided in 1892 at thirty-one that a fortune was to be made in chewing gum, something then unheard of in the United States.

The history of this phenomenon oddly enough began with an arch foe of America, Mexican dictator Santa Anna, who had been long deposed and was vacationing on Staten Island in 1868. The strutting military leader was

163

William Wrigley, Jr., who promoted the chewing of gum into a vast fortune. (UPI)

seen on the beaches breaking off pieces of chicle to chew. One gaper,
Thomas Adams, later ordered 5,000 pounds of chicle, invented a machine
that would produce the chicle in long, thin strips notched so that store owners
could break off penny lengths, and sold the product under the label of Adams
New York Gum.

A Louisville druggist, John Colgan, found Adams's gum chewy but taste-
less so he added tolu balsam to the chicle and put out his own Taffy-Tolu
brand. William Wrigley, Jr., who had sampled the product, decided to go
into the gum business. He visited a gum manufacturer. A stickler for prompt-
ness, Wrigley had bragged long and loud how he had never been late for an
appointment. When the manufacturer kept him waiting for more than ten
minutes, Wrigley stalked out, tardiness which cost the manufacturer at least
$40 million a year, the annual business Wrigley brought to another manufac-
turer who interviewed him at the appointed minute.

Wrigley's sales genius soon established him as the predominant figure in his
field—inside of forty-five years his firm produced and sold more than 113
billion sticks of gum, paying out more than $185 million in dividends. (Wri-
gley named his first gum Lotta, meaning that his customers got a lot of value
for their pennies.)

The enormous success of Wrigley's gum allowed the extrovert in the man
to run rampant. He always bought flaming red cars, stating that they were

easier to find. The interviews he gave always accentuated his own sense of achievement. He bragged to the press that he could sell anything, "including pianos to armless men in Borneo." He was forever hustling, especially his own sales force, an enormous army of pitchmen who, after all, had a monopoly in the gum business. In 1902, Wrigley wanted to inspire his salesmen with the loftiest image he could muster—his own photograph. He personally autographed 12,000 pictures of himself and shipped these off to his representatives, asking that they return similarly signed photos to him.

For the potential customer, Wrigley was willing to do much more. Twice he shipped off his popular gum free to every name listed in every telephone book in America. Wrigley ordered an outdoor sign that was three miles long constructed next to the Trenton–Atlantic City Railway. He had a bevy of scribes rewrite the Mother Goose stories, inserting chewing gum into the nursery jingles, and distributed 14 million copies of these blatantly revisionist editions throughout the land.

The gum tycoon from Chicago soon had more than 10 percent of the public chewing away on his prosaic product (39 sticks per capita in 1914, 100 in 1925, 130 in 1947). His son, Philip K. Wrigley, proved to be as potent a promoter as his father, though more reserved in his approach. Deciding to devote his time to his baseball enterprises—the Chicago Cubs and the franchise he owned in Los Angeles—dynamic William turned over his gum

Gum magnate P.K. Wrigley, shown on Catalina Island in the 1930s; he died in 1977.

empire to his son P. K. in 1925. Young Wrigley immediately sailed across the Pacific and, in a short time, converted the Chinese into avid gum chewers.

P. K. Wrigley was no laggard in supporting the nation's military during World War II. Following the Japanese sneak attack on Pearl Harbor, Wrigley ordered the million-dollar electric sign advertising his gum in Times Square dimmed. The elaborate floodlight system that had made the Wrigley Building in Chicago light up like a birthday cake was then dismantled and turned over to the navy. He had long viewed the Japanese threat as real. Nine months before Pearl Harbor and before aluminum was prohibited to civilian manufacturers, P. K. voluntarily turned over to government agencies his entire five-hundred-thousand-pound inventory of aluminum ingots used for wrapping-foil. Of course, Wrigley did benefit from his patriotism; his firm got the job of wrapping army rations. Moreover, Wrigley's gum found a whole new generation of chewers in the ranks of the GIs who spread the product throughout the world. It was during this period that Wrigley's firm issued an unforgettable slogan aimed at American workers in war plants (italics added):

YOU AMERICAN WORKERS are showing the world what production really means. Yes, and you know how it helps to chew gum *while you work*. You know that chewing Wrigley's Spearmint Gum keeps your mouth moist—helps relieve monotony *and nervous tension*.

Tension among the Wrigleys was always relieved on Catalina Island, twenty-six miles off the coast of southern California, a barony that rivaled Hearst's San Simeon. William Wrigley had purchased the entire twenty-two-square-mile island (except the town of Avalon) for about $3 million in 1919. The Wrigley estates dominate Avalon today, perched on towering hills above beautiful Avalon Bay. Here the grade-school dropout, his son, and his grandson have peered over tranquil Pacific waters undoubtedly marveling in the dynasty produced by their dirt common product, a wafer-thin piece of magic without enemies, except one, the venerable Emily Post who deliberately shunned any mention of gum in the many editions of her *Etiquette*. The immense popularity of the Wrigley product finally compelled the grandiose arbiter of taste to write publicly, "It is still impossible to imagine a lady walking on a city street chewing gum."

Nothing, on the other hand, was impossible in the imagination of another Chicago business mogul, John Warner Gates, better known to the gambling worlds as Bet a Million. Flamboyant, extravagant, a plunger to the last penny, Gates, like Wrigley, was a hard-nosed salesman who built his fortune on profits from barbed wire, the bane of the cowboy and the cattle baron, the fortress of the farmer. By 1890, Gates had put together one of the most powerful trusts in America, consolidating all the manufacturers of barbed wire in his monopoly. He did this simply by buying out the patents of business opponents. Those who resisted Gates saw the ruthless side of an iron-willed competitor.

Reluctant owners of some barbed-wire patents were invited by Gates to a special suite in Chicago's Wellington Hotel. Bet a Million wasted no time. He offered $400,000 for the patents. Still the representative of some owners held out. Gates, chomping on a cigar, put his face up close to the man and stared into his eyes, saying, "Mister, we're going out to Billy Boyle's to eat. When we get back, I might make one more offer. You tell that to your bosses. If you take it, all right. If you don't we'll push you to the wall and ruin you!" The offer was accepted and Gates formed the Columbia Patent Company. By March 1900, Gates was head of the powerful American Steel and Wire Company. Though many times a millionaire, Gates could never resist a new venture, despite the fact that he might not fully understand the workings of a new enterprise. In 1905, he attempted to corner May wheat in Chicago's commodity markets and lost more than $7 million within weeks. He then plunged into the production of costly Broadway extravaganzas and lost millions on those ventures. But he battled Gould and Harriman, pulling off vastly successful business coups at the expense of these easterners. The one man he could not beat, J. Pierpont Morgan, ultimately finished John W. Gates as a financial power in the U.S. In 1907, Morgan forced a panic in the sale of the stock of Gates's powerful southern combine, the Tennessee Coal and Iron Company, costing the firm more than $60 million and compelling Gates's partners to be absorbed into the U.S. Steel firm. Though associated with Republic Steel after that, Gates, nevertheless, was finished as one of the nation's business leaders.

Few of the thousands of workers in his plants were sorry to see him go; Gates was tighter with a dollar than Carnegie, stingy to the point of meanness to his employees, cold-hearted, and uncaring. He once shut down a plant throwing 4,000 employees out of work, even though immense orders for steel and iron products were waiting to be filled. Gates's decision remained inexplicable even when the press questioned his reasoning. His only statement was "Our company is running this business, without any need of explaining, and we shut down and open our mills when we see fit." At the time, Gates was paying his top workers $11.70 a week. He insisted that his workers be identified only by numbers, not their own names, a policy that caused the press to accuse him of treating his employees as convicts.

One of Gates's critics responded to the lockout by typifying him as "a man without the bowels of compassion," but added that "in the domestic relations he is a model son and father." Bet a Million did not run around with pretty, young women; he was a loyal family man devoted to his wife. But he had two vices that were for him obsessive—gambling and his errant son Charlie.

Gates spoiled his son rotten which was public knowledge. Nothing Charlie Gates did provoked his father's considerable wrath. Once, when Charlie was in his late teens, he staggered drunk into the resplendent Gates mansion at 2944 South Michigan Avenue. Bet a Million took his offspring by the arm, sat him down, and understandingly patted him on the head telling the youth in a soft voice that Demon Rum would be the end of him (Gates had interrupted a business meeting to coddle his boy while financial leaders sat in silent shock.)

"Son," Gates told Charlie, "I'll make you a proposition. You stay sober until you're twenty-one. Don't get drunk this way and be a good boy. You do that and on the day you're twenty-one, I'll deposit a million dollars in the bank in your name."

Charlie Gates might have been an apprentice alcoholic but he was nobody's fool. He took the deal, stayed sober until turning twenty-one, and, the minute he collected the million dollars, went on a wild and drunken spending spree that even shocked the Levee, Chicago's roaring red-light district. He was always the same after that, always broke, and always given more fortunes to squander by his father.

Bet a Million was almost as indulgent of his pet dog, a Boston bull terrier named Blondie, as he was of son Charlie. He took the dog with him wherever he went, insisting, much to the chagrin of headwaiters, that the dog be seated next to him in America's exclusive restaurants. In the three-story mansion Gates called home in Chicago, a special chair was built for the dog and this chair was always next to Bet a Million's place at the dining table. Blondie would squat in the chair gobbling freshly ground meat while Gates and family ate their chef-prepared meals.

John W. Gates was not religious, although he donated large sums to charities and even founded the St. Charles Training School for wayward boys. He had a deep resentment for orthodox churches, having been barred from attending church as a youngster after being accused of stealing from the poor box. This seething anger surfaced years later during Gates's heyday when some ministers headed by Charles E. Baller came to the millionaire to seek funds in establishing a new Methodist church in West Chicago.

Gates studied the group of respectful clergymen assembled before his enormous desk who were staring about at the magnificent offices. He then settled his gaze on Baller and snarled, "Not a damned cent, Charlie. I was thrown out of that Sunday school for something I wouldn't think of doing—stealing pennies! I've done a lot of mean things in my life, but nothing that low. You boys don't get a red cent!" The tycoon promptly tossed the religious leaders out of his office, enjoying his vengeance thirty years later.

Bet a Million was never thrown out of any gambling den he frequented and he was a regular visitor to the most lavish gambling casinos the world over. He would, it was said, play anybody at almost any game; his fascination for poker never abated. One story, undoubtedly apocryphal, had it that he would bet on anything which earned him his sobriquet. An oft-told canard had it that Gates was dining with another multimillionaire and, after watching a fly buzz about his table, pointed to the insect and said, "I'll bet a million that that fly lands on the sugar bowl." The bet was made and Gates won, naturally.

Other legends about Gates were certainly true. He did, indeed, in a marathon head to head poker game at the Waldorf-Astoria Hotel in New York, beat fellow tycoon Joseph Leiter to the tune of almost a half million dollars. His insatiability for gambling was never at more of a fever pitch than when he strolled into the fabulous casino owned and operated by the mysterious, elegant gambler Richard Canfield. He lost fortunes at Canfield's tables but always paid up without a whimper. His one great desire was to beat Canfield. To that end he battled Canfield's faro tables one night (after losing that very afternoon $325,000 at a nearby racetrack). He asked that the stakes be raised from the average $500 on case cards and $1,000 on doubles to $2,500 and $5,000. The dealers made special allowances for Bet a Million, making the limits four times higher than anywhere else in the world, including Monte Carlo. Still the stakes were not high enough for Gates. He asked for higher limits to be given to him.

Canfield himself, impeccably attired, cool, reserved, walked to Gates's private gaming room. "What limits are you now playing?" he asked the millionaire.

"Twenty-five hundred to five thousand."

"How high do you wish to go?"

"Five and ten."

Canfield never blinked, saying, "You may have it." He then added wryly, "Are you sure that's high enough?"

It was. Gates played faro all night and won more than $400,000, thereby cutting his losses to less than $75,000. He emerged from the gaming room flushed with victory. Seeing Canfield strolling across the lobby of his lavish emporium, Gates could not resist gloating. He marched up to the prince of gamblers and announced, "I've beaten you, Canfield. I've taken $400,000 from your establishment."

Richard Canfield smiled pleasantly. He shook Gates's hand. Without a quaver in his voice at having lost a fortune to his arch gambling foe, he said, "So glad you enjoyed your visit. Perhaps you'll win big next time." As Gates stared unbelievably at the nerve of the man, Canfield calmly went into another gaming room to greet other guests.

"I don't think," Bet a Million intoned to a friend standing nearby, "that I'll ever speak to that fellow again as long as I live."

Hog Butcherers

Philip Danforth Armour was another of those "self-made and proud of it" men who put his brand on Chicago society as surely as he did the beef that passed through the enormous stockyards. Born in 1832 in New York State, this farm boy journeyed to the goldfields of California, scooped up a modest strike, and returned East only to drift back to the Midwest, settling in Milwaukee where, with John Plankinton, he began his career as a meat packer. He soon moved to Chicago once he realized that that city was becoming the nation's hub of the railway systems.

It was in Chicago that Armour's wealth grew to enormous proportions. He was a tireless worker, demanding and driven only to enlarge his estate and coffers. When once asked what his pastime was, Armour dryly replied, "Making money. It is my vocation and my avocation." He more than any other individual was responsible for the success of Chicago's sprawling Union Stockyards.

The pork packer was easily angered at the thought of those who did not slave as he did to earn their money. When he heard that Marshall Field did not leave his home for the office until 9:00 A.M. (and left his office before 4:00 P.M.), Armour became enraged, snarling, "No Chicagoan should indulge in such leisure!" Armour always got up at 5:00 A.M. on the dot, breakfasted within an hour, and was behind his office desk by 7:00 A.M. waiting "for the boys with the polished nails to show up." He would leave the office at 6:00 P.M. and, without variation, head straight to his mansion at 2115 Prairie Avenue where he would eat a large home-cooked meal and retire, also without variation, at 9:00 P.M. That was his life, period.

Once, while in the company of his fellow magnates Field and Pullman, Armour's rigid schedule was challenged. Though it was nearing 9:00 P.M., Field suggested a game of cards. Bristled Armour to Field: "I have not broken my retiring hour for Mrs. Armour and I see no reason to do it for you. It must be wonderful to have a business like yours—and keep bankers' hours!"

The meat packer was an enigma to the press. A group of reporters cornered Armour one day, one bold newsman stating, "You've made your pile—why not clear out?"

The normally succinct Armour was shocked at such a question. "I have no other interest in life but my business," he answered with injured pride. "I do not want any more money. As you say, I have more than I want. I do not love the money. What I do love is the getting of it. What other interests can you suggest to me? I do not read. I do not take part in politics. What can I do?" (According to writer James Burnley, Armour was so busy that he "never watched a parade in Chicago," in fact, he never once even walked to his office window to view men marching in the street below.)

Armour's attitude toward women, or the only woman in his life, his wife, Malvina Belle Ogden of Cincinnati, was similar to his view of good livestock. He once admitted that he "looked around for a long time for a good mother with daughters, and I found her in Cincinnati. I went down there and picked out the youngest and prettiest of the girls."

Through shrewd manipulation of pork prices during the Civil War, Armour established a gigantic fortune. He had an uncanny ability to determine the value of young companies seeking investment. After studying the growth of Midwest railroads, he felt that the St. Paul line was a major opportunity. He bought $4 million worth of stock in the line at $65 a share and saw the stock skyrocket to $95 a share in a short period of time.

The meat packer demanded unswerving loyalty at all times from his employees and business associates. Calvin Favorite, his private stockbroker on the Chicago Board of Trade, had a son who began a new firm. Hearing of this Armour called Favorite.

"What's this I hear, Calvin, about your son forming a new company?" grilled Armour.

"I guess that's true," replied Favorite.

"I hear that he is taking some Armour men along with him."

"I guess that may be true," admitted the broker. "But I don't see how I can stop that."

"I don't see how you can either, Calvin," seethed Armour. "But I do know that if you don't, you and I part company." He got his way.

Nothing, however, angered Philip Armour more than the mention of his chief competitor and fellow meat packer Gustavus Franklin Swift. Upon hearing that his executives were studying Swift's business tactics, Armour exploded with indignation, issuing the following decree: "I have ordered a rule posted in our House that anyone who refers to business in the future, and says that we ought to do so and so because Swift is doing so and so, will be shot!"

When Armour died on January 8, 1901, he left his empire and $30 million to his two sons, Jonathan Ogden Armour, the heir apparent, and Philip Danforth Armour, Jr. The old man's funeral was huge, all of his thousands of employees lining the route of his hearse. Among the crowd was a junior executive who remembered the boss well. It had been the custom of Philip Armour, Sr., to reward his office help with new suits, cheaper outfits given to younger office helpers. When Armour had seen the junior executive ordering a costly suit at the meat packer's expense, one that did not fit the young man's position, Armour had growled, "I have killed a lot of hogs, but this is the first time I ever dressed one."

J. O. Armour had his father's penchant for empire and the ego to go with it. He bought the Chicago Subway Company to "clear the streets of traffic," he told a friend, and, in that way, have more room for his own car. He reveled in his fortune, snorting to his advertising director, "J. P. Morgan may have more money, probably has, but I believe I have more power than any other man in the world."

His local power in Chicago was enormous and, according to the Illinois Tax Reform League in its 1909 report, scandalous in that Armour, who

Actress Sarah Bernhardt's fascination for Chicago's slaughterhouses caused her to order members of her troupe to witness the bloodletting.

Singer Mary Garden, who once terrorized J.O. Armour in his office.

headed the Beef Trust, held personal property worth $30,840,000 and was assessed each year on only $200,000. J. O. was certainly not the world-beater his father had been. He often shunned public appearances, stating that his father knew how to make speeches but he did not. "He was," according to one Chicago historian, "the classical example of the rich man's son who didn't know what to do with himself."

He also appeared helpless in cleaning up the horrid sanitary conditions in his meat-packing plants, either inept, or worse, indifferent. Again, he relied upon the philosophy of his father: "I like to turn bristles, blood, and the inside and outside of pigs and bullocks into revenue." It was this very credo that caused muckraker Upton Sinclair to pen his classic novel *The Jungle* in 1906, a book that shocked President Theodore Roosevelt, and, more than any other factor, brought about the passing of the Pure Food and Drug Act. ("I aimed at the nation's conscience," moaned Sinclair later, "but all I did was hit its stomach.")

Though his pride and pocketbook were hurt in cleaning up his plants, J. O. Armour delighted in showing off his slaughterhouses, ordering that tours be conducted. Sarah Bernhardt, the great prima donna of the theater, a burly, aggressive sort, so much enjoyed the slaughterhouses—she spent hours watching with fascination the pigsticking—that she ordered her entire troupe, including ingenues who wept at the bloody sight, to witness the killing. In 1910, opera singer Mary Garden took the tour after meeting J. O. at lunch. Some strange urge was undoubtedly ignited by the bloodletting, for she showed up in J. O.'s office a few hours later and refused to leave. Heavily perfumed and displaying a shocking amount of silk-stockinged leg as she sat perched on Armour's desk, she terrified the tycoon by blowing smoke in his face from a cigarette in a long holder. Rushing into the office to rescue their boss from this vamp, Armour's executives found J. O. cowering in a corner.

Mrs. Armour, the former Lolita Sheldon, played out the role of grande dame in Chicago, surrounding herself with hundreds of well-to-do yes-women, all, of course, from her own class. Her notion of a picnic was to spread a damask tablecloth on a marble table not more than fifty yards from her front door on her estate grounds, and to be served with silver by the butler and several footmen. She had the hobby of collecting shoes, the most expensive made, and boasted that at all times she had not less than 100 pairs of white ones alone.

By 1922 the Armours had lost their millions, the company stock had been bought up and the estates had vanished as the great plantations of the South had. J. O. Armour paid off his creditors to the last penny; they would not, however, accept some oil rights which they considered worthless. The Armour luck proved to be intact. Some years later the oil rights were valued at $8 million.

The lifelong and most dogged competitor of the Armour empire was

Gustavus Franklin Swift, a taciturn 190-pound, 6-foot business tycoon who
devoted almost as much of his waking hours to the meat-packing industry,
and his many other investments, as did the irascible P. D. Armour. It was
Swift who was accused of making his fortune off meat by-products. He did
not deny it, telling reporters, whom he would seldom see, that he could not
tolerate waste. It was Swift who famously quipped, "Now we use all of the
hog, except the grunt." If he could have packaged the grunt, the Swift label
would have gone onto it.

Swift, also a farm boy like Armour but from Massachusetts, came to
Chicago in 1875, also the year in which Armour arrived from Milwaukee. He
was never the plunger into fields other than meat packing that Armour was,
devoting most of his time to Swift & Company. He sought to save money at
every turn. Swift felt that middlemen buyers of cattle inflated the prices, so he
traveled west at every chance to buy his own cattle and arrange for shipment
to the Chicago stockyards. He did everything but ride the cattle cars back
home.

He watched his plants like a hawk and any time he spotted workmen with
hammers and nails he called in the plant manager. (He was adamant about
not making repairs.) On one occasion he thundered, "Whenever you see a lot
of mechanics at work anywhere you are in charge, fire 'em!"

"But sometimes they are needed, Mr. Swift," came the manager's reply.

"They'll find their way back, then. They're a luxury. We can't afford
luxuries. It isn't only the high wages you pay 'em—it's the lumber and nails
and brick and hardware they use too. No, sir, when you see a gang of 'em
around and you don't know that you have to have 'em around, be on the safe
side and fire 'em. That's the way I always work it."

Once Swift decided to pay an unscheduled visit to one of his remote plants,
entering by the back gate. A vigilant security guard challenged him with,
"Hey, you, where are you going?"

"Isn't this Swift & Company's plant?"

"Yes, but you can't come in this way," the guard told Swift. "You have to go
around the front."

"I'm going in this way," said the obstinate bewhiskered old man.

"No, you're not."

"I certainly am. It's shorter to go through than to go around."

"You won't go through this gate. Now get out of here!"

"Say—do you know who I am? I am G. W. Swift!"

"I don't care who you are. My orders are that nobody comes through here
unless it's part of his job. You can't go through here even if you are Mr.
Swift—and I don't think you are."

Swift stared at the guard, studying his face. "What's your name?"

"Bateman."

"All right, Bateman. You'll hear more of this."

The guard smirked and closed the gate in the old man's face. Swift, his face red, walked to the front of the plant and within minutes was standing before the startled plant manager.

"You've got a guard on the back gate named Bateman?"

"Yes—yes, sir," stammered the manager.

"Good man. He wouldn't let me in. Better raise his wages. A man like that will save us a whole lot more than he costs."

Everybody and everything in the world of G. W. Swift had to pull his or its own weight, even his prize horse. One morning while driving into the stockyards, the horse slipped on ice and fell. Several men ran to the horse to help lift it on its feet. Swift leaped up in the buggy, cracking his whip in the air, shouting, "Let him alone! Let him alone! If he can't get himself up, I don't want him!" The horse struggled upright, vindicating the thorny demands of its owner.

Swift, like his erstwhile competitor Armour, was a devoted family man, one who told reporters that living in Chicago was better for maintaining wedded bliss than living in the wicked old East. "The New Yorker who says Chicago is a city of no luxuries is probably one of that constantly growing number who are insatiable in their greed for the softer things in life. To those men who have families and who find in their homes the greatest of their pleasures, Chicago offers all that New York offers, and, in my opinion, more."

When not at work for his meat packing empire, G. W. Swift was in his home, playing boss, of course. His domicile was nothing like the ostentatious mansions of Armour, Field, Palmer, McCormick, and Gates. He, his wife Ann, and his sons lived in a comfortable but nondescript home at the corner of Emerald and 45th streets, close to the stink of the stockyards, which is where Swift insisted they stay. Not until the close of his career did Swift give in to his wife's pleas and move the family to another house, somewhat larger but still nowhere near resplendent, at 4848 Ellis Avenue.

After moving in, his wife told Swift that "everything was ordered except the draperies and laces."

The mere mention of such luxuries caused the old man to catch his breath. "Draperies and laces?"

Ann Swift nodded. "Draperies for the doors, lace curtains for the windows."

The tycoon shook his head. "We're not going to have any of those fool things for the windows!"

"I think we are," his wife said firmly.

"But, I hate curtains!"

"I know you do."

"Well, I won't have them in my house and that's that!"

Ann Swift was silent for a moment, then said, "I think you will have to find someone else to live with you in *your* new home, and that's that."

Marshall Field I, the dry goods king, all business and grace. (UPI)

G. W. Swift looked at his wife in complete shock. "What do you mean?"

"Exactly what I say. I've lived more than thirty years inside houses that were as you like them, Gustavus, or, at least, not as I liked them."

The meat packer only glanced at his wife's narrowed eyes to know he was beaten, probably for the first and only time in his life. "I don't have to have them in the bedroom, do I?" he asked meekly.

"No," smiled Ann Swift.

Swift had the soul of an accountant and was forever attempting to teach his children arithmetic at an early age, especially at dinner. One night he selected little George Swift, age five, to tally the figures he threw out. "How much is twelve plus thirteen, George?"

"I don't know," the boy shrugged.

"Sure you know," G. W. insisted, giving his son his businessman's stare.

George began to wither beneath his stern parent's glare, whimpering, "I don't know—that's too hard for a little boy."

G. W. would not give up. "Now you listen, George! If you had twelve cents and I gave you thirteen cents, how much would you have?"

The five-year-old lifted his eyebrows, grinned widely and blurted the Swift philosophy, "Oh, a quarter, of course! Why didn't you say you meant *money*?"

The Second Family

Marshall Field I, as a maker of fortunes, a breaker of men, and the dynastic founder of what has always been considered Chicago's "second family" in the hierarchy of high society, was no garish drumbeater when he first came to Chicago from Massachusetts. He was born in Conway, Massachusetts, in 1834. (Like Swift, Field descended from Pilgrim fathers.) Tall, blonde, handsome, Field was absorbed with the work ethic, taking a clerical position with the wholesale dry-goods firm of Cooley, Wadsworth & Company. He managed to save half of his first year's salary of $400 by sleeping on the store's counter.

Charming manners and a soft voice made the young man appealing to his superiors, an attitude that overlapped into his business philosophy when dealing with customers and still does throughout the Field department stores. Yet, as Ernest Poole once said of him, Field could be "cold-souled and courtly." While working for Cooley, Field spent most of his conscious moments memorizing the stock on hand. According to his older brother Joseph, Field "carried purchasing and selling prices in his head or in a small black book kept carefully in an inner pocket." He was a genius at turning over stock, selling off lines rapidly, and acquiring new ones. He brought such profit to his firm that he was taken in as a partner in January 1860 when he was only twenty-five years old.

Three years later Field was a comparatively rich man with enough means to afford a good marriage. To that end he met twenty-three-year-old Nannie Douglas Scott of Ohio at a social and promptly fell in love with her. He was either too reserved or too shy to propose but he did follow the lovely to the train station. Just as the train was pulling out, Field yielded—perhaps the only moment in his life—to a compulsion; he leaped aboard, raced to Nannie, and asked that she be his wife. The romantic woman accepted.

Field turned back to business with a vengeance. In 1867 he and Levi Zeigler Leiter pooled their funds (Field borrowed $100,000 from his onetime employer John Farwell) and bought out the vast dry-goods operations of Potter Palmer.

Field's title of The Merchant Prince, a sobriquet bestowed by the press and one he abhorred, seemed to be justified with the opening of his grand, great store at Washington and State streets on October 12, 1868, when Field was but thirty-four years old and the city of Chicago only one year older. A great throng, all of the best families in the city, appeared at the doors, for Field and Leiter had ballyhooed the fact that their emporium would be the finest in the world, offering the best goods that could be purchased anywhere—and that meant New York.

Gushed the *Chicago Tribune*: "The attendance of wealth, beauty, and fashion . . . was something unparalleled in Chicago's history. One would have thought that the opening was an adjourned meeting of the Charity Ball, judging from the long line of carriages filled with the cream of the avenues. The attractions were unusual—a drygoods store in a marble palace."

Field inspected his first grand store (and the one rebuilt after the Great Chicago Fire of 1871) with ritual, checking his clerks and looking over the quality of his merchandise. On one occasion Field stood behind a pillar listening to idle clerks singing a chorus. He stepped into view after allowing them to finish their song and said, "Sing it again, boys, but this time a little softer." When he spotted one salesman hiding dirt and wastepaper behind a counter, he pointed to the debris and said to the embarrassed clerk, "What are you getting ready to do here? Raise potatoes?"

It was rare for the department store tycoon to praise any employee. When hearing that his ace carpet salesman James O'Malley had had a particularly good outing in Indiana, Field told him, "I am very proud of you, Jimmy."

"You don't tell me that very often, Mr. Field."

"That might cost me too much money," Field said without a smile.

As time went on, Field realized that he must rid himself of his truculent Dutch partner Levi Leiter. Horrible reports reached Field after his return from long business trips; his partner was losing a great deal of business with his brusque, mostly insulting, manners. One customer, Field learned, had entered the store and ordered $700 worth of goods. Leiter ran up to him and shouted, "No! You cannot have these goods."

"But I'm going to pay cash for them," the customer begged.

"That makes no difference," Leiter said, shoving the man toward the door. "Your record is bad!"

Any customer who failed to purchase an item as promised was on Leiter's permanent no-good list. One such patron was accosted by Leiter as he was about to buy an item with cash. Leiter grabbed the item and put it back in the rack, shouting, "You promised to return for something last week and you did not do it, so get out! Hurry—or I will have the porter throw you out!"

Leiter's quirks were outright bizarre. He suspected the worst of anyone who dyed his hair. He barred the way of one patron, shaking his head and pointing to the door.

"But I have made some purchases," said the customer, "and I've come to pick them up."

"No, you don't!" Leiter bellowed. "You are a thief! Your mustache is dyed—so get out of here!"

Finally, Field had had enough. He canvased his salesmen and clerks, telling them he intended to either buy out Leiter or sell to him; he simply could not go on in partnership with such a self-destructive person. His employees said that they would stay or leave with him, which is what Field had hoped and planned. He next went to Leiter and told him that he would name a price for the buy-out and Leiter had twenty-four hours to accept it. If he chose to buy out Field, he would have to pay the same amount. Field then named a very modest price. Leiter nodded agreement feeling he would not be bought out for such a paltry sum, that he could wait and buy Field out the next day. During the allowed time period, however, Leiter went to the employees and discovered that if he bought the enterprise they would all quit, leaving him destitute. He was compelled to take Field's offer the following day, outfoxed by one of the shrewdest men to ever stroll the streets of Chicago. From that moment on, Marshall Field I had the department store empire virtually to himself. Field was labeled a ruthless tyrant by his severest critics, a tyrant who unconscionably abused his employees, especially the thousands of sewing women, weavers, and others on several continents who produced his wholesale goods. It was accurately estimated that Field, during his heyday, made a personal income of between $500 and $700 an hour while he paid his workers $2 a day, working them in sweatshops fifty-nine hours a week. "Pay your employees as little as you can, and sell your goods for the highest price you can get" was the Field philosophy, as summed up by historian Gustavus Meyers, who also felt that Field's much-vaunted generosity to the poor and needy was mythical. Boomed Meyers , "The amounts that Field gave for 'philanthropy' were about identical with the sums out of which he defrauded Chicago in the one item of taxes alone."

The Field enterprises grew astronomically during the 1880s. The company grossed $30 million in 1884, $50 million a year by 1901. By 1895, Field and his onetime partner Levi Leiter owned $319 million worth of land in Chicago's South Side alone.

The claim that Field "had been nothing more than a persistent tax evader," was based on the tycoon's habit of insisting that he be assessed on not more than $2,500,000 worth of personal holdings in Chicago. If city officials dared to raise the assessment, Field threatened to leave the city, moving his residence to another locale where municipal authorities would appreciate getting what they could from his personal holdings. Stubborn assessors in 1908, however, insisted that $1,730,000 be paid the city of Chicago in back taxes. (This was an incredibly low estimate, utter generosity on the part of city officials.) The Field estate compromised and sent John R. Thompson, treasurer of Cook County, a check for $1 million, which was accepted without question. The deal saved the Field estate a staggering fortune. To quote Meyers, "If the compound interest for the whole series of years during which Field cheated in taxation were added to the $1,730,000, it would probably have been found that the total amount of his pocketing of tax money reached several million dollars."

At least Field did pay *some* taxes during his lifetime, unlike the scores of magnates who completely ignored dues to the government. In 1905 Marshall Field was reported to be the individual who paid the highest amount of taxes in the United States. Moreover, Field's interests were vast, almost unknown except to the inner core of his executive circle. The sleeping-car empire of George Pullman, for instance, was in Field's hip pocket according to one newspaper account appearing in 1901. "In the popular mind," read the account, "George M. Pullman has ever been deemed the dominant factor in that vast and profitable enterprise." The account labeled this belief a lie and that "Field is, and for years has been, in almost absolute control. Pullman was little more than a figurehead. Such men as Robert T. Lincoln, the president of the company, and Norman B. Ream are but representatives of Marshall Field, whose name has never been identified with the property he so largely owns and controls."

According to the executors of Field's twenty-two-thousand-word will (the most comprehensive and airtight such document ever recorded in a Chicago court), the department store tycoon owned 8,000 shares of Pullman stock, then valued at $800,000, just after his death on January 6, 1906. Field had at the time of his death about $4.5 million in various banks, another $8.5 million due him from the store, vast real estate holdings in Chicago and New York, stocks, bonds—an overall fortune of more than $140 million. His staggering estate was the only Chicago holding that rivaled that of the Astor, Rhinelander, and Goelet fortunes of New York.

With more than five thousand persons flocking to Chicago's auditorium, few not employed in Field's enterprises, Congressman George Adams addressed the silent throng. "What poor man has the right to complain of Mr. Field's millions?" bellowed the congressman. "Who has the right to envy his success? All the world knows how it was won—all the world knows that the patient, intelligent industry and square dealing which made Mr. Field one of the richest men in the world are just the qualities by which a right-thinking poor man strives to better his condition and make life easier for his family."

Marshall Field's dynasty, with his son Marshall Field II dead from gunshot wounds (as described in an earlier chapter), fell to his grandsons Henry and Marshall III, fortunes that were left to them in five-year stages, beginning with their twentieth and twenty-fifth birthdays respectively, Marshall getting the lion's share.

Marshall Field III was raised in England, returning to America in 1914 on the *Lusitania* which would be sunk by German torpedoes the following year. On that boat trip Field fell in love with Evelyn Marshall of New York. They were married the following year. Despite his wealth, Field enlisted in the army as a private in 1917; his newspaper rival of two decades later, the bellicose Colonel Robert McCormick, also enlisted—as an officer on Pershing's staff.

Following the war, Field settled down in a luxurious Long Island, New York, estate rather than return to Chicago. The huge estate Caumsett—all of 1,630 acres, purchased in 1921 for $1.5 million—was staffed with eighty-five servants and provided guests with all sorts of amusements, including seaplaning and indoor tennis. Field occupied some of his time with investment banking but paid more attention to the hundred registered Guernseys grazing on his land. He had two daughters and a son, Marshall IV.

In 1930, Field divorced. He married again, this time to Audrey Coats, goddaughter of King Edward VII. The couple spent most of their time yachting about the world. Field divorced again in 1934 and underwent intensive analysis by Dr. Gregory Zilboorg. Field's third marriage took place in 1936 when he wed Ruth Pryn Phipps, with whom he had two more daughters.

The eccentric Dr. Zilboorg urged Field to enter a new business, the world of newspapering. He first bought *PM* in New York, and later the *Chicago Sun*, the *Chicago Times*, and the *Chicago Daily News*. The *Sun* and the *Times* were later combined to combat the morning behemoth the *Chicago Tribune*. Field's heirs lost the *News*, or rather collapsed it, in 1978 through what many considered cold-blooded indifference, discarding one of the greatest newspapers in the country, one whose walls sagged under the weight of Pulitzer Prizes. The *Sun-Times* continues but the inglorious end of the *News* marked the final dream of Marshal Field III.

During World War II, Field was lambasted by the jingoistic Colonel McCormick in one of the *Tribune*'s most disgraceful editorials, undoubtedly written by Colonel Bombast himself. The 1942 attack read: "Field is of age to volunteer. He cried for war before it came. Now that it has come, he lets men like MacNider and O'Hare do the fighting while he skulks in his clubs, night and otherwise. No one would suggest that he is indispensable to *PM*, or to anything else. The term to fit to him and to all the herd of hysterical effeminates is coward."

Field did not respond; he seldom reacted to criticism. He rarely made a public statement and when he did the words were puzzling. Before his death in 1956, Field's most controversial remarks had to do with the wealth of the Field empire: "I happen to have a great deal of money. I don't know what is going to happen to it and I don't give a damn."

This prompted John D. Rockefeller, Jr., to respond with "I don't care what happens to Marshall Field's money, but I do care what happens to mine."

But Field money is still present in Chicago and so too are its family members, all in low profile. The great fortune of $140 million left by the founding father, once thought to be an incomprehensible sum, dwindles in the imagination today when compared with the $240 million left in 1980 by the murdered ex-Beatle John Lennon. But in its day, the Field money was real, its taxes negligible, and opportunities for it to effectively control the destiny of Chicago unlimited.

Where the Fields of Chicago have always been considered perhaps Chicago's richest family, the McCormicks have been the city's most prestigious, or rather the first of the great dynastic families. They have certainly proved in the past to be the most provocative, some of its members, like the unforgettable Colonel McCormick, donning their own heads with royal crowns a la Henry VIII. And some of the McCormicks were on the decidedly wacky side, if not outright certifiable.

The First Family

The dynasty began with Robert McCormick, a Virginia farmer-inventor. With his son Cyrus Hall McCormick providing most of the creativity, the two invented the reaper in 1835, a device that revolutionized farming the world over and made Cyrus McCormick one of the wealthiest men on earth. Actually, hundreds of inventors had been attempting to create the reaper but it was Cyrus's version—he was the forty-seventh person to obtain a reaper patent—that proved to be the most universally effective.

When Cyrus McCormick was running for Congress from Chicago in 1864, the *Chicago Tribune* (ironically, the paper to which a branch of the McCormick family would later be umbilically bound) attacked Cyrus, stating that he had stolen the invention from a Cincinnati candlestick maker named Obed Hussey. It is true that Hussey invented a machine crudely similar to McCormick's; Hussey filed suits against McCormick but lost. The Hussey machine, as it was later used, in principle was essentially a lawn mower.

McCormick's success lay in the Midwest, his reaper initially rejected by the more conservative farmers of the East. He settled in Chicago in 1847, establishing his first manufacturing plant with the encouragement of the city's first citizen William B. Ogden. Other plants were constructed that literally formed a ring around the Midwest's breadbasket, and in this way, reasoned McCormick, farmers could be serviced better with parts for his reaper. A good businessman, McCormick allowed his customers to pay for his reaper in installments, knowing their livelihood depended upon seasonal crops; if the crops were poor, McCormick deferred payments.

The wealth poured in and McCormick began investing in Chicago real estate and railroads—anything that could turn another dollar. Before the close of the Civil War he was estimated to be worth more than $5 million, his income averaging $2,000 a day. He joined hands with Pullman in 1867 to garner most of the stock of the giant Credit Mobilier Company. A little more than fifty years later, the McCormick family of International Harvester and *Chicago Tribune* fame would be listed tenth in the breakdown of America's wealthiest families with an estimated gross fortune of $211 million.

A worker, McCormick delighted in rolling up his sleeves and laboring alongside his men in his plants whenever any machines broke down. He was tireless and, on occasions, incredibly stubborn. Once, when he missed his New York to Chicago train with his wife Nancy "Nettie" Fowler (whom he married in 1858 when he was almost fifty), McCormick exploded upon learning that not only had his luggage been sent on without him but that he had been overcharged $8.70 for "excess weight." McCormick carried on a twenty-year suit over the lost baggage and the overcharge, taking his case all the way to the U.S. Supreme Court. Though all the witnesses to the insignificant event were by then dead, except McCormick and his wife, the reaper tycoon won.

The millionaire had a sumptuous mansion built on Rush Street where he roamed through dozens of high-ceilinged rooms, firing servants on the spot who did not suit him. Somehow the noise and wailing of his five children never bothered him. He was totally absorbed in business, watching every penny. Once McCormick was traveling by stage and tried to haggle the driver's fee of $21 down to $15. He lost. In France, he underwent a serious operation for the removal of carbuncles. When he complained of the doctor's fees, he was curtly told that the operation had saved his life.

A year before his death, the seventy-four-year-old reaper king still worked an exhausting day in his office and plants. He exhausted everyone around him. Traveling to one of his plants, McCormick stopped in a country hotel to take breakfast. Within the hour he was storming out, thrusting a note into the hand of a startled headwaiter. The memo read: "Ordered oatmeal with sweet milk—sent to me cornmeal mush. Waited then & received cracked wheat— had ordered balance of breakfast in 20 mins. from first order and finally this breakfast was brought to me in about ½ hr., after the time it was to be here, thus losing ½ hr. of my time in waiting."

Even on his deathbed McCormick thought of nothing but his empire. When he died on May 13, 1884, at age seventy-five, his last words were "Work—work."

Though the mantle of directorship for the McCormick financial empire fell to Cyrus Hall McCormick II, there was never any doubt who really ran things. "I was elected president," the McCormick son later stated, "but you may believe me when I say that, in fact, I was not the president at all. My mother was the real president of the company, and she gave me my instructions on all points and all problems."

Nettie McCormick ran the harvester works as if she were maintaining the ark of the covenant. This deeply religious woman eventually turned over great fortunes to various religious organizations, giving almost a half million dollars to the Presbyterian church. Great cash gifts were made to other religious institutions, including the establishment of the McCormick Hall at the Theological Seminary dedicated in honor of Cyrus McCormick I.

Others in the McCormick family, however, were disinclined to honor the inventor of the reaper. In 1885 the inventor's brother Leander McCormick published a booklet entitled *Memorial of Robert McCormick* in which he stated that his father, not Cyrus, was solely responsible for the reaper, and that his greedy brother, who had "promised to make all the family rich if he ever made anything out of it," literally stole the invention. The family split into two warring factions over this impossible claim, creating the bitterest feud in the history of American capitalism, one that exists to this day.

Many of the McCormicks proved to be flamboyant, eccentric, and weird. There was William Sanderson McCormick, brother to Cyrus I, whose investment acumen was less than visionary. He turned down a request from Marshall Field I to back the first great department store, thereby losing millions. When Field's store proved to be a great success, William McCormick's nerves shattered. He took several medical cures and wound up in the State Hospital for the Insane in Jacksonville, Illinois, where he died; the cause of death was officially listed as typhoidal dysentery. "The Cyrus McCormicks," wrote Arthur Meeker, a family friend, "—we might as well face it—were noted for a certain not undistinguished goofiness. . . . Old Madam McCormick [Nettie] was subject to some form of circular dementia, and obviously should never have had children." Meeker went on to state that of Cyrus's five children, one son and a daughter were hopelessly insane and were kept in luxurious retirement in southern California all their adult lives. Another daughter, who became Mrs. Emmons Blaine, daughter-in-law of James G. Blaine, inherited $40 million, but acted as if she were Apple Annie, walking the streets of Chicago dressed like a tramp, supporting crank causes. She wandered aimlessly about Chicago, her purse threadbare, the heels of her ancient shoes breaking off.

Another son, Harold Fowler McCormick, at first seemed as steady as his rock-ribbed father. He married Edith Rockefeller, a grande dame of Chicago society for decades, but then became enamored of a Polish opera singer, Ganna Walska, who was no singer at all and brought nothing but ridicule to the McCormick clan. (It was the relationship between Harold McCormick and Walska, his second wife, that was most assuredly depicted in Orson Wells's *Citizen Kane* and affixed to the Hearstian legend like a shabby talisman.)

Ganna Walska, a dark, heavyset woman who was more vamp than artist, a female predator, spotted millionaire Harold and decided to snare him. At the time, Edith and Harold McCormick were the chief sponsors of the Chicago Opera Company. With such interests, McCormick, as naive as a twelve-year-old, was easily convinced by Walska that she was the greatest singer in the world after their first meeting in 1920. Ganna Walska, at the time, had but one operatic appearance in her scrapbook and she dared not mention even that. She had been with the Havana Opera Company in 1917; her debut was in *Fedora*. She was so terrible in her performance that she was all but hissed from the stage. The following night the audience showered the stage and the singer with rotten eggs and vegetables. Walska read her reviews, all acid-dipped and damning, and walked out on her own debut.

Harold Fowler McCormick and his bizarre Polish opera singer Ganna Walska; her eccentric career undoubtedly served as the inspiration for the heroine of *Citizen Kane*.

A view of the grand foyer of the Civic Opera House at the time of Ganna Walska's "near" performance.

She sang for Harold privately and soon convinced him that, in addition to her physical charms (for which he later divorced Edith and married her) she possessed a voice the world had to hear. "She clearly marked him as her prey and meant to devour him," wrote one society historian. "Worse, he was crazy to be devoured. I've no idea how many of his millions she managed to swallow too, during the years they spent together. Besides what he gave her in cash, jewels and real estate, he was forever hiring halls for his wife, subsidizing opera companies, making ill-advised attempts to bolster up a mythical talent."

Harold McCormick hired the best singing coaches in Europe to hammer a sense of music into Walska's head. Frances Alda was given $10,000 by McCormick to teach his paramour, but it was a futile attempt. So bad was the diva that she even appeared under aliases, but nothing could disguise that awful voice.

McCormick would not give up. He insisted that Walska appear at the Chicago Opera in the lead of Leoncavallo's *Zaza*. It was a disaster from the outset. (At the time Walska was the wife of multimillionaire sportsman and carpet tycoon Alexander Smith Cochran and McCormick was still married.) The opening was scheduled for December 21, 1920. The house was sold out in advance; Harold McCormick (like Orson Welles' Kane) saw to that. But there was no opening; Ganna Walska saw to that.

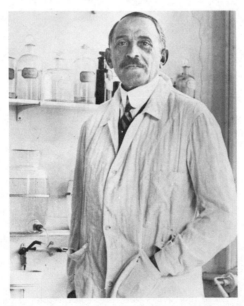

Dr. Serge Voronoff, whose monkey glands theories Harold McCormick accepted as reality. (UPI)

For Director Gina Marinuzzi the rehearsals were nightmares. The director insisted that the so-called soprano project her voice beyond the orchestra pit. Walska told the director what she thought of such insolence. As a result, the director gave up, turning over the production to Pietro Cimini. The new director could make nothing from nothing when it came to Ganna Walska's talent. At the dress rehearsal for *Zaza*, three days before the opera was scheduled to open, Cimini begged Walska to sing louder. Still the soprano's voice was barely audible. Finally, the exasperated Cimini called a halt and said to Walska, "Madame, please sing in your natural voice."

Walska sauntered to the footlights, glared down at Cimini and snarled, "Pig! You would ruin my performance!" As the director's mouth fell open in shock, Walska turned on her heel and marched from the stage, abandoning *Zaza* altogether. She went immediately to the business office, storming up to Herbert Johnson and Marinuzzi, shouting, "Gentlemen, I am packing my bags. At the end of this season you will be packing yours!"

Walska left for Europe and the Chicago Opera Company announced with much embarrassment that the production of *Zaza* was "postponed indefinitely." Harold McCormick was undaunted by this brazen act of mad ego; he continued to pursue the wild Walska who apparently convinced him that he was sexually inadequate. Harold's answer to that was, he believed, in the clinic run by Dr. Serge Voronoff, an infamous crackpot who had recently informed the world that he could rejuvenate any male, for the proper prices, through the transplanting of thyroid glands from monkeys. Harold McCormick underwent this operation, but it apparently failed from most reports.

Ganna Walska later discarded McCormick, as she had a half dozen other wealthy lovers, and moved into an enormous mansion in Santa Barbara, ironically, close to the Pacific estate of another retired prima donna, a real one, Lotte Lehmann. McCormick married a third time before his death, this time playing it safe by wedding his trained nurse.

The one McCormick who never played it safe and seldom held his tongue was the unpredictable, colorful Colonel Robert Rutherford McCormick who, in addition to the *Chicago Tribune* to which his name will be forever linked, established a broad empire in communications. Born in Chicago, the son of Robert Sanderson McCormick, the Colonel grew to 6-feet 4-inches and weighed (generally) around 215 pounds. He was fond of blood sports and engaged in boxing, polo, even riding to hounds on his Wheaton estate where he was later to erect the Cantigny Museum, adorning the landscape with World War I artillery pieces and inviting a not-too-eager public to walk through lifelike trenches while the sounds of warfare boomed and blasted on tapes. He wore a bristly mustache, British-tailored suits, shaved with an old-fashioned straight razor till the day of his death, and *always* ate a hearty meal, his dinners washed down with Scotch.

The editor of the *Tribune* also gardened and while at these chores he would sing his favorite ditty:

A family affair—Colonel McCormick's wedding picture in 1944 included (from left to right), Joseph Patterson, best man; Mrs. Chauncey McCormick; the Colonel; his bride, Mrs. Maryland Mathison Hooper; and Chauncey McCormick in whose lavish home the wedding took place. (UPI)

Pa ain't got no peas and corn,
Pa ain't got potaters,
Pa ain't got no lima beans,
But Jeesus—what tomaters!

McCormick literally ran everything at the *Tribune*. After he went to the Chicago Athletic Club one day in 1909 and found the *Tribune* treasurer signing checks in the steam room, he became the treasurer. Towering behind his red-and-white marble desk in the *Tribune* building, McCormick bellowed his orders to editors, advertising executives, and circulation and production chiefs who sweated under his glare in two lengthy meetings a day. He was an absolute dictator with all employees but he paid them well, awarded high bonuses, and provided dental and medical coverage, all of which, of course, kept his people from unionizing, or chiefly, kept the Newspaper Guild out of the *Tribune*; McCormick always paid his editorial personnel the same or more than Guild scale. No one, including the Guild, was going to tell Robert R. McCormick, Bertie to his intimate friends, what to do or say.

The Colonel thought he could merely point his finger at anyone who worked for him and convert him into a good newsman. One such nonwriter was promoted to foreign correspondent by the Colonel for mysterious reasons. The correspondent sent back incoherent copy to the desk in his travels, almost every word having to be rewritten. Then a piece arrived from the same correspondent that was near perfect. Suspicious, the copy editors checked and found that the correspondent had plagiarized the entire piece from the *Encyclopaedia Britannica*. When this was brought to McCormick's attention, he merely snorted, "Well, I'm glad the son of a bitch can read!"

Many asked if McCormick could read, or if he read his own newspaper. The distinguished critic Claudia Cassidy had been working for the *Tribune* for almost two years, her byline appearing almost every week. After she wrote a critique of *Good Night, Sweet Prince*, McCormick sent the following note to his editors: "Fine review. Why haven't we had this woman before? RRMc."

He was forever asking his editorial staff questions, some ridiculous, some inexplicable. He would call from London tying up the phones merely to ask what kind of weather Chicago was having. He set the staff on its ear once by calling to inquire "How much would be added to the known area of the world if the ocean bottoms were made into land?" Since the ocean bottoms have never been explored, the question was impossible to answer, but the Colonel expected answers. The reporter assigned to the task guessed that

Colonel Robert Rutherford McCormick, who ran the *Tribune* with an iron hand and issued his verbal autobiography over the WGN airways. (UPI)

there were twenty-million-odd square miles to the ocean bottoms (later confirmed as an appropriate estimate by the *National Geographic*), but no one ever found out why McCormick required such strange information.

McCormick was a superpatriot and a political gadfly, forever lambasting Washington. He was moody and changable when it came to politicians. He backed Herbert Hoover but, upon reading the president's inaugural address to be delivered the following day, he sent a wire to his Washington Bureau, imperially stating, "This man will not do."

During the gangster years, McCormick's personal fear for his life resulted in armed *Tribune* guards being placed everywhere in the Tower, machine guns hidden throughout offices, guard dogs trained to protect the boss. The Colonel kept an axe and telephone in his office toilet in case he was attacked.

His fear, of course, was of Al Capone, crime warlord of the twenties in Chicago, a fear which was barely evident in the words the Colonel broadcast in 1954. He purchased radio station WGN in 1924, changing its call letters from WDAP; it is still *the* giant among Chicago radio stations. In one of his chatty broadcasts at WGN three decades later, McCormick related how *he* backed down Capone one dreadful night. "There was talk of a strike and the publishers called a meeting to hear the demands. I arrived late. As I entered an outer office, I saw several swarthy, evil-looking men who eyed me

In his last years, McCormick wandered the streets of Chicago wearing dark glasses and being led by a German Shepherd, pretending to be a blind man.

coldly. Inside, I saw to my amazement that Al Capone brazenly had invaded the meeting with the aim of terrorizing those present. I ordered Capone to leave and to take his plug-uglies with him. I knew his reputation but I also knew he had never killed anyone himself [a gross misconception] and I didn't think he'd start then. Capone got out. He didn't muscle in on the newspapers. We continued to expose him." Nevertheless, McCormick, according to writer Ferdinand Lundberg, continued to "fear assassination," and was "driven like a Chinese war-lord in an armored car between his office and his Wheaton, Illinois estate."

McCormick's WGN was the first to broadcast "Little Orphan Annie," adapted at the Colonel's direction from the *Tribune*'s comic strip. In the early 1930s, the ever-tyrannical Colonel made it a policy that only his *Tribune* advertisers would be allowed to take commercials on WGN, a policy which showed his unusual understanding for restraint of trade.

His whims, fancies, and preferences were always catered to at the *Tribune* and at WGN. McCormick would call in and speak to the WGN orchestra director requesting his favorite tunes. Naturally these were played, repeatedly. Sometime in the late 1930s, the era in which the big bands were at their zenith, McCormick sent a memo to WGN which read, "The term 'swing music' has come to my attention. What is it? Should we have some of it on WGN?"

Like Harold McCormick's, the Colonel's taste ran to opera and so he featured this music on his Chicago Theatre of the Air, always followed by his own chatty talks. He was never able to find a sponsor for the program. Although informative, the Colonel's talks were, in a word, dull. He essentially began his oral memoirs on WGN. Listeners did not respond with a deluge of mail.

In the Colonel's first broadcast, he began with "I was born on July 30, 1880. My first vivid recollection is the day that the anarchists were hanged in Chicago, November 11, 1887 [four of the Haymarket rioters]. Children were not allowed out of doors because riots were feared. The police were armed with rifles. The widow of one of the men, Miss Van Zandt, who married the anarchist [August] Spies by proxy after his conviction, lived in our neighborhood. We were deathly afraid of the poor woman and I am afraid I shouted at her on the street. My older cousin, Robert Hall McCormick, had a high bicycle. I used to ride on the step behind him. One day her pug dog ran out and we rode over it, but fortunately did not kill it."

Irrespective of McCormick's self-indulgence, he continued to not only build up the *Tribune* and its communications groups, but invested in firms and real estate until he accumulated financial holdings of $100 million. His estate was valued at more than $20 million when he died in 1955.

Upon the death of this most spectacular man, it was recalled that the Colonel had the strange habit in his last years of roaming the Near North Side of Chicago, disguised as a blind man, wearing smoked glasses and clutching a leather harness, being lead by his favorite watchdog, a German shepherd. He would always wind up at the same address—150 East Ontario Street, his birthplace. He was known to the doorman and the manager of the nightclub that occupied the address as Haroun-al-Raschid, and was always treated with the greatest kindness. So courteous were these nightclub people that he decided to give them the treat of their lives. Under his alias, he arranged for an after-hours party which was attended by all of the nightclub's help. He treated them to dinner and drinks, finally rising, whipping off his dark glasses, and toasting the famous man who had been born on the sacred premises, Colonel Robert R. McCormick. Then he stared at the group and, thinking to shock his audience into awe, announced, "And I am that man!"

Everyone remained silent, smiling. They had known that all along.

8

Elegant Egomania

Most of Chicago's millionaries preferred to spend their fortunes in their own lifetimes, many dying close to broke. The traction king Charles Tyson Yerkes, Jr., the fat thief who ran the street railways of Chicago, reveled in corrupting aldermen, spending his tainted money, and shocking his fellow millionaires. "The secret of my success," Yerkes once whispered with a smile to the dour Marshall Field I, "is to buy up old junk, fix it up a little, and unload it upon some other fellows."

"Why don't you run more street cars during rush hours?" someone once asked Yerkes.

"Shush," Yerkes responded, putting a finger to his lips. "It's the strap-hangers who pay the dividends!" He delighted in the role of robber baron, once declaring, "Let us take the land anyway and apologize afterward."

Yerkes, who had misappropriated funds in Philadelphia in 1871 and served two years in prison for the deed, established a large brokerage house in Chicago, cornering the stock sold in the city's streetcar holdings. When he learned that a newspaper in town planned to reveal his prison record, Yerkes went directly to the paper's editor, telling him, "The publication of that article will hurt me. It will hurt me a great deal. It will hurt me personally. I shall be down and out. There will be nothing for me to do. I tell you all this so that you may not underestimate the consequences to me. I also inform you that if you publish it, I, myself, personally, will kill you, sure! Good morning!" The article was not published.

A voluptuary on all levels, Yerkes spent his fortune of $30 million on women, lavish balls, parties, and art. He was finally driven out of town by Mayor Carter Harrison, going to London where he died in 1901 with only $2.1 million in his depleted estate, not enough to begin the resplendent art museum in New York which Yerkes had decreed in his will should be established in his honor.

193

Samuel Insull, the utilities magnate, began his career in Chicago with $250,000 borrowed from Marshal Field I. (His son was later quoted as saying—given the disgrace heaped upon the family name after the Insull empire collapsed—that he'd "rather be injected with smallpox" than borrow money.) Insull was not a party-giver, preferring private soirees and purchasing yachts. At one time Insull was the president of fifteen corporations, the chairman of the board of fifty-six other firms, and a member of the board of eighty-one other companies.

During the Crash of 1929, the Insull empire began to totter, and to bolster it, Insull wildly attempted to buy up his own stock, throwing away his millions. Although the pyramid of holding companies Insull controlled was shattered, Commonwealth Edison and Peoples Gas were not harmed, contrary to public belief. To quote one business columnist, "The loss to the public on all its investment in Insull companies was less than twenty-five percent."

Insull, no longer able to stem the tide of debt that engulfed his holding companies, fled on a yacht to the Mediterranean. He was told to anchor his ship elsewhere by the Greek government. He sailed to Turkey where officials turned him over to U.S. authorities; he was wanted to answer charges in Chicago of using the mails to defraud.

Once back in Chicago, the depressed old man was placed in the Cook County jail next to a thirteen-year-old-boy charged with kidnapping and murdering a two-year-old girl. The press made much of the new company that the onetime tycoon was then keeping, but Insull was undaunted, telling the press, "I still think I did right by leaving Chicago when I did, and I would do the same thing again under similar circumstances."

He was acquitted of all charges and, thoroughly ashamed, left for Paris, where, in the summer of 1938, the great Insull stepped aboard a subway and died of a heart attack in a rush-hour crush. He had about 40¢ in his pockets and was wearing monogrammed underwear. He left an estate of less than $1,000 and debts spiraling beyond $14 million. He was remembered little by his own generation, except with criticism. "His idea of conversation," recalled a peer, "was a tediously insolent monolog."

The author once met Insull's grandson in a Chicago pub. He was every inch the gentleman, but at the mention of his grandfather's name, the grandson's bow tie almost popped, a wild look came into his eyes, and he bolted to the street without another word.

Socially, Marshall Field's onetime partner, Levi Z. Leiter and his wife purposely adopted an attitude similar to Insull's, but for different reasons. They traveled abroad a good deal but never told a soul in the European pleasure spas they visited that they were from Chicago, always insisting that they were residents of Washington, D.C. Mrs. Mary Theresa Carver Leiter was, at best, an oddball, whose mansion she claimed was full of "statutes, spinal staircases, and sexual bookcases." Her malapropisms and quirks paled next to that of her husband who left $25 million when he died in 1904. Leiter felt that for some reason his body might be stolen by ghouls so he ordered that his tomb, surrounded by four thousand square feet of ground, be the most formidable in the country. His corpse to this day reposes in Washington's Rock Creek Cemetery, protected by tons of concrete and steel.

Death among the Rich

Chicago's wealthy have not only died in style but in everlasting memory of their money. One trip to Graceland Cemetery to view the incredible monuments in this burial ground of the rich will convince the reader that these strutting citizens did, indeed, take it with them.

At the time Marshall Field opened his first glorious emporium, Walter Loomis Newberry was told by doctors that he had but six months to live and was ordered to sail for the south of France and to keep a nurse in attendance at all times. He sailed, but without the nurse, saying, "I can't afford it." He died almost on schedule while sailing back to America, shunning the cost of medical attention and leaving an estate of more than $4 million. The body of the founder of Newberry Library was almost tossed overboard after he died in his cabin aboard the *Persia*. A fellow traveler intervened with the ship's captain, saying, "No, Walter belonged in Chicago. He would want to be buried there." Newberry's body was sealed in a cask of rum to preserve the remains and shipped on to the city that had made him wealthy; he was buried in an impressive tomb at Graceland, cask and all.

Many of the rich could not bear to see their fortunes disappear before they did. William F. Coolbaugh, who had been the president of the Union National Bank of Chicago for fifteen years, became depressed when he learned that his property was declining in value during a particular panic. On the morning of November 14, 1877, he dressed in his finest clothes and went to the statue of his best friend Stephen A. Douglas where he put a silver-plated revolver to his head and blew out his brains, staining the base of the statue with his millionaire's blood.

Real estate millionaire Dr. D. K. Pearsons never intended for any relative to enjoy his fortune. Before he died, Pearsons had his own magnificent marble monument erected in a Hinsdale cemetery. He next gave away all his money when he knew the end was near, calmly stating, "I desire to have my affairs all arranged before I die so that I shall have only to lie down and rest."

In 1912, Arthur Ryerson, scion of the Chicago steel fortune, learned of the death of a relative while vacationing in Europe and caught the next boat home. Since he insisted upon traveling elegantly, Ryerson made sure he sailed aboard the finest ship in the world, the *Titanic*, and he is undoubtedly still aboard in his suite at the bottom of the Atlantic.

Medill McCormick met his end in preferred seclusion. (UPI)

Medill McCormick, removed from the editorship of the *Tribune* in 1910, went on to become a Republican senator. Rich, but a solitary figure, McCormick hemorrhaged in his Washington, D. C., apartment in February 1925. Since he preferred total seclusion, there was no one present to prevent him from bleeding to death.

Frederick H. Prince, who was virtually the outright owner of the Chicago stockyards by the late 1920s, thought about death constantly. Ultra germ-conscious, Prince refused to use a telephone, insisting that the invention conveyed the Black Death. He died of a cold.

Potter D'Orsay Palmer, whose mother was the very epitome of high society in Chicago for decades, never gave a thought to death, instead wedding any pretty girl in sight. He married four times, the last being a roadhouse waitress. (The last Mrs. D'Orsay Palmer was asked if she really loved her husband and her reply was "Sure, I'm his wife, ain't I.") Palmer died in 1939, his life reckless to the end, from wounds received in a fist fight at a stag picnic.

Nearing age 100 in 1960, Mrs. G. Alexander McKinlock, onetime social lioness in Chicago, bemoaned the passing of the rich, particularly Chicago's wealthy, saying, "In the old days, everything was private. There were private houses and private parties and private balls and private yachts and private railroad cars and private everything. Now everything is public—even one's private life. [Today] everything is in such a hurry. Look at the *Saturday Evening Post*. It comes on Tuesdays. And people are like puppy dogs. They get married for a few minutes!" Mrs. McKinlock died privately.

Railroad magnate George Pullman, whose name adorns one of America's most violent and repressive strikes on record, was also buried at Graceland Cemetery. Fearing that union leaders would steal his corpse, Pullman ordered that he be entombed in total secrecy. His body was spirited out of his mansion in the middle of the night, his coffin wrapped in tar paper to disguise it. It was lowered into a pit the size of his own living room then filled with cement, tons of it. A magnificent tomb was then constructed above this death fortress.

The entire scheme was in keeping with Pullman's idea of self-sanctity. Asked once if he ever had dreams while he was a lowly youth that he would some day become a multimillionaire and head of a railroad dynasty, Pullman snapped, "No, I did not. If I had dreamed them, I'd be dreaming still!" Pullman's greatest dream, fully realized, was the building of his model mill town on Lake Calument for his employees. The chief architect of this project was a man named Beaman who went to Pullman saying that the place ought to be named after him since he had designed the model city. George Pullman nodded, smiled, and said, "I'll tell you what we'll do. We'll take the last half of your name and the first half of mine—and we'll call it Pullman."

Flaunting It

Chicago's rich were forever linking themselves with noble ancestry, some even claiming to be related to one John Billington, a charter passenger on board the *Mayflower*. The fact that Billington was the first official murderer in America, killing his neighbor in 1630 over some cleared land, did not daunt those desperately clinging to any kind of Pilgrim ancestry.

The wealthy spent fortunes on tracking down *some* sort of family history, paying genealogists enormous amounts to pinpoint any kind of European predecessor of worth, ordering coats of arms that could be mounted on impressive shields to adorn office buildings, mansions, cars, yachts. The Crane family of the plumbing concern, it was reported by Cleveland Amory, once requested a coat of arms and the shield professionals suggested including the emblems of bathtubs, sinks, and toilets with a hand pulling a chain and the motto *Apres moi le deluge*. The Cranes were disinclined to accept the shield.

If distinguished forefathers were not available, the rich reasoned that marriage into royalty was the next best thing. Many a daughter of Chicago's superrich married into aristocracy, chiefly the British peerage since that group of impoverished noblemen required the most money.

With few exceptions, whenever a hard-working business entrepreneur struck it rich in Chicago, he built a towering mansion and began competing with his or her rival rich in giving the most talked-about parties. (This notably excluded Ferdinand Sulzberger, the millionaire meat packer whose chief enjoyment was drinking beer with his butchers in saloons near the yards.)

Marshall Field I, ever tasteful, actually set the pattern in superparties by financing an extravaganza called the Mikado Ball at his mansion at 1905 Prairie Avenue near the end of 1885. The party was to honor his two children—Marshall, then seventeen, and Ethel, age twelve. Field had the sets of the original *Mikado* production brought from the Fifth Avenue Theater in New York and reconstructed on the first and second floors of his sprawling mansion.

More than 400 children from the country's uppercrust—from Baltimore, Boston, and New York—attended the grand ceremonies. Johnny Hand's orchestra was hidden in a small pagoda and the young ladies were given party favors designed by James McNeill Whistler. The cost of this party remained a secret but it was rumored to have caused Field to write a six-figure check.

The McCormick's, of course, had begun this tradition of costly celebrations in honor of their children. Cyrus McCormick spent a fortune five years earlier to herald his son's coming of age, gathering two hundred of Chicago's social cream in the home of railway magnate Perry Smith at 675 Rush Street.

There, in the second-floor theater, the orchestra of Julius Fuchs, hired for the occasion, performed Goldmark's *Rustic Wedding*, then heard for the first time in Chicago. Dancing and a banquet of gourmet dishes followed.

George Pullman and his wife, Harriet Sanger Pullman, would not be outdone by anyone. Their soirees were the most lavish of all. His $250,000 Prairie Avenue home was forever ablaze with party lights. Following one fete, the *Tribune* gawked, "The gardens of Cashmere were not more beautiful than the superb apartments of the Pullman residence, caught as it seemed, in a shower of roses."

Pullman used his palatial train cars to transport guests to the elegant theater he had constructed in the housing area named after him. One such excursion in the winter of 1883 was reported by the *Inter-Ocean*, which reported that the train loaded with wealthy passengers en route to the model city "rivaled the drawing rooms of the palace homes when they are thrown open on grand occasions. This train, beautiful without and elegant within, furnished with the loveliness of a great city, rolled out of the dingy depot into the storm, but there was all gaiety on board, and none heeded the howling wind and the driving snow."

The two grandes dames of Chicago society were unquestionably Mrs. Edith McCormick, first wife of the eccentric Harold McCormick, and the reigning queen herself, Mrs. Potter Palmer. Both women were astounding egotists who fairly dripped with the most expensive jewelry in the Midwest,

Grand dame of Chicago society, Mrs. Edith Rockefeller McCormick in her heyday. (painting by Frederich August Von Kaulbach)

perhaps the country, at the time. Mrs. McCormick had the larger, showier jewels, most experts agreed.

Harold had given her a $2 million rope of pearls. Her emerald necklace was valued at more than $1 million. This necklace also contained 1,657 small diamonds. It was also rumored that she possessed some of the crown jewels of Russia spirited out of that country after the fall of the czar.

Mrs. McCormick's parties and balls were lavish but rigidly structured as was her own life. She never spoke to her scores of servants but had her orders transmitted by her secretary and the household's first steward. After they were grown, her own children could only see her by appointment. Four butlers served her meals, whether she dined alone or not.

The society queen spent most of her time redecorating her huge mansion at 1000 Lake Shore Drive, the grounds running a full block north and south, an estate which Edith transformed into her private park. She once gave a massive party in this park, demanding that her hundreds of guests wear authentic eighteenth-century costumes and wigs. In the middle of this lavish affair, however, a gale wind blew in off the lake sweeping away wigs and tearing brocaded gowns to shreds.

Edith McCormick spent a great deal of time analyzing a select group of high society friends. She had learned her psychiatry from Carl Jung in

Switzerland and considered herself an excellent analyst. She had even ana-
lyzed herself many times, she later claimed. She also believed strongly in
reincarnation, stating on several occasions that she had, in a former life, been
the mother of Egyptian King Tutankhamen.

Following her divorce from Harold, Edith Rockefeller McCormick undertook some risky stock investments and was all but wiped out in the Crash of
1929. Her brother John D. Rockefeller, Jr. came to her rescue, providing a
living fund for the once regal woman. She moved out of her palatial estate, its
belongings later auctioned off, and took a suite in the Drake Hotel where she
died in 1932 at age sixty. She had tried to cure her own cancer through
self-analysis and failed.

A prominent Chicago businessman bought Mrs. McCormick's old limousine, "an amazing, long black vehicle that looked like a cross between a
hearse and a gondola." The owner's wife rode around in this monster for a
few seasons before telling her husband, "I can't bear to ride in it anymore—I
feel like I'm sitting in the lap of Edith's ghost."

Edith McCormick's only rival as Chicago's queen bee was the stunning,
autocratic social empress Bertha Honore Palmer, a Kentucky-bred girl whom
Potter Palmer made into a Chicago monarch, building for her a turreted
Rhenish castle for an untold fortune. (It was forever known as Palmer

Mrs. Potter Palmer as a young woman; she fairly staggered under the weight of her jewelry.
(painting by George P. Healy)

Mrs. Potter Palmer shown greeting guests on her throne-like platform insider her mansion's ballroom during the 1893 reception for the Spanish Infanta.

The roof garden of the Palmer Houe, a magnficent hotel Potter Palmer built to glorify his wife, Chicago's social Queen Bee.

Castle.) Palmer, who began to accumulate his wealth with the dry-goods store he later sold to Marshall Field, opened the finest hotel in Chicago, the Palmer House, and spent almost every dime he earned on his wife. Said one of Palmer's friends: "He loaded her with jewelry and he loved to see her wear his gifts. I remember him saying proudly, 'There she stands with two hundred thousand dollars on her.' When they went abroad, he slept with her diamond tiara under his pillow."

Palmer left his great fortune almost wholly to his wife, no conditions attached. When his lawyer pointed out to him that Bertha might remarry, Palmer only nodded, "If she does, she'll need the money."

Bertha Palmer was a collector of art, acquiring a great number of Impressionist paintings, a collection rivaled and exceeded only by the Ryerson collection of Renoirs that covered the walls of the steel tycoon's Drexel Boulevard mansion. Ryerson left two-ninths of his $6 million estate to the Art Institute; Bertha's son Potter Palmer, Jr. became president of the Art Institute.

Mrs. Palmer's most noteworthy gems included her famous dog collar which was studded with 7 large diamonds and 2,268 pearls. She was seldom photographed without her neck being encircled by this incredible necklace. When wearing this and her diamond tiara and other gems at grand functions she seemed to stagger visibly from the weight of the jewelry. Always, she pretended her gems were mere baubles; she once lost a $40,000 teardrop emerald at a party in Paris and cooly stated to the hostess, "Someone will return it. If they don't, they need it more than I do."

Another time in Paris, Evalyn Walsh McLean, then a child, befriended Mrs. Palmer who dazzled the teenager with her gems. "She let me finger to my heart's content her necklace of emeralds and diamonds," Mrs. McLean remembered, "and seemed to understand the passion in my eyes as I looked at them." Mrs. McLean would later be married to a newspaper tycoon in Washington and would be the owner of the hapless Hope Diamond.

Although Mrs. Palmer ruled the roost in Chicago, visiting dignitaries did not always treat her with the deference she demanded, conduct the queen bee always remembered. The Infanta Eulalia of Spain arrived in Chicago in George Pullman's private car paying an unofficial visit to the city. She breakfasted with Mayor Harrison and his wife and went to dinner with the Harlow Higinbothams, but she was reluctant to lend her august presence to a reception Mrs. Palmer gave in her honor, saying, "I prefer not to meet this innkeeper's wife." She did attend the reception, however, and Mrs. Palmer treated her royally, even after hearing the remark.

Some years later, Mrs. Palmer was in Paris where she was asked to attend a reception for the Infanta. Bertha Palmer sent along a precise note to the hostess which stated, "I cannot meet this bibulous representative of a degenerate monarchy."

More than any other woman of her day, Mrs. Potter Palmer looked every

inch the social leader Chicago envisioned as a society queen bee—tall, with a
gray marcelled coiffure, her dark eyes penetrating and commanding, always
posed as Titania in her portraits. Her ornate castle at 1350 Lake Shore Drive,
in addition to the heavily framed masterpieces of the Barbizon school adorning its walls, boasted a maroon velvet ballroom where all of the social queen's
functions were held. To be invited into this ballroom and be received by Mrs.
Palmer was to be annointed, blessed, accepted. "It must also, I conjecture,"
wrote Arthur Meeker, "have been a subtle asset that her very name sounded
like the sort of person she aspired to be; after all, in the Eighties nothing
typified elegance more indubitably than the potted palm."

Mrs. Palmer was tirelessly energetic. She reigned as president of the Board
of Lady Managers of the Chicago's World Fair of 1893. Her charitable work
was staggering and she never hesitated to goad her rich friends to aid the
needy, to operate baby clinics and hospitals, and, above all else, to raise the
cultural level of Chicago. She died in 1918 and for decades Chicago society
was lacking a majestic social leader; it still is, even though a write-in contest in
the 1950s was held in which Chicago society was asked to name a successor to
Mrs. Bertha Palmer as its leading social matriarch. Mrs. Chauncey
McCormick, and Mrs. Edward L. Ryerson were among the many nominated
but no one really won. Like Babe Ruth's immortal No. 3, that tiara is
permanently, and thankfully, retired.

9

Author, Author!

The rich have always made it their special avocation to support *certain* fine arts in Chicago, chiefly those controllable according to the tastes of the socially elite—opera, painting, sometimes, if the artist is not too obstreperous, sculpture—albeit the middle-class audiences of today are more supportive of opera and the Chicago Symphony than in earlier times; they are, quite naturally, more enlightened and as selective as today's low-profile millionaires. Still, Chicago at the dawn of the 1980s is as woefully threadbare of broad-based support of the fine arts as it was before the Great Fire of 1871; a recital by any of the world's leading pianists in this city of millions still commands only an audience of a few hundred.

Jazz, on the other hand—and any aficionado does consider this a fine art—is extremely popular today, almost as popular as it was in the early 1920s when the Austin High Gang—the McPartland Brothers, Dave North, Bud Freeman, Frank Teschemaker, and Dave Tough—along with Leon Bix Beiderbecke, visiting King Oliver, Louis Armstrong, and others created that unmatchable Chicago style of jazz that is now legendary the world over.

Early Scriveners

Lowest of the low on Chicago's totem pole of fine arts (and many of its most erstwhile denizens will argue that it is no fine art at all) is the field of writing. Its proponents too have developed since the 1870s what can loosely be termed a Chicago style in writing—hard, somewhat cynical, always exciting prose. Unlike New York and others points east, Chicago never developed any literary salons sponsored and patronized by the rich, for the rich have always been the mortal enemies of Chicago writers, in spirit and philosophy, and the writers have always been considered to be proletarian muckrakers by the city's social elite. The writers have always been a tough,

A caricature of Oscar Wilde at the time of the poet's sensational visit to Chicago. (sketch by E. Jump)

uncompromising lot, the best ones, at least, loners for the most part, even when making reluctant appearances in so-called literary renaissances. There never has been and probably never will be a literary "set" in Chicago, even though the activity, mostly drummed up by Ben Hecht and company between 1910 and 1925, gave out the sound of a thundering herd stampeding east for New York theaters and publishing companies.

In the beginning, after the Great Fire, Chicago's stockyard mentality resisted any idea of having the city play host to a literary subsociety. The closest thing to aesthetes were the newsmen and these were largely unschooled though talented cynics. These roughneck gentlemen turned with a vengeance on the British poet Oscar Wilde when he visited Chicago in the gaslight era; by then his much publicized homosexual liaisons and utter aestheticism made him a happy target for Chicago's press. An anonymous *Daily News* reporter penned the following verse, under the title, "Balaam, the Ass-thete," to welcome the poet to the city:

He comes! The simpering Oscar comes.
The West awaits with wonder,
As bullfrogs listen to beating drums,
Or hearken to the thunder.

The women pause with bated breath,
With wild and wistful faces,
And silent as the halls of death
Seem all our public places.

Here in the energetic West,
We have no vacant niches
For clowns and pansies in the vest
Or dadoes on the breeches.

We do not live by form or rule,
We love our wives and lassies;
We like to look at Western mules
But not aesthetic asses.

Wilde's response to this open insult was never recorded, but he did live up to expectations by holding a press conference upon his arrival at the Drake Hotel where he greeted sneering newsmen while lying on a sofa, a tigerskin drawn to his chin and a roaring fire close by to warm his cold blood. A reporter of the *Inter-Ocean* reluctantly shook the poet's hand and later stated that it felt "like the clinging of a vine."

The British poet was dismissed, most of the press preferring to give its

Illustration from *The Cliff Dwellers* by Henry Blake Fuller, one of Chicago's first best-selling novels.

coverage to the reigning champion of boxing John L. Sullivan who was also visiting the city. Wilde, the newsmen noted, wore white gloves, along with breeches tied at the knee, black silk stockings, and pumps when he lectured at the Central Music Hall. On the other hand, the great John L. brandished only his mighty bare knuckles, a sight thought to be much more appealing than "some fop from London."

Few of Chicago's early-day writers and authors were independent of the many daily newspapers. The newsmen always formed (and still do) the nucleus of Chicago's literary core. But there were rare exceptions who managed to make a living as authors alone.

The books these men wrote were drawn from the lower- and middle-class elements of Chicago society, grass-roots literature that did not include intellectual stances. They were more like back-country yarn spinners dedicated to regionalism than chroniclers of the nation at large. The most successful of Chicago's homegrown authors in this early period was Henry B. Fuller who penned a successful novel *The Cliff-Dwellers* which portrayed the Chicago native coping with new skyscrapers on the prairie and the peculiar transition from small town to metropolis. Fuller wrote another Chicago epic *With the Procession* then, establishing an unbroken tradition, moved off to New York and Europe to develop "larger themes."

Coming from Massachusetts in 1893, Robert Herrick devoted much of his literary labor to trying to make sense out of Chicago businessmen, obsessed as he was with the tumultuous tycoons of Chicago. His novel *Memoirs of an American Citizen* depicted the life of a Chicago meatpacker. He enlarged this theme in *One Woman's Life*, the story of an adventuress in Chicago. The only urbane and sophisticated novelist of this period was the polished Hobart Chatfield-Taylor who wrote *With Edge Tools* which was not a success.

The newsmen, on the other hand, were born hustlers of their work, especially the gangling, 6-foot Opie Read who published *The Arkansaw Traveler*, a humorous weekly, and whose down-home novel *The Jucklins* was purchased by more than a million streetcar riders, making Opie so rich that he promptly retired and played the role of author in residence. Another popular author with stronger themes, but still of the mean streets, was Indiana-born George Ade who became a reporter for the *Chicago Record* in 1890 and for seven years wrote a column entitled *Stories of the Streets and the Town* which was later put into book form. Eugene Field, of course, was the dean of newspapermen-authors, the forerunner of the so-called literary journalist whose "Sharps and Flats" column appeared in the *Daily News*. Field spent most of his spare time in McClurg's bookstore at Wabash and Monroe streets. Here he was lionized by the owner who gave him a corner of the bookstore where Field held forth with a polyglot literary circle which included the Reverend Frank Gunsaulus who had written an obscure novel called *Monk and Knight*. The minister's presence caused Field to dub his spot

George Ade toward the end of his life in 1936 in Florida; his Chicago stories of the 1890s brought him fame.

A caricature of Eugene Field, lampooning the newsman for turning from journalism to poetry.

in the bookstore the Saints and Sinners Corner—Field undoubtedly thought he himself represented the sinners.

There were other places where Chicago's hard-pressed literati gathered— The Whitechapel Club, Billy Boyle's English Chophouse, the Press Club. Often in attendance were Finley Peter Dunne, creator of Mr. Dooley; Knut Hamsen; Joseph Kirkland; Mary Hartwell Catherwood; and sometimes Mrs. John Kinzie, whose novel *Waubun*, a tale based on early life at Fort Dearborn, was Chicago's first big literary success before the 1880s.

Shang Draper was never asked to this group but then Shang's literary output was decidedly lower than pedestrian. Draper published a weekly in which he graphically described the delights awaiting any male wishing to visit the bordellos in the red-light district. He wrote stories about prostitutes, his most popular novella being *Little Nell, the Life and Times of a Wicked Woman.*

By the turn of the century, novelists began flocking to Chicago to write of its wild and woolly ways. Theodore Dreiser arrived and, fascinated with the life and times of the corrupt Charles T. Yerkes, converted this colorful thief into the protagonist of his novels *The Financier* and *The Titan.* Upton Sinclair used the stockyards for his social horror story *The Jungle.* Frank Norris took one look at the frantic grain manipulators of the Chicago Stock Exchange and penned *The Pit.* American classics were beginning to emerge, scenes and characters wholly drawn from Chicago and set down by basically Chicago natives. Inside the offices of the Fine Arts Building on Michigan Avenue, another classic was created by Frank Baum and artist Arthur Denslow—*The Wizard of Oz.* The Fine Arts Building, a generation later, would house one of the most remarkable literary periodicals ever published in America, run by an even more remarkable woman, Margaret Anderson.

The Poignant Periodicals

The idea of little magazines or literary periodicals was not new to Chicago. *The Dial* had been published for a number of years, sponsored by McClurg & Co., a book firm, but it was rather stiff and unadventurous, a posture that was to assure its death by hardening of the arteries thirty-eight years after its inception when the magazine was moved to New York. The venerable *Poetry Magazine*, established by the indefatigable Harriet Monroe, actually paid poets for their verses which made the likes of Carl Sandburg and Edgar Lee Masters leap for joy. Miss Monroe was always ladylike, even though some of the material she published compelled her to skip quickly over the page. Sandburg attacked evangelist Billy Sunday with the following in her hallowed magazine: "You slimy bunkshooter . . . I like to watch a good four-flusher work, but not when he starts people puking and calling for the doctors."

Harriet Monroe, founder of *Poetry Magazine*.

The colorful Margaret Anderson, Chicago's one-woman Renaissance, and founder of the magnificent *Little Review*.

Religious zealot Billy Sunday was the target for Carl Sandburg's wrath while writing in *Poetry Magazine*.

Margaret Anderson's tent home at Braeside beach, 1914.

Margaret Anderson arrived in Chicago in 1912, the same year in which the folksy Carl Sandburg showed up. Ben Hecht, future novelist of *Eric Dorn* as well as a host of other books, was already a working newspaperman by then, having become a resident a year earlier. Margaret was only twenty-one when she entered Chicago, pawning some of her clothes for train fare since her wealthy parents in Columbus, Indiana, disapproved of her leaving home.

She argued Francis Browne into giving her a clerical job in Browne's bookstore, located in the Fine Arts Building, and was soon the book reviewer for Browne's periodical *The Dial*. She was even paid for reviewing books, after a fashion. "In those days," Margaret was to recall in her autobiography *My Thirty Years' War*, "books were published at lower prices. All novels sold for a dollar and a half. When you finished reviewing them you took them to McClurg's and sold them for seventy-five cents each. This was your salary."

Margaret thought *The Dial* stuffy. She had ideas of her own, definite ideas. Full of anarchist thought—she was a devotee of Emma Goldman—Miss Anderson's idea to start her own magazine dedicated to the "seven arts" came as a result of fitful slumber. "I had been curiously depressed all day. In the night, I wakened. First precise thought: I know why I'm depressed—nothing inspired is going on." She decided to provide that inspiration with the *Little Review*.

Pitching tents at Braeside near Ravinia on Chicago's North Shore, Margaret lived the Bohemian life and encouraged all who were bold, who wished to experiment with poetry, prose, music, art, anything of creative effort that could be printed, to come to the *Little Review*. Ben Hecht, poet and wild man Maxwell Bodenheim, and others would steal out to Margaret's tent camp on the beach and pin poetry to the flap which she could read with her morning breakfast. And she read everything, believing that "an artist is an exceptional person. Such a person has something exceptional to say. Exceptional matter makes an exceptional manner. This is 'style'! In an old but expressive phrase, 'style is the man.' "

November's winds and snow drove Margaret and her sister Lois into an apartment unfurnished except for two beds and a baby grand piano which Margaret had wheedled a dealer into letting her use in the hope of one day selling it to her. Lois Anderson's stay with her literary sister was brief; the swarm of literary figures soon proved too much for her and she returned home to Indiana. Her place was taken by a strange creature Jane Heap whose mannish haircut and clothes made her appear even stranger. She refused to speak in anything but monosyllables. Jane became Margaret's second in command at the *Little Review*.

Emma Goldman, Margaret's idol, visited the editor but only after the dedicated anarchist was assured that Miss Anderson's apartment was empty of capitalistic furniture. Emma listened attentively, squatting on the bare floor, while Margaret played the piano. When Miss Anderson finished, Emma

Anarchist Emma Goldman listened to Margaret Anderson play the piano and pronounced her a great artist. (Wide World)

The eccentric Jane Heap, Margaret Anderson's associate editor of the *Little Review*.

stood up, brushed herself off, and headed for the door, pausing only for a moment to say, "My dear, you are a great artist."

The fires of anarchy were banked deep inside Margaret Anderson, or they were during her Chicago years. When she learned that an anarchist in Utah had been condemned for blowing up mines, Margaret wrote an editorial asking, "Why doesn't someone shoot the Governor of Utah?" This prompted federal agents to put Margaret under surveillance, but someone told the agents that Miss Anderson was nothing more than a flighty society girl gone a little berserk and the watchdogs departed.

Brazen, not berserk, would be a more apt word; without a dime to her name Margaret leased Room 917 in the Fine Arts Building which served for years as the offices of the *Little Review*. She published her elegant magazine on the proverbial shoestring; it is now a collector's item, any single copy bringing a heavy price. The newspapermen, fellow artists, even wealthy people who refused to give their names, contributed for the upkeep of Margaret and her magazine. The poet Eunice Tietjens gave her a diamond ring telling her, "I don't want this any more. Sell it and bring out an issue." She did.

She was less fortunate with the management of the Fine Arts Building. A Mr. Greene was forever pestering her for her back rent. One day the courteous Greene stood before her and sheepishly said in a low voice, "Miss Anderson, we really must have a check."

"You really want a check?" she replied.

"Yes, for thirty dollars."

Margaret wrote out the check and gave it to Greene. He was back inside of four days, his face wearing a sour look. "There must be some mistake," he said, embarrassed. "The bank says this check is no good."

"But I didn't say it was good."

The printer was forever demanding payment for previous issues of the *Little Review*. Margaret would listen for his footsteps, then run into a large, long closet in her office, closing the door. The little man would enter the office and pace. Margaret would sit in the closet at a small desk editing her magazine beneath the glare of a naked light bulb. When she ran out of space she made her notes on the closet wall, including references to a new writer sending submissions from Europe, one James Joyce. (Margaret was to go on to publish in installments *Ulysses*, the major work of this literary genius, the first publisher to do so in the United States—for which she was branded a criminal by the courts—more than a decade before Bennett Cerf at Random House began taking bows as the champion of that work.)

When that printer threatened to cease printing the *Little Review* unless he received some sort of payment, Margaret called the frustrated man and told him she was mailing him all the cash she had on hand. With that she prepared an elaborate envelope and posted the sum total of her cash reserve—five cents.

A page proof of James Joyce's *Ulysses* with the author's massive editorial corrections before publication in the *Little Review*.

Chicago critic Burton Rascoe promoted Margaret Anderson's *Little Review* at every opportunity.

But Margaret and her publication were never destitute for long. She became the darling of the newsmen. Burton Rascoe, Floyd Dell, Vincent Starrett, and a score more thumped her cause in their columns and drummed up contributions to keep her going. And the writers kept flocking to her. Edgar Lee Masters, who was devoted to slapstick comedy and whose *Spoon River Anthology* poems had appeared in *Poetry*, showed up at any hour of the day at the *Review's* tiny office to tell witless jokes and play practical jokes; he often pretended to be the building manager standing outside the door and shouting for the entire floor to hear that "Margaret Anderson is a deadbeat!"

Another writer of budding genius Sherwood Anderson arrived. He wrote for the *Review* with flexing pride in Chicago's tough-town image, as he did in *Mid-American Chants*: "You know my city—Chicago triumphant; factories and marts and roar of machines—horrible, terrible, ugly and brutal. Can a singer arise and sing in this smoke and grime? Can he keep his throat clear? Can his courage survive?"

Anderson left his copywriting job in a Chicago advertising agency to write his later powerful *Windy McPherson's Son* and his immortal *Winesburg, Ohio*. He became such a success that he moved to New York and then on to Europe to squander his time and talent (as did Ernest Hemingway for a short while) in salons run by Gertrude Stein and company. By the time Anderson wrote *Dark Laughter*, most of his onetime Chicago friends agreed that he was no longer the great writer he had been in the Chicago days of the *Little Review*. The author, at least, went out in style of sorts. He swallowed an hors d'oeuvre at the captain's table on a transatlantic crossing and neglected to remove the toothpick, which killed him.

Another ardent supporter of the *Review* was the lean and laughing poet Vachel Lindsay. The pronunciation of his name became so mangled by the public at large that, for Margaret's September 1914 issue, he penned the following:

> My Middle Name
>
> My middle name rhymes not with satchel,
> So please do not pronounce it "Vatchel,"
> My middle name rhymes not with rock hell,
> So please do not pronounce it "Vock Hell,"
> My middle name rhymes not with hash hell,
> So please do not pronounce it "Vasch Hell,"
> My middle name rhymes not with bottle,
> So please do not pronounce it "Vottle,"
> My middle name is just the same as Rachel.
> With V for R;
> Please call me Vachel.
>
> Nicholas Vachel Lindsay

Lindsay too would vanish into the East, and one fine day of deep depression in 1931, commit suicide by swallowing an entire bottle of Lysol.

Editor of *December*, Curt Johnson (extreme left) at an editorial conference in 1964 in Chicago's O'Rourke's Pub; second from left with pipe is poet David Pearson Etter.

Nelson Algren, standing, with bookdealer Aileen Wimmer, witnessing columnist Mike Royko autographing one of his books.

"He Waved Whenever I Saw Him"

Hecht joined with his fellow newsman Charles MacArthur to write Broadway plays, gleaning an enormous success from *The Front Page* which portrayed his wild Chicago days. He would eventually be the highest paid screenwriter in the history of Hollywood. Margaret Anderson herself would be gone by 1917, moving her *Little Review* to New York then on to Paris where it died in 1923. (The little magazines of Chicago continued to thrive piecemeal long into the 1960s. The author contributed *Literary Times* from 1961 to 1970. R. R. Cuscaden published *Midwest*, a unique poetry journal. Probably the best of the independent little magazines of that time and continuing to this day is Curt Johnson's *December*. The magazine *Poetry* essentially died with its great founder Harriet Monroe when she perished while climbing a mountain in Peru in 1936 at age seventy-seven. None of the university-backed "literary" publications have ever been of note except to promote professorial credos and echo precious, fake standards in literature promoted by the New York cognoscenti. Fine novelists still struggle in the city—Marc Davis, Jim McCormick, Curt Johnson, Harry Mark Petrakis, Richard Stern, Bill Granger, John Powers, Norbert Blei—the list is staggering. And, of course,

Ernest Hemingway as he looked just before he returned to Chicago from the Italian Front in World War. I.

we still have Mike Royko, a one-man avatar among newsmen, literary or otherwise.

Almost all the prominent writers of the *Little Review* period would join the exodus to the East by 1925, and that certainly included Ernest Miller Hemingway. Born in Oak Park, Hemingway ran off to Kansas City to work for the *Star* before enlisting in the Italian Ambulance Service during World War I. He returned in January 1919 carrying so many tiny fragments from a bomb in his body that he was called by one New York newspaper in a headline the "Most Wounded Man of the War." At first he lived at his father's summer resort in Horton's Bay, Michigan, recuperating and trying to forget a nurse who had tended him in a Milan Hospital and had thrown him over for an Italian officer. (This same nurse would be the role model for the heroine of *A Farewell to Arms*.) At the urging of his good friend William D. Horne, Jr., who had also served in the ambulance corps, Hemingway went to Chicago, moving in with Horne at 1030 North State Street.

He met and liked Sherwood Anderson who was to help in furthering his career. (Hemingway would repay this kindness, as he did with most others, with a sneer, lampooning Anderson in his second novel, *The Torrents of Spring*.) He also met Ben Hecht and neither liked the other.

"Hemingway was not a likeable fellow," Hecht told the author in 1962. "Too much concerned with his own 'art' and not enough with living. I invited him to have lunch with the boys but he never showed up. You would see him with Swatty [Hecht's nickname for Anderson] sometimes. He kept to himself. He waved whenever I saw him but that was it. It seemed to me as if he couldn't wait to get the hell out of Chicago."

Hemingway and Horne moved into the great Victorian mansion owned by advertising executive Y. K. Smith (over whom a young lover, Wanda Stopa, would commit murder a few years later). The advertising mogul thought of himself as a patron of the arts and he allowed Hemingway and Horne to live practically rent free. Smith introduced Hemingway to Anderson. According to an interview the author had with Horne in 1969, the young Hemingway was in awe of Anderson. "Sherwood was a helluva nice guy," Horne recalled. "Even before Hemmy and I moved over to Y. K. Smith's we visited there and Sherwood was there and we would have an evening where we would sit around and talk high-mindedly about literature and art. Sherwood, after reading Hemingway's stories, was very impressed by this new, young kid just coming along as a writer. Hemingway took his criticism very well. Sherwood was a god. He was enormous! Ernie was unpublished; he was only editing a magazine."

Hemingway worked as an editor on the *Cooperative Commonwealth* magazine owned by Harrison Parker, whose farmer's cooperative organization came under heavy scrutiny for its shady dealings. Hemingway wrote and edited human interest stories but, after all, according to Horne, "It was a potboiling job, it was keeping him alive.

Hemingway at the zenith of his literary career.

"We used to go over to Kizo's on the corner of State and Division streets. It was a wonderful Greek restaurant. We got soup, steak and green peas, and apple pie for sixty-five cents and that's what we ate there night after night after night. And for a few months I banked that and then Ernie got this job running the *Cooperative Commonwealth* and then he paid me back—I wish to hell I had never taken the money."

Hemingway discovered what kind of deal he was involved in with Harrison Parker's great business scheme and wrote an exposé of the organization. "And he tried to peddle the story to every paper in Chicago." Horne recalled. "And they wouldn't touch it. Who was Ernest Hemingway compared with Harrison Parker?"

The young war hero (he had been given the Italian Medal for Valor for his role at Fossalta) also tried to get jobs on the newspapers but he was rejected. "He was a great God-gifted reporter," Horne emphasized. "The material that had appeared in the *Kansas City Star* and the *Toronto Star* was some of the greatest journalism ever written. Why some city editor could not recognize this genius and glom on to him is beyond the imagination."

Hemingway, around this time, was a regular visitor to Kid Howard's gym where he worked out. "He sparred with me one time in Smith's apartment," Horne said while rubbing his jaw nostalgically. "I learned that day never to lay yourself open with a right cross without getting yourself covered. He clipped me on the side of the jaw and I was out standing up."

Chicago author James T. Farrell, whose *Studs Lonigan* became a classic.

Poet Gwendolyn Brooks presenting Jack Conroy with the first (and only) Literary Times Award for literary achievement in 1967.

Horne and Hemingway, despite the clip on the jaw, moved from the Smith house to 100 East Chicago Avenue for the summer of 1920 and then moved back to Smith's in the fall. It was at this time that Hemingway met his first wife.

"Smith's sister Kate," Horne related, "had a girl friend named Hadley Richardson and they met. Ernie and Hadley fell in love and it was like falling off a pier. It was terrific, stupendous! They got engaged and then we all went up to help them get married at Horton's Bay." Horne was an usher at the wedding.

Hemingway and his bride lived in Chicago for a few months. He was then contacted by the *Toronto Star* and was sent to Paris as a foreign correspondent (a part-time job, really, at $35 a week, but it was enough to live on, if you killed pigeons in the *bois* and took them home for supper, which is what Hemingway did to survive). He was never to return to Chicago, except on "passing-through" visits.

The novelist wrote little of his birthplace, Oak Park, and hardly at all about Chicago, where he failed to find a job, and it is our good fortune that he did not. In 1952, Hemingway stated, "I had a wonderful novel to write about Oak Park and would never do it because I did not want to hurt living people."

When Hecht and company cleared out of the city in the mid-1920s, the

Chicago author Saul Bellow at the time of *The Adventures of Augie March.*

literary fronts were mainly held down by working newsmen and their subject matter, what with the success of the Chicago gangster, was basically crime oriented. Fred Pasley of the *Chicago Tribune* wrote the memorable *Al Capone, The Story of a Self-Made Man.* A young college student named W. R. Burnett studied the activities of the old Glorianna Gang and wrote *Little Caesar* which spawned a massive gangster cycle in the movies.

The 1930s were dominated by a return of young proletarian authors who dealt with ethnic and Depression themes, the most heralded of these being James T. Farrell who forever linked his classic *Studs Lonigan* to Chicago history. Jack Conroy moved from Missouri to Chicago to write his great novel *The Disinherited* and begin his little magazine *The New Anvil* in which he published for the first time Nelson Algren, who submitted his first novel to the magazine in installments calling it *Somebody in Boots.* It is common knowledge that without Jack Conroy, there might have been no Nelson Algren, a fact that Nelson Algren would undoubtedly contest, for he, like Hemingway, showered little gratitude upon his supporters before moving in a huff to a New Jersey residence in the mid-1970s.

In the 1940s, Chicago entered the literary doldrums. Aside from the excellent writings of Algren and Willard Motley, perhaps the only significant writer of this period was the black poet Gwendolyn Brooks, now the poet laureate of Illinois. (It is true that Nobel Prize winner Saul Bellow resides in Chicago and has for a great deal of time, but he has never been considered anything but a product of the Academy. His public appearances in Chicago have consisted of walking his dog on the far North Side of the city.) During the 1950s Algren reigned supreme as Chicago's literary lion; he had climaxed his writing career with *Man with the Golden Arm.* After several stormy years, Algren retreated into obscurity, moving into a third-floor walk-up at 1958 West Evergreen. By the 1960s he appeared embittered, carping at any imagined slight to his reputation. "It took a quarter of a century for my books to get in the Chicago Public Library," he told writer Irwin Saltz. At the time he displayed a puerile resentment of other writers, especially those who had made money, and yet he has always contended that he never intended to write solely for money, but for art. "I see where Harold Robbins is going to buy this casino in Monte Carlo. And I think, 'Is he a better writer than me?' Hell no, I'm better than he is. He's got forty million dollars and I'm just trying to find my bookie so I can collect the seventeen-sixty he owes me."

The author had plenty of time and experiences to witness the temper tantrums of the late Nelson Algren before he departed the city. He was, when in public, sore and mean to any and all other writers, young, old, lame, and energetic. He could not seem to tolerate the thought of any other writer in his territory which might explain his hostility toward James T. Farrell and Ben Hecht, both friends of the author. The word perhaps that best fits this very creative man is *niggardly.* His close friend was Studs Terkel, but then Studs is

AUTHOR, AUTHOR! 225

not, in the real sense, a writer but a marvelous interviewer, not someone who might have truly threatened Algren's possessive sense about Chicago, a sense that crazily insisted that he was the only Chicago author worth reading. All of it is sadly reminiscent of the Chicago Cubs of a decade ago when all they had was Ernie Banks, a cheerless scoreboard, and a very depressed Jack Brickhouse. Like Banks, Algren was a star alone, and even before that star faded, the crowd left, pocketing its roar.

10

The Bully Boys

Chicago has always loved Carl Sandburg because he, quite simply, summed up the attitude of the city from its swampy beginnings to its present-day skyscrapers; a city that loves to brawl and cherishes its strongman leadership, which is why its citizens have overwhelmingly elected a good balance of sinners and strong-man reformers. Chicagoans have been noted for their fair play. When any administration becomes too sanctimonious the public response has been to "throw the rascals in." Nowhere in America has reform and corruption been as proudly embraced as in this volatile, unpredictable city. Long John Wentworth, who had served six years in Congress as a Democrat, won two terms as a Republican mayor. (Lincoln had seen to the rise in power of Republicanism, especially in his Chicago stronghold.) The real reason for Wentworth's election was the disgraceful conduct of his predecessor Mayor Thomas Dyer who chose to decorate his inaugural parade with cartloads of whores accompanying his marching patronage workers.

Wentworth, who proved to be a courageous and honest mayor, changed all that, and in his typical style, ignoring all other authority but his own, trampled upon law to bring order. In his first term of office, Wentworth's initial order of business as mayor was to direct his police force—fifty-some officers patroling a city of one-hundred thousand—to root out all prostitutes posing as mothers of large families. This was a ruse by which whores convinced authorities to pardon their "husbands" who were serving time in jail. Next, Long John went after the Sands, the most corrupt, vice-ridden area in the city, a sprawling sinkhole next to the shores of Lake Michigan that consisted of scores of tumbledown buildings teeming with gamblers, pimps, whores, and thieves. The *Tribune* had reported that the area was "decidedly the vilest and most dangerous place in Chicago. For some years past it has been the resort or hiding place of all sorts of criminals, while the most

The piled signs and boxed goods of Chicago merchants from Long John Wentworth's 1857 raid.

Police ushering prostitutes to the station near the armory and gas works, 1866; raids like this were begun by Major Long John Wentworth.

wretched and degraded women and their miserable pimps congregated there in large numbers. A large number of persons, mostly strangers in the city, have been enticed into the dens there and robbed, and there is but little doubt that a number of murders have been committed by the desperate characters who had made these dens their homes. The most beastly sensuality and darkest crimes had their homes in the Sands."

Long John told these unsavory citizens to get out of the area by April 20, 1857, promising to destroy the terrible district. The Sands residents merely laughed, jabbing the ribs of their political sponsors at such ridiculous posturing. True to his word, Wentworth, accompanied by his volunteer fire department and a huge posse under the command of the sheriff, appeared in the Sands on the appointed day. Shrewdly, Long John had arranged through friends to have dogfights staged at the Brighton Race Track that day, an event that lured away most of the worst male inhabitants, including Dutch Frank, Mike O'Brien, and others, leaving the prostitutes and bartenders alone.

"Move your furniture into the street," bellowed the behemoth mayor. "You have a half hour!" The terrified inhabitants were still scrambling to save belongings when Long John ordered his firemen to set every building in the Sands afire. The entire area was blazing within minutes amidst the shrieks of fleeing prostitutes. It was ashes by sundown when the startled male denizens returned. They could do nothing except to slink off to other Chicago hellholes on the South and West sides. Charges were later brought forth that most of Wentworth's firemen were drunk during the Sands raid. Long John denied the allegation, stating that his men, most of whom were volunteers from the best families in Chicago, had been given only one shot of whiskey each to fortify them. "I know this to be a fact," Wentworth proclaimed. "I poured the drinks!" Wentworth continued his war on the vice districts throughout his two administrations, sending his club-wielding officers many times into Conley's Patch which contained the "dirtiest, vilest, most rickety, one-sided, leaning forward, propped-up, tumbled-down, sinking fast, low-roofed and most miserable shanties."

The mayor always led his men personally on these raids. He was absolutely fearless. Once, when raiding Burrough's Place, a terrible nest of gamblers, Wentworth sent his policemen through the windows and back doors, driving the inhabitants out the front and into his own huge arms. He helped to book the gamblers, dragging them to crude police wagons. When their lawyer appeared, Wentworth hammerlocked the attorney and tossed him into jail.

Anything that annoyed the mayor brought prompt action. When walking through the downtown district, Wentworth kept bumping his head against low-hanging signs and awnings—he was 6-foot-6—which the merchants had put up to advertise their wares. Long John would also stumble on the display crates and boxes on the walkway. These "obstructions" had to go, Wentworth decreed, and, on June 18, 1857, his entire police force swept through the

downtown area tearing down every awning and sign and carrying away all
the goods lying in boxes on the street. These were taken to Randolph
and State streets and made into a huge pile. The incensed merchants were told
that they could retrieve their property at that point but they were to take "this
debris" and store it. If the signs went up again, they would be torn down
and burned.

Goaded by some of the merchants, but mostly by the crime bosses, the
Illinois legislature moved in 1861 to curb Long John's autocratic use of
Chicago police. They enacted a law in which the police would henceforth be
controlled by a commission. Long John exploded and called his force to a
City Hall meeting on the night of March 21, 1861, and fired every man. For
twenty-four hours the city was without any protection, but since Wentworth
had acted with such haste, the criminal element had no idea that the streets
were unpatrolled; only two burglaries occurred. The force was reorganized
by the commission the following day.

Long John Wentworth typified almost every mayor Chicago ever had:
independent, headstrong to the point of creating public chaos, and with a
total disrespect for authority beyond his own powers. This was never more in
evidence than in 1860 when Long John played host to the Prince of Wales
who was later to become Edward VII. With his huge arm about the future
monarch of England, Long John lead his royal visitor to a hotel balcony to
look out over a sea of uplifted faces in the street. "Boys!" boomed Long John.
"This is the Prince of Wales! He's come to see the city and I'm going to show
him around! Prince, these are the boys!"

The Wide-open Politicians

In its fits of repression, the Chicago public has historically turned away
from its sins, electing reform mayors. This was the case, in the 1850s, of Dr.
Levi D. Boone, a mayor who proved to be a disaster. Boone, a fanatical
member of the Know-Nothing party, a hater of all people and things foreign,
was a strange selection by the electorate in that Chicago has always been a
city of great ethnic populations, having huge segments of Irish, Swedish, and
German immigrants, to name just a few of its burgeoning nationalities. The
xenophobic Mayor Boone, in office not more than a few days, got it into his
head that the drinking of beer was anti-American and banned the brew. The
Germans, not to mention the Irish, went wild and rioted, resulting in a pitched
battle in front of City Hall. This imbecilic confrontation was to go down in
the city's history as the Lager Beer Riot, but it should have been named after
its perpetrator Boone. Later mayors indulged in different excesses, ones
profitable to their own coffers. Gambling and all manner of vice were
tolerated through the administrations of the 1870s and 1880s, although reform
Mayor John A. Roche suppressed gambling during his term. His successors

Reformer W.T. Stead and wife; the British reformer was shocked at the roaring vice and gambling in Chicago during the World's Fair; Stead went down with the *Titanic* in 1912.

The scene outside the Ashland Avenue mansion of Chicago Major Carter Harrison I on the night of his assassination, October 9, 1893, at the hands of Patrick Eugene Prendergast (inset).

DeWitt C. Cregier and Hempstead Washburne found it convenient to look the other way as payoffs from the gamblers were sent along to City Hall.

When Carter Harrison, Sr., was elected for his fifth term in 1893, the gamblers virtually took over the city, and with Harrison's blessing. The mayor had been financed in his last run for office through a campaign fund which had been collected by the real boss of the city, supergambler Big Mike McDonald. In the lofty words of reformer W. T. Stead, Harrison "took pains to recoup those patriots who had supplied him with the sinews of war."

The stakes were enormous, for Chicago was about to play host to the World's Fair in the summer of 1893. A great White City of huge pavilions boasting Grecian columns and man-made lagoons, exquisite fountains and statuary, had been prepared for the hundreds of thousands of visitors to the city. In praise of this colossal enterprise, Harrison declared that "genius is but audacity. Chicago has chosen a star and, looking upward to it, knows nothing it cannot accomplish." The audacity was Harrison's umbilical union with McDonald and the gamblers. What they accomplished was a wide-open city where every imaginable form of gambling and vice went abetted by authorities and the police. This is essentially what Harrison had promised—as would Big Bill Thompson years later—a wide-open town.

Harrison held his pockets open wide and into them the gamblers and brothel owners dumped a fortune. Everybody in the administration got rich right on down to street cleaners like Big Jim Colosimo, who became the crime czar of the city, his career sponsored by alderman Bathhouse John Coughlin and Hinky Dink Kenna. From Colosimo's reign came Johnny Torrio, then Capone, then the national crime syndicate, all of it in direct lineage from Mayor Carter Harrison, the Greedy.

Of this period, historian Herbert Asbury was to say: "Chicago was the most wide-open town that America had ever seen, or probably will ever see. And it was also, with the possible exception of New York in the days of Boss Tweed, the most corrupt, and, for that matter, had been for a decade. Everyone in Chicago capable of reasoning knew that virtually all departments of the city government reeked of graft and bribery, but nobody felt called upon to do anything about it." To support this claim was the worst gambling den in the city, which also served as a whorehouse, an establishment that was operated directly above the saloon owned by Alderman John Powers.

A visitor to the World's Fair was Englishman W. T. Stead, a church reformer who was shocked at conditions under the Harrison regime. He investigated and soon found that the mayor was the chief crook in Chicago who gleaned millions from all illegal activities encouraged by his administration. "This sum," Stead was to write, "which amounted during the World's Fair, in some districts to a colossal fortune, was divided. Many people had a finger in the pie before the residue reached Mr. Harrison. But however many there were who fingered the profit en route, there was enough left to make it well worth the Mayor's while to allow the houses to run."

Mayor Carter Harrison in caricature revealing the magnificent World's Fair in Chicago; Harrison also let loose widespread corruption, graft and vice, working hand-in-glove with Chicago's crooks.

A view of the Grand Court, World's Columbian Exposition, 1893.

Stead went on to state that the city council, with two exceptions, was corrupt. "There are sixty-eight aldermen in the City Council," he charged, "and sixty-six of them can be bought; this I know because I have bought them myself."

Rubber-stamped franchises paid aldermen handsomely according to news accounts. When the corrupt Charles Yerkes wanted to establish a streetcar monopoly, he paid four aldermen $25,000 each and $8,000 more to those aldermen who voted the franchise to his firm. Another alderman instrumental in passing an ordinance that would benefit one of Chicago's overnight tycoons was paid $100,000 in cash and received two large tracts of land.

One alderman learned that his fellow grafters had received $5,000 payoffs to push through a measure in the city council, where he had only been given $3,500. His reaction, according to the *Chicago Record* was to "weep in anger before going over to the opposition, assisting in the final overthrow of the deal."

Harrison used his veto to any measure that was being bought as a blackmail tool. He would usually get half of what the deal was worth. Council members who passed an ordinance over the mayor's veto charged 25 percent more than usual payments, one alderman explaining, "We have to charge more if the mayor gets mad at us."

Harrison's big boodle scheme came to an end, at least for him, on the night of October 9, 1893. The World's Fair had closed and Harrison was resting—if not counting his kickbacks—in the library of his Ashland Avenue mansion. One of the problems facing the mayor was his much publicized crusade to convert the railway system into an elevated construction that would encircle the downtown district (this would become Chicago's famous El, the tracks encircling the downtown area known as the Loop). Harrison faced a battle in the city council in pushing the plan through.

The mayor's doorbell rang and, as was his custom, he answered the door himself. A pale young man, his hands nervously twitching, stood before Harrison, mumbling words the mayor could not hear. The mayor began to say something when the caller suddenly jerked forth a revolver and emptied it into Harrison, who pitched forward onto the front porch, dead. His assassin Patrick Eugene Prendergast then sat down on the front steps to wait for the police.

Prendergast was a political oddity; he had purchased a fifty-cent pamphlet entitled *Every Man His Own Lawyer* and had gotten the notion that he was suddenly equipped to handle the job of corporation counsel for Harrison's proposed elevated train project. He petitioned City Hall for this position but was rebuffed as a crackpot. Prendergast brooded over the rejection and finally, in frustration, took vengeance on Harrison.

Harrison may have been gone but his corrupt regime went on. "He was a good man," cooed Michael "Hinky Dink" Kenna, boss of the red-light district,

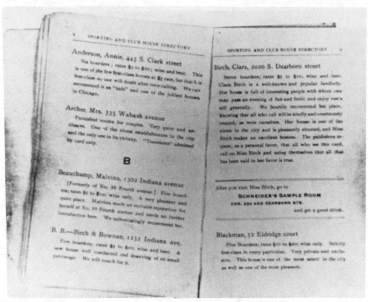

The Club House Directory which evaluated Chicago's scores of brothels for visitors to the Exposition.

Alderman Bathhouse John Coughlin of the notorious First Ward as drawn by John McCutcheon.

Alderman Michael "Hinky Dink" Kenna of the First Ward as drawn by John McCutcheon.

A red-light whore entertaining the rowdy guests during the First Ward Ball, 1908. (sketch by John McCutcheon)

to his pal Alderman Bathhouse John Coughlin, "but we gotta think of the future." He meant, of course, their pocketbooks.

Hinky Dink and the Bath

Coughlin and Kenna were the bosses of the Levee, the terrible First Ward which was also the city's roaring red-light district. Under their leadership, the grand brothels and gambling hellholes flourished. Everybody kicked back to them for protection against the police or police raids. The only time the police raided any Levee hellhole from 1893 to 1911, when Carter Harrison II, then mayor, closed down the district, was because they either forgot or ignored the payments. No tally was ever taken, but it is certain that both men became millionaires through their blatant graft and bribery. They were a total disgrace which, of course, is why they are looked back upon with fondness by many a Chicagoan remembering the free and easy times they allegedly represented.

Bathhouse John Coughlin got his nickname after working for several years in Turkish baths as a "rubber." A tall, buffoonish-looking man with a beer paunch and a glad hand, Coughlin opened the Silver Dollar Saloon in his native First Ward during the era of William Jennings Bryan. He was elected to the city council in 1892. He wrote terrible poetry and sappy ballads which he thought were good; the cynical reporters of the day encouraged him to make a fool out of himself by asking him to recite and sing his own works in public at every opportunity. Coughlin's childish vanity was touched and he complied.

One of the alderman's major works was entitled "Dear Midnight of Love," written in 1899. Not having much to do at a city council meeting that year, Kenna suddenly stood up and announced to members that his opus would be performed at the Chicago Opera House, sung by Miss May de Sousa, and that "everybody's invited." Council members leaped to their feet and cheered, most in derision.

Reporters attended the rehearsals. One asked the Bath how he came to possess such creativity. "There's nothing to it," Coughlin said with a grin. "I'm certainly the best there is, the best anybody ever looked at. I'm doing a stunt right here now that no alderman can touch, no alderman in the world. The orchestra's all right. The singer's all right—and I ain't swelled a bit because I got it coming to me."

May de Sousa stepped to the footlights in rehearsal and warbled into the song, if one could call it a song. A sample chorus:

When silence reigns supreme and midnight love fortells
If heart's love could be seen, there kindest thoughts do dwell.
If darkness fancies gleam, true loving hearts do swell;
So far beyond a dream, true friendship never sell.

Listening in the back of the theater, Michael "Hinky Dink" Kenna made a sour face, turned, and ran into the street, yelling, "Help! Help! I need a drink!"

But Coughlin's personal band, all members of the Cook County Democratic Marching Club, finished playing the song and then, in triumph, lifted the beaming Coughlin to their shoulders and marched about with him on stage.

The production ran for a week and the newspapers lampooned it, one reviewer writing under the name of Inspired Idiot. Commented the *Journal's* critic: "That settled it. From now on, it's Bathos John."

Mayor Carter Harrison II was in attendance at one of the performances and remained speechless in his private box. In the next box sat Coughlin's mentor, a much embarrassed Hinky Dink, gripping the rail in fright, his face ashen. Harrison later asked Kenna, "Tell me, Mike—do you think John is crazy or just full of dope?"

"No," retorted Hinky Dink. "John isn't dotty and he ain't full of dope. To tell you the God's truth, Mr. Mayor, they ain't found a name for it yet."

Coughlin never lived down the production of his song, but then again, he didn't care. He had all the money he could spend and the power he could wield. He merely shrugged each succeeding year when John Kelley of the *Tribune* wrote half-witted verses such as "Why Did They Build Lake Michigan So Wide" and signed Coughlin's name in print on each anniversary of "Dear Midnight of Love." No one could erode his fame, he thought, as he referred to himself as "the poet lariat of the First Ward."

The real boss of the First Ward, however, was Michael "Hinky Dink" Kenna, elected to the city council in 1897. Shrewd and crafty, it was Kenna who had the contacts at City Hall and within the hierarchy of the police force. Through these, Kenna kept the brothels and gambling dens going full blast in the First Ward. He also had the guts of a burglar. Called in by Mayor Harrison II to answer for a precinct captain who wasn't taking orders from City Hall, Kenna stood up for his handpicked man, telling Harrison, "You got him all wrong, Mr. Mayor. He never understood the orders. If you give him another chance you'll never need to complain. He's one of our best captains. I can always count on him. He's a good conscientious son of a bitch, even if he does run a whorehouse!"

When Harrison obliquely mentioned Kenna's payoffs from his red-light district supporters, Kenna drew his small frame stiff, snapping to the mayor, "I never took a dollar from a woman! No house ever paid me for protection!" When he calmed down, he admitted to Harrison, "Of course, I'd just as soon run a poker game, but a faro bank of a big kind, in a hotel room for high-fliers to play, no suckers. You know, men that love to play and can afford to pay. I'm strong for that!"

Kenny and Coughlin not only bullied the mayor about but reveled in their

Thieves, prostitutes, and police captains at the First Ward Ball. (sketch by John McCutcheon)

unchecked power by giving an annual First Ward Ball. Every pimp, prostitute, sneak thief, pickpocket, bank burglar, gambler, and crook in the Levee attended, along with those police captains in favor with Bathhouse and Hinky Dink. The affair grew to colossal proportions, more than 15,000 of the city's worst elements jamming into the Coliseum in 1908. For this event, Bathhouse John wrote the following poem (printed on thousands of leaflets and distributed through the throng):

> On with the dance
> Let the orgy be perfectly proper
> Don't drink, smoke or spit on the floor
> And say keep your eye on the copper.

The ball was always a huge success, a way in which Kenna and Coughlin showed their respects to the denizens of the most notorious ward in America and one that had made the aldermen rich. But the boom faded when Carter Harrison II was forced by civic leaders and reformers to close down the Levee in 1911. The aldermen wielded some power after that through their handpicked crime czar Big Jim Colosimo, but when Colosimo was killed by Capone in 1920 at Johnny Torrio's orders, the aldermen were shunted to the sidelines, although they lingered long and shook sorry heads at the gang wars of the 1920s; in their day they would never have allowed things to get so out of

Hinky Dink Kenna, still pugnacious in old age, 1943.

hand. But the new day belonged to Big Bill Thompson, mayor of Chicago, who first took office in 1916 as a Republican, held on for another term, and was thrown out by reform Mayor Dever's Democratic machine, then returned to become Al Capone's tool.

Big Bill

As Capone had said, "Nobody's on the legit." He could have been pointing at Thompson and most of the city's residents would have agreed. As a young man, Thompson began, paradoxically enough, as a reformer, but soon backed corrupt politicians, such as Mayor Fred Busse, who campaigned for "Sunday Saloons and a wide-open city," a slogan Thompson would later adopt with a vengeance.

Thompson was backed, or rather shoved, into office by Senator Billy Lorimer, his political mentor, during the campaign year of 1915. It was done with torchlight marches, free-beer picnics and a song written expressly for Big Bill by Mrs. Frank Catlin.

We want a great and fearless mayor!
Thompson's the man! Thompson's the man!
One who is on the square.

Al Capone, shown fishing off his Florida estate in 1929, used Mayor Thompson like a puppet.

While the thugs are plying, the grafters trying,
We want a cleaner city
Where the good can thrive and shine.
No more picking pockets!
No more graft skyrockets
This must go out! They're put to rout!
Bill Thompson's the man for me!
There's a man in the heart of this old town
With a heart that is big and free.
He'll pull the crooks and grafters down.
Bill Thompson is the man for me!

Instead of pulling the grafters down, Bill Thompson gave them the green light. He had been elected even though he was known to be corrupt—he had admitted that he had patronized Levee brothels—and in the face of such an endorsement, Thompson felt he could act with impunity and did. The Republican machine that put Thompson in office became all-powerful, as much as the Democratic machine under Richard J. Daly would be three decades later. The ward bosses knew their voters down to the last man, dead or alive. During this election, Oscar Depriest, a former Negro alderman, was going over the votes in an all-Negro ward which had cast 272 votes, 271 being for Thompson. Depriest turned to a cohort and barked, "I know who double-crossed here! Go out and find Mose Jackson and give him a raking over the coals!"

Bill Thompson controlled all of Cook County for years to come following the Republican sweep of the States Attorney's Office, and the election machinery through the election of his handpicked Cook County judge. Running for a second term, Thompson appealed to the uneducated, the vice-ridden, the tens of thousands who thought to share in illegal booty. His 1919 campaign was all banner and slogan. Thompson organized the Chicago Boosters Club which put up huge posters everywhere reading, "A booster is better than a knocker." He extorted more than $1 million from business leaders for his war chest—he said it was "to help publicize Chicago"—by threatening not to renew their licenses. He led dozens of marches down the main streets while his paid henchmen gave out the roaring chant, "All hats off to our mayor, Big Bill the Builder." He won.

Thompson's second election was also a big win for Johnny Torrio and Al Capone, who had contributed large sums to his campaign and had forced thousands to join the William Hale Thompson Republican Club, which was little more than an organized gang of thugs and could have served as a role model to Hitler's Brown Shirts in Germany three years later.

The worst race riots in twentieth-century America occurred in Thompson's Chicago in 1919. He looked the other way as usual. The mayor, however, was defeated by reform candidate William Dever in 1923. This forced Capone and Torrio to move their headquarters to Cicero, but Thompson still worked on the gangster's behalf. During Dever's helpless administration, Thompson ridiculed the mayor and his supporters at every turn. He rented a theater and brought two live rats in a cage on to the stage, labeling the rodents with the names of his political opponents and debating them, an act that won him instant notoriety the world over. He defied the federal law, Prohibition, promising booze to the electorate if he were reelected (Capone would supply the hootch). He screamed from one stage: "Read Bill Thompson's platform—you can't find anything wetter than that in the middle of the Atlantic! It's the only wet platform in the campaign!"

The massive, towering Thompson saw to it that he was always near an American flag, almost draped in it. Not having a clear-cut issue in his 1927 campaign, Thompson speciously attacked King George of England, saying that if the king ever dared to come to Chicago, he would "punch him in the nose." He added: "I want to make the King of England keep his snoot out of America! That's what I want! I don't want the League of Nations! I don't want the World Court! America first and last and always! That's the issue of this campaign! That's what Big Bill Thompson wants!"

But Thompson and Capone only wanted one thing—the return of political power in Chicago. Capone, to assure Thompson's reelection, sent more than 1,000 goons into the city on primary day. They broke arms and legs, shot

George "Bugs" Moran, the only survivor of his gang which was slaughtered on St. Valentine's Day, 1929 by Capone machinegunners, an act which brought about the end of Major Thompson's lurid reign.

down Thompson's political foes, and threw so many hand grenades into polling areas where Thompson was expected to do badly that the whole, terrible event was labeled the Pineapple Primary. It was the same on election day. Thompson won both times, thanks to Al Capone.

He thanked Capone by letting the mobster literally rule Chicago. He was paid handsomely to travel abroad, sunning himself in foreign pleasure spas. The city government was actually in Capone's hands anyway, according to most reports, after Daniel A. Serritella, a Capone henchman, was appointed by Thompson to the post of City Sealer. When Thompson was at home, he busied himself with bribes and kickbacks. According to interviews conducted by the author with onetime Missouri gangster and bagman for Boss Pendergast, James Henry "Blackie" Audett, Thompson received enormous payoffs from the kingpin of Kansas City. Audett once delivered about $50,000 in cash to Big Bill so that Thompson would stump for federal legislation that would help the Missouri machine. "I took it right into his office," Audett insisted, "and he counted out every bill in the bundles. Then he smiled and thanked me."

Big Bill was less cordial with critics. When Judge John H. Lyle, one of the few public officials who was honest at the time, courageously stated that

Thompson was in league with Capone, Thompson exploded, stating, "I don't care about name-calling, but he has attacked my integrity and I'd like to knock this loony judge down, kick him in the face and kick hell out of him!" He then sued Lyle for $1 million, a suit that came to nothing.

Fed up with gangsters, grenades, and machine guns, the Chicago electorate finally turned on Thompson, replacing him with reform Mayor Anton Cermak. (Most agreed that Capone's slaughter of the Bugs Moran gang on St. Valentine's Day, 1929, was the last bitter pill the Thompson-Capone combine forced down the public throat, and this event, more than any other, contributed to Thompson's final defeat.)

The *Chicago Tribune* reveled in Thompson's ouster, publishing one of the most stinging editorials in the newspaper's history: "For Chicago, Thompson has meant filth, corruption, obscenity, idiocy and bankruptcy. . . . He has given the city an international reputation for moronic buffoonery, barbaric crime, triumphant hoodlumism, unchecked graft, and a dejected citizenship. He nearly ruined the property and completely destroyed the pride of the city. He made Chicago a byword of the collapse of American civilization. In his attempt to continue this he excelled himself as a liar and defamer of character. He's out.

"He is not only out, but he is dishonored. He is deserted by his friends. He is permanently marked by the evidence of his character and conduct. His health is impaired by his ways of life and he leaves office and goes from the city the most discredited man who ever held place in it."

Yet Big Bill Thompson, "the Builder," continued to reside in Chicago, as did his criminal sponsor Capone. Scarface also continued to have only three large portraits on the walls of his massive office inside the Metropole Hotel: Washington, Lincoln, and William Hale Thompson. By 1933, Capone was sent to prison on tax evasion. Thompson, according to later reports of his illegal wealth, should have been Capone's cellmate.

Big Bill, however, died in bed on March 19, 1944, at age seventy-seven. His estate was originally estimated at a modest $150,000, but some days later, his loot was uncovered in safe-deposit vaults, an overall sum of $2,103,024, two-thirds of this in old gold certificates, cold Capone cash.

Managing the Machine

Following the fall of Big Bill, the Republicans were through as a force in Chicago; never again would they take charge of Cook County politics. Mayor Anton Cermak was accidentally assassinated in Florida by Joseph Zangara in 1933. (Zangara was aiming at President-elect Roosevelt when Cermak got in the way.) He did not represent the Chicago mob in attempting to remove the reform mayor, as rumor later had it. Nevertheless, Cermak began the Democratic dynasty that has run Chicago to the present, its most

Chicago iron-man Mayor Richard J. Daley (second from right), leading his favorite parade on St. Patrick's Day.

powerful figure being Richard Joseph Daley who ruled Chicago with an iron hand and a massive patronage system from the mid-1950s until his death in 1977.

The tyrannical Daley ran the last all-powerful political machine in America, one no less corrupt than its predecessors. Daley pummeled the press, cold-shouldering reporters with the arrogance of a feudal lord. He was a master of malapropism who spoke witlessly and with all the articulation of one afflicted with chronic spasms. His fractured grammar was thought to be cute by his supporters, and these were legion. His oppressive manner and bully-boy tactics created a permanent iron gray atmosphere in Chicago.

Daley lived inside plain, double-breasted suits, and as far as he was concerned, Chicago had no ills, no problems. In fact, when the rest of the country long realized that it was being plundered by the national crime syndicate, Daley refused to admit the existence of any such cartel in Chicago. In 1962, Mayor Daley said of the *Outfit*: "What crime syndicate? There is no such thing in the good city of Chicago." He had apparently never heard of Tony Accardo, Sam Giancana, and others who headed the crime syndicate in Chicago, although these names made up everyday headlines in Chicago newspapers throughout Daley's reign. But then, Richard J. Daley was a cute man.

Though Daley was never proved to be a crook, his most intimate associates in Chicago politics spent a good deal of time in jail. His onetime backer, former Governor Otto Kerner, was convicted of bribery in a racetrack scandal and sent to prison. Daley's press secretary for nineteen years Earl Bush was convicted of mail fraud. Alderman Thomas E. Keane, his closest friend and adviser, the second most powerful man in Chicago, was convicted of mail fraud and sent to prison. Alderman Paul I. Wigoda, Keane's legal associate, was convicted of extortion. Edward J. Barrett, who had taken over from Daley the position of the Clerk of Cook County in 1955, was convicted of soliciting and taking payoffs in 1973. Clarence Brasch, Police Traffic Chief, was convicted of extortion in the same year. The list could go on and on, but Richard J. Daley's name remains pure.

Many would argue that, for politicians, there is no such thing as guilt by association. Yet it is inconceivable that Richard J. Daley was not aware, as he insisted to the end, of the illegal operations of his closest confidants, unless one is to believe that he was nothing more than a political idiot savant or non compos mentis who ruled through stumbling fortune the destiny of a great city without the muck of his friends besmirching his own august presence. Dick Daley was too shrewd and tough and calculating to fit that mold.

He knew.

Bibliography

Thousands of books, periodicals, pamphlets, and reports, as well as newspapers and the author's own notes and various interviews over the years as a reporter and editor in Chicago, were employed in researching this work. What follows proved to be the most helpful of published material.

Books

Allen, Edward J. *Merchants of Menace—The Mafia.* Springfield, Illinois: Charles C. Thomas, 1962.
Allen, Frederick Lewis. *The Big Change.* New York; Harper & Bros., 1952.
———. *Only Yesterday.* New York: Harper & Bros., 1931.
———. *Since Yesterday.* New York: Harper & Bros., 1940.
Allen, Lee. *The American League Story.* New York: Hill & Wang, 1962.
———. *The National League Story.* New York: Hill & Wang, 1961.
Allsop, Kenneth. *The Bootleggers.* London: Hutchinson, 1961.
Amory, Cleveland. *Who Killed Society?* New York: Harper & Bros., 1960.
Anderson, Margaret. *My Thirty Year's War.* New York: Alfred Knopf, 1930.
Andrews, Wayne. *Battle for Chicago.* New York: Harcourt, Brace and Company, 1946.
Asbury, Herbert. *Gem of the Prairie.* New York: Alfred A. Knopf, 1940.
Asinof, Eliot. *Eight Men Out.* New York: Holt, Rinehart and Winston, 1963.
Axelson, G. W. *Commy.* Chicago: Reilly & Lee Co., 1919.

Barrow, Edward Grant, with James M. Kahn. *My Fifty Years in Baseball.* New York: Coward-McCann, 1951.
Bartlett, Arthur. *Baseball and Mr. Spalding.* New York: Farrar, Straus and Young, 1951.
Bent, Silas. *Strange Bedfellows.* New York: Horace Liveright, 1928.
Boettiger, John. *Jake Lingle.* New York: E. P. Dutton & Co., 1931.
Bradley, Hugh. *Such Was Saratoga.* Garden City, New York: Doubleday Doran, 1940.
Bright, John. *Hizzoner Big Bill Thompson.* New York: J. Cape & H. Smith, 1930.
Buchanan, Lamont. *The Story of Football.* New York: Stephen-Paul, 1947.
Bullough, Vern L. *The History of Prostitution.* New Hyde Park, New York: University Books, 1964.
Burnley, James. *Millionaires and Kings of Enterprise.* Philadelphia: Lippincott, 1901.
Burns, Walter Noble. *The One-Way Ride.* Garden City, New York: Doubleday Doran, 1931.
Busch, Francis X. *Enemies of the State.* New York: Bobbs-Merrill, 1954.
Butterfield, Roger. *The American Past.* New York: Simon and Schuster, 1947.

248 PEOPLE TO SEE

Carlson, Oliver. *Brisbane, A Candid Biography*. New York: Stackpole Sons, 1937.
Casey, Robert J. *Chicago, Medium Rare*. New York: Bobbs-Merrill, 1952.
Cassin, Herbert N. *Cyrus Hall McCormick*. Chicago: McClurg, 1909.
Caughey, John Walton. *Their Majesties the Mob*. Chicago: The University of Chicago Press, 1960.
Chaetetz, Henry. *Play the Devil*. New York: Clarkson N. Potter, 1960.
Chenery, William L. *So It Seemed*. New York: Harcourt, Brace and Company, 1952.
Churchill, Allen. *A Pictorial History of American Crime*. New York: Holt, Rinehart and Winston, 1964.
Cipes, Robert M. *The Crime War*. New York: New American Library, 1967.
Coblentz, Edmond D. *William Randolph Hearst*. New York: Simon and Schuster, 1952.
Cohn, Art. *The Joker Is Wild*. New York: Random House, 1955.
Collins, Frederick Lewis. *Glamorous Sinners*. New York: Long & Smith, 1932.
Considine, Robert B. *The Unreconstructed Amateur*. San Francisco: Amos Alonzo Stagg Foundation, 1962.
Cook, Fred J. *The Secret Rulers*. New York: Duell, Sloan and Pearce, 1966.
Cooper, Courtney Riley. *Ten Thousand Public Enemies*. Boston: Little, Brown, 1935.
Corey, Herbert. *Farewell, Mr. Gangster!* New York: Appleton-Century-Crofts, 1936.
Crockett, Albert Stevens. *Peacocks on Parade*. New York: Sears, 1931.
Crowinshield, Francis W. *Manners for the Metropolis*. New York: Appleton, 1908.

Danzig, Allison. *The History of American Football*. Englewood Cliffs, New Jersey: Prentice-Hall, 1956.
Davis, Ronald L. *Opera in Chicago*. New York: Appleton-Century, 1966.
Dedman, Emmett. *Fabulous Chicago*. New York: Random House, 1953.
Demaris, Ovid. *Captive City*. New York: Lyle Stuart, Inc., 1969.
Dennis, Charles H. *Victor Lawson, His Time and His Work*. Chicago: The University of Chicago Press, 1935.
DeVoto, Bernard. *The Course of Empire*. Boston: Houghton-Mifflin, 1952.
Dibble, Roy Floyd. *Strenuous Americans*. New York: Boni & Liveright, 1923.
Dobyns, Fletcher. *The Underworld of American Politics*. New York: Dobyns, 1923.
Duke, Thomas S. *Celebrated Criminal Cases of America*. San Francisco: James H. Berry Co., 1910.
Durocher, Leo, with Ed Linn. *Nice Guys Finish Last*. New York: Simon and Schuster, 1975.
Durso, Joseph. *The Days of Mr. McGraw*. Englewood Cliffs, New Jersey: Prentice-Hall, 1969.

Enright, Jim. *Chicago Cubs*. New York: Collier Books, 1975.
Erbstein, Charles E. *The Show-Up: Stories Before the Bar*. Chicago: Pascal Covici, 1926.

Farr, Finis. *Chicago*. New Rochelle, New York: Arlington House, 1973.
Farrell, James T. *My Baseball Diary*. New York: A. S. Barnes, 1957.
Federal Writer's Project—Illinois—Work Project Administration. *Baseball in Old Chicago*. Chicago: A. C. McClurg & Co., 1939.
Flinn, John T. *History of the Chicago Police from the Settlement of the Community to the Present Time*. Chicago: Police Book Fund, 1887.
Furer, Howard B. *Chicago: A Chronological and Documentary History, 1784–1970*. Dobbs Ferry, New York: Oceana Publications, Inc., 1974.

Gage, Nicholas. *Mafia, USA*. Chicago: Playboy Press, 1972.
Gilbert, Paul Thomas, and Charles Lee Bryson. *Chicago and Its Makers*. Chicago: The University of Chicago Press, 1929.
Gosnell, Harold F. *Machine Politics, Chicago Model*. Chicago: F. Mendelsohn, 1937.
Green, Laurence. *The Era of Wonderful Nonsense*. Indianapolis: Bobbs-Merrill, 1939.
Grimm, Charlie, with Ed Prell. *Jolly Cholly's Story, Baseball, I Love You!* Chicago: Henry Regnery, 1968.
Grund, Francis J. *Aristocracy in America*. New York: Harper & Bros., 1959.

Harper, Robert S. *Lincoln and the Press*. New York: McGraw-Hill, 1951.

Harrison, Carter. *Growing Up With Chicago*. Indianapolis: Bobbs-Merrill, 1944.
———. *Stormy Years*. Indianapolis: Bobbs-Merrill, 1935.
Hecht, Ben. *Charlie, The Improbable Life and Times of Charles MacArthur*. New York: Harper & Bros., 1957.
———. *A Child of the Century*. New York: Simon and Schuster, 1954.
———. *Gaily, Gaily, The Memoirs of a Cub Reporter in Chicago*. New York: Doubleday, 1963.
Hirsch, Phil, ed. *The Killers*. New York: Pyramid, 1971.
Holbrook, Stewart H. *The Story of the American Railroads*. New York: Crown, 1947.
Hoover, J. Edgar. *Persons in Hiding*. Boston: Little, Brown, 1938.
Horan, James D. *The Desperate Years*. New York: Crown, 1962.
House, Brant, ed. *Crimes That Shocked America*. New York: Ace Books, 1961.
Hynd, Alan. *Murder, Mayhem, and Mystery*. New York: A. S. Barnes, 1958.

Ickes, Harold L. *America's House of Lords, An Inquiry into the Freedom of the Press*. New York: Harcourt, Brace and Company, 1935.
Irving, Henry Brodribb. *A Book of Remarkable Criminals*. New York: George H. Doran, 1918.

Jackson, Joseph Henry, ed. *The Portable Murder Book*. New York: Viking Press, 1945.
Johnson, Malcolm. *Crime on the Labor Front*. New York: McGraw-Hill, 1950.
Johnston, James P. *Grafters I Have Met*. Chicago: Thompson & Thomas, 1906.
Josephson, Matthew. *The Robber Barons*. New York: Harcourt, Brace and Company, 1934.

Katcher, Leo. *The Big Bankroll: The Life and Times of Arnold Rothstein*. New York: Harper, 1959.
Kefauver, Estes. *Crime in America*. New York: Doubleday & Co., 1951.
Kingston, Charles. *Remarkable Rogues*. New York: John Lane, 1921.
Kobler, John. *Capone*. New York: G. P. Putnam's, 1971.
Kobre, Sidney. *The Yellow Press and Gilded Age Journalism*. Tallahassee, Florida: Florida State University, 1964.
Koenigsberg, M. *King News, An Autobiography*. New York: F. A. Stokes Co., 1941.

Lait, Jack, and Lee Mortimer. *Chicago Confidential*. New York: Crown Publishers, 1950.
Landesco, John. *Organized Crime in Chicago*. Chicago: The University of Chicago Press, 1968.
Leech, Harper, and John Charles Carroll. *Armour and His Times*. New York: Appleton-Century, 1938.
Lewis, Lloyd and Henry Justin Smith. *Chicago, The History of Its Reputation*. New York: Harcourt Brace and Company, 1929.
Lieb, Fred. *Baseball As I Have Known It*. New York: Coward, McCann & Geoghegan, 1977.
Linn, James Weber. *James Keeley, Newspaperman*. New York: Bobbs-Merrill Co., 1937.
Lord, Walter. *The Good Years*. New York: Harper & Bros., 1960.
Louderback, Lew. *The Bad Ones*. New York: Fawcett, 1968.
Lucia, Ellis. *Mr. Football: Amos Alonzo Stagg*. New York: A. S. Barnes, 1970.
Luckman, Sid. *Luckman at Quarterback*. Chicago: Ziff-Davis, 1949.
Ludlow, Fitzhugh. *The Heart of the Continent*. New York: Hurd and Houghton, 1870
Lundberg, Ferdinand. *Imperial Hearst*. New York: Equinox Cooperative Press, 1936.
Lyle, Judge John H. *The Dry and Lawless Years*. Englewood Cliffs, New Jersey: Prentice-Hall Inc., 1960.

Mann, Arthur. *Baseball Confidential*. New York: David McKay, 1951.
Mayer, Harold M., and Richard C. Wade. *Chicago: Growth of a Metropolis*. Chicago: The University of Chicago Press, 1969.
McClellan, John L. *Crime without Punishment*. New York: Duell, Sloan and Pierce, 1962.
McConaughy, John. *From Caine to Capone, or Racketeering down the Ages*. New York: Brentano's, 1931.
McPhaul, John J. *Deadlines and Monkeyshines*. Englewood Cliffs, New Jersey: Prentice-Hall, 1962
Meeker, Arthur. *Chicago With Love*. New York: Knopf, 1955.
Merriam, Charles E. *Chicago*. Chicago: The University of Chicago Press, 1929.

Merz, Charles. *The Dry Decade*. Garden City, New York: Doubleday, Doran, 1931.
Messick, Hand, and Burt Goldblatt. *The Mobs and the Mafia*. New York: Ballantine Books, 1973.
Millar, Mara. *Hail to Yesterday*. New York: Farrar & Rinehart, 1931.
Moore, Edward C. *Forty Years of Opera in Chicago*. New York: Horace Liveright, 1930
Moore, William T. *Dateline Chicago*. New York: Taplinger Publishing Co., 1973.
Myers, Gustavus. *History of the Great American Fortunes*. New York: Modern Library, 1936.

Nash, Jay Robert. *Almanac of World Crime*. New York: Doubleday, 1981.
———. *Bloodletters and Badmen: A Narrative Encyclopedia of American Criminals from the Pilgrims to the Present*. New York: M. Evans, 1973.
———. *Look for the Woman*. New York: M. Evans, 1981.
———. *Murder America: Homicide in the United States from the Revolution to the Present*. New York: Simon and Schuster, 1980.

Orth, Samuel P. *The Boss and the Machine*. New Haven, Connecticut: Yale University Press, 1920.
O'Sullivan, F. Dalton. *Crime Detection*. Chicago: O'Sullivan, 1928.
Owen, Collinson. *King Crime*. New York: Holt, 1932.

Pasley, Fred D. *Al Capone, The Biography of a Self-Made Man*. New York: Ives Washburn, 1930.
———. *Muscling In*. New York: Ives Wasburn, 1931.
Peterson, Virgil. *Barbarians in Our Midst*. Boston: Little, Brown, 1952.
Pierce, Bessie L. *As Others See Chicago*. Chicago: The University of Chicago Press, 1933.
———. *A History of Chicago*. New York: Alfred A. Knopf, 1937.
Pinkerton, Matthew Worth. *Murder in All Ages*. New York: A. E. Pinkerton & Co., 1898.
Poole, Ernest. *Giants Gone*. New York: Whittlesley House, 1943.
Porges, Irwin. *The Violent Americans*. Derby, Connecticut: Monarch Books, 1963.
Powers, Francis J. *Life Story of Amos Alonzo Stagg, Grand Old Man of Football*. St. Louis, Missouri: C. C. Spink & Son, The Sporting News Publishing Co., 1946.

Quinn, John Philip. *Fools of Fortune*. Chicago: W. B. Conkey, 1890.

Radin, Edward D. *Crimes of Passion*. New York: G. P. Putnam's, 1953.
Rascoe, Burton. *Before I Forget*. Garden City, New York: Doubleday, 1937.
Reckless, Walter, *Vice in Chicago*. Chicago: The University of Chicago Press, 1933.
Rice, Grantland. *The Tumult and the Shouting*. New York: A. S. Barnes, 1954.
Roberts, Howard. *The Chicago Bears*. New York: G. P. Putnam's Sons, 1947.
Robertson, Mrs. Harriet M., ed. *Dishonest Elections and Why We Have Them*. Chicago: Published by the author, 1934.
Roe, Clifford. *Panderers and Thier White Slaves*. Chicago: Revell Publishing Co., 1910.
Rogers, Agnes, and Frederick Lewis Allen. *I Remember Distinctly*. New York: Harper & Bros., 1947.
Ross, Ishbel. *Ladies of the Press*. New York: Harper & Bros., 1936.
———. *Silhouette in Diamonds*. New York: Harper & Bros., 1960.
Ross, Robert. *The Trial of Al Capone*. Chicago: Robert Ross Publishing Co., 1933.

Sann, Paul. *The Lawless Decade*. New York: Crown, 1957.
Schlesinger, Arthur Meier. *The Rise of the City, 1878-1898*. New York: Macmillan, 1933.
Sedgwick, Henry Dwight. *In Praise of Gentlemen*. Boston: Little, Brown, 1935.
Sinclair, Andrew. *Era of Excess*. New York: Harper & Row, 1964.
Skinner, Emory Fiske. *Reminiscences*. Chicago: Vestal Printing Co., 1908.
Smith, Alson J. *Chicago's Left Bank*. Chicago: Henry Regnery Co., 1953.
———. *Syndicate City*. Chicago: Henry Regnery Co., 1954.
Smith, Henry Justin. *Chicago's Great Century, 1833-1933*. Chicago: Consolidated Publishers, 1933.
———. *Deadlines and Josslyn*. Chicago: Sterling North, 1934.

Sondern, Frederic, Jr. *Brotherhood of Evil*. New York: Farrar, Straus and Cudahy, 1959.
Spalding, Albert G. *Baseball*. New York: American Sports Publishing Co., 1911.
Spink, J. G. Taylor. *Judge Landis*. New York: Thomas Y. Crowell, 1947.
Stagg, Amos Alonzo. *Touchdown!* New York: Longmans, Green & Co., 1927.
Stead, William T. *If Christ Came to Chicago*. New York: Living Books, 1964.
Steffens, Lincoln. *Shame of the Cities*. New York: McClure, Phillips & Co., 1904.
Stone, Irving. *Clarence Darrow for the Defense*. Garden City, New York: Doubleday, 1941.
Stuart, William H. *The Twenty Incredible Years*. Chicago: M. S. Donahue, 1935.
Sullivan, Edward Dean. *Chicago Surrenders*. New York: Vanguard Press, 1930.
―――. *Rattling the Cup on Chicago Crime*. New York: Vanguard Press, 1929.
―――. *The Snatch Racket*. New York: Vanguard Press, 1932.
Sullivan, Mark. *Our Times*, vols. I–VI. New York: Charles Scribner's Sons, 1926–35.
Swanberg, W. A. *Citizen Hearst: A Biography of William Randolph Hearst*. New York: Charles Scriber's Sons, 1961.
Swift, Louis F., and Arthur Van Vlissingen. *The Yankee of the Yards*. Chicago: A. W. Shaw, 1927.

Tebbel, John. *An American Dynasty*. New York: Doubleday, 1947.
―――. *The Compact History of the American Newspaper*. New York: Hawthorn, 1963.
―――. *The Life and Good Times of William Randolph Hearst*. New York: Dutton, 1952.
―――. *The Marshall Fields*. New York: Dutton, 1947.
Tully, Andrew. *Era of Elegance*. New York: Funk & Wagnals, 1947.

Waldrop, Frank C. *McCormick of Chicago*. Englewood Cliffs, New Jersey: Prentice-Hall, 1966.
Wardman, Cy. *The Story of the Railroad*. New York: Appleton, 1911.
Warshow, Robert. *Bet A Million Gates*. New York: Greenberg Publishers, 1932.
Washburn, Charles. *Come into My Parlor*. New York: Knickerbocker Publishing Co., 1936.
Wecter, Dixon. *The Saga of American Society*. New York: Scribner's, 1937.
Wendt, Lloyd, and Herman Kogan. *Bet A Million!* Indianapolis: Bobbs-Merrill, 1948.
―――. *Big Bill of Chicago*. Indianapolis: Bobbs-Merrill, 1953.
―――. *Lords of the Levee*. Indianapolis: Bobbs-Merrill, 1943.
Weyand, Alexander M. *Football Immortals*. New York: The Macmillan Co., 1952.
―――. *The Saga of American Football*. New York: The Macmillan Co., 1955.
Whyte, William Foote. *Street Corner Society*. Chicago: The University of Chicago Press, 1943.
Wilson, Samuel Paynter. *Chicago and Its Cesspools of Vice and Infamy*. Chicago: N.P., 1910.
Winkler, John K. *William Randolph Hearst, A New Appraisal*. New York: Hastings House, 1955.
Winwar, Frances. *Oscar Wilde and the Yellow Nineties*. New York: Harper & Bros., 1941.

Zorbaugh, Harrey W. *The Gold Coast and the Slum*. Chicago: The University of Chicago Press, 1929.

Periodicals

"After Ten Years." *Newsweek*, December 24, 1956.
"Again, Chicago." *Time*, May 1, 1944.
"All the Strings." *Newsweek*, January 13, 1964.
"All Unquiet on the Chicago Front." *The Literary Digest*, June 28, 1930.
Ashbury, Herbert. "The St. Valentine's Day Massacre." *Forty-seven The Magazine of the Year*, September 1947.
"At the Garden Gate." *Time*, June 20, 1955.

"Back to the Carnival." *Time*, March 23, 1959.
"Bad Boy of Baseball." *Newsweek*, May 17, 1921.
"Ban Johnson, The Theodore Roosevelt of Baseball." *The Literary Digest*, March 6, 1919.
"Baseball: Another Business Facing Change." *U.S. News & World Report*, August 12, 1963.
"The Baseball Scandal." *The Nation*, October 13, 1920.
"Baseball's Grand Old Man." *The Literary Digest*, May 6, 1922.
Bent, Silas. "Newspapermen—Partners In Crime?" *Scribners Magazine*, November 1930.

Blanshard, Paul. "Who Killed Jake Lingle?" *The Nation*, July 2, 1930.
Boyle, Robert H. "Off Year for the Chicago Cubs." *Sports Illustrated*, August 6, 1962.
"Bullets from the Bloc." *Time*, February 18, 1952.

"Chewing Gum is a War Material." *Fortune*, January 1943.
"Chicago as Seen by Herself." *McClure's Magazine*, May 1907.
"Chicago Cycle." *Newsweek*, May 27, 1946.
"Chicago Finally Gets Het Up." *Life*, March 3, 1952.
"The Chicago Rackets." *Life*, November 29, 1948.
"Chicago's Fabulous Collectors." *Life*, October 27, 1952.
"Chicago's Police Scandal." *The Literary Digest*, January 27, 1917.
"Chicago's Trials with 'Grand Opera'." *The Literary Digest*, February 21, 1925.
"Chicago: Whiskey Sour." *Newsweek*, April 21, 1947.
"The Coach." *Time*, June 16, 1952.
"The Coach." *Time*, Marcy 26, 1965.
"The Comiskey Dynasty." *Newsweek*, July 31, 1939.
Cook, Gene, and Robert Hagy. "Gangland Stirs Again." *Life*, May 15, 1944.
"Council Corruption." *Newsweek*, February 9, 1953.
Crisler, Herbert O. "My Most Unforgettable Character." *Reader's Digest*, December 1962.
"Curtains for Roe." *Newsweek*, August 18, 1952.

Davidson, Bill. "How the Mobs Control Chicago." *Saturday Evening Post*, November 3, 1963.
Davidson, Bill, and Sandy Smith. "Panic in Chicago's Mafia." *Saturday Evening Post*, May 21, 1966.
"Death in the 24th Ward." *Time*, March 8, 1963.
"Death of a Businessman." *Time*, August 14, 1944.
"The Demise of a Don." *Time*, June 30, 1975.
"Double Dealer's Death." *Time*, January 7, 1974.

"Election of a Queen." *Newsweek*, December 28, 1953.

"Fair Grounds Saved." *Time*, March 17, 1941.
Fay, Bill. "The Meanest Man in Football." *Collier's*, November 25, 1950.
"Fireside Message." *Time*, May 26, 1958.
Fitzgerald, Harold A. "Slick Tricks With a Football." *Saturday Evening Post*, October 8, 1938.
"The Flaw In The Diamond." *The Literary Digest*, October 9, 1920.
Flynn, John T. "These Our Rulers." *Collier's*, July 6, 1940.
Flynt, Josiah. "In the World of Graft—Chi, an Honest City." *McClure's Magazine*, February 1901.
"For Honest Baseball." *The Outlook*, October 6, 1920.
"Foul Wind from Chicago." *Time*, July 28, 1958.
Frank, Stanley. "The Decline and Fall of the Cubs." *Saturday Evening Post*, September 11, 1943.
Frank, Stanley, and Edgar Munzel. "A Visit with Bill Veeck." *Saturday Evening Post*, June 6, 1959.
Fullerton, Hugh S. "Charles A. Comiskey." *American Magazine*, May 1911.
Furlong, William. "P. K. Wrigley: Baseball Magnate." *Saturday Evening Post*, Summer Edition, 1972.
"Furore in Fight World." *Life*, January 9, 1959.

"Gang Guns in Chicago." *Newsweek*, October 9, 1950.
"Gangland's Brazen Challenge to Chicago." *The Literary Digest*, June 21, 1930.
"The Gang's Still Here." *Time*, June 1, 1962.
"Grand Old Man." *Time*, November 21, 1938.
"Gridiron Shake-ups That Enliven the Fall." *The Literary Digest*, October 29, 1932.
Griswold, J. B. "You Don't Have to be Born With It." *American Magazine*, November 1931.

Haig, John Angus. "A Business Version of the Fuller Life." *Nation's Business*, September 1938.

Halas, George. "73-0." *Saturday Evening Post*, December 6, 1940.
———. "My Forty Years in Pro Football." *Saturday Evening Post* (series), November 23 and 30, December 6, 1957.
Hallgren, Mauritz A. "Chicago Goes Tammany." *The Nation*, April 22, 1931.
Hammond, Mary K. "Corruption in Chicago." *Current History*, December 1951.
"Hard Days for Halas." *Newsweek*, January 5, 1970.
Higdon, Harold. "The First 100 Years Are the Hardest." *Today's Health*, July 1962.
"Hold Spalding Up." *The Literary Digest*, September 25, 1915.
Holman, C. T. "Coach Stagg to Retire." *Christian Century*, October 26, 1932.
"How Ban Johnson Came Back." *The Literary Digest*, March 27, 1926.
"How 'Red Grange' Trains By Toting Ice." *The Literary Digest*, October 10, 1924.
"Hustler's Return." *Newsweek*, December 22, 1975.

"I'm Awfully Hot." *Time*, October 9, 1950.
Irwin, Will. "The First Ward Ball." *Collier's*, February 6, 1909.
"The Island Kingdom of P. K. Wrigley." *Forbes*, November 11, 1970.

Johnson, Ban. "Making the American League." *Saturday Evening Post*, March 22, April 12, 1930.
Johnston, Richard W. "Future Bears." *Sports Illustrated*, December 9, 1974.
"Judge Landis, The New Czar of Baseball." *The Literary Digest*, December 4, 1920.
"Just Like Papa Played." *Time*, December 6, 1963.

Kennedy, John B. "Lords of the Loop." *Collier's*, April 3, 1926.

Landesco, John. "The Criminal Underworld of Chicago in the Eighties and Nineties." *Journal of the American Institute of Criminal Law and Criminology*, May-June 1934, March-April 1935.
Lardner, John. "Washington Eyes a Millionaire." *Newsweek*, August 29, 1955.
"The Law of Kenesaw." *Newsweek*, December 6, 1943.
Leitzell, Ted. "Chicago, City of Corruption." *The American Mercury*, February 1940.
Lucia, Ellis. "Gridiron Stagg Line From Coast to Coast." *Oregonian*, November 9, 1947.
———. "Football's Grand Old Man." *Classmate*, October 23, 1955.
"Lucky Ted." *Time*, August 18, 1952.
"Lundin and Thompson of Chicago." *The Literary Digest*, March 3, 1923.

"Making the 'Black Sox' White Again." *The Literary Digest*, August 20, 1921.
Mangil, William. "Torrio, 'The Immune'." *True Detective*, September 1940.
"Man Without an Enemy." *Newsweek*, February 18, 1952.
Martin, John Bartlow. "Al Capone's Successors." *American Mercury*, June 1949.
McWilliams, Carey. "Chicago's Machine-Gun Politics." *The Nation*, March 15, 1952.
"Murder—And $350,000." *Newsweek*, April 15, 1957.
"Muscleman's Money." *Time*, July 21, 1958.

Nash, Jay Robert. "Earnest Hemingway, The Young Years." *Chicago Land Magazine*, August 1968.
———. "Heyday!" *Mankind Magazine*, October 1972.
"Newspaper Criminals in Chicago." *The Nation*, July 23, 1930.

"Once More Chicago Has a Queen." *Life*, January 25, 1954.

"Papa Bear Steps Aside." *Newsweek*, June 10, 1968.
"The Parting of Papa." *Time*, June 7, 1968.
Peterson, Virgil W. "Chicago: Shades of Capone." *Annals of the American Academy of Political & Social Science*, May 1963.
"The Players' League Starts." *Collier's*, June 12, 1909.

"Quarterbacking A New Industry." *Nation's Business*, December 1966.

Randolph, Col. Robert Isham. "How to Wreck Capone's Gang." *Collier's*, March 7, 1931.
"The Rest Is Silence." *Time*, December 24, 1965.
"Return of the Rub-Out." *Time*, March 8, 1963.
Rice, Grantland. "All-American Makers." *Collier's*, December 6, 1941.
————. "Rich Men's Toys." *Collier's*, July 27, 1927.
————. "The First Fifty Years." *Collier's*, December 9, 1939.
"R.I.P." *Time*, December 6, 1943.

Saltz, Irwin. "Nelson Algren on the Make." *ChicagoLand Magazine*, May 1970.
"Same Old Sam." *Time*, December 4, 1944.
Sargent, Kate. "Chicago, Hands Down." *The Forum*, December 1927.
Scully, Frank, and Norman L. Spear. "Too Old to Retire." *Reader's Digest*, February 1944.
Shepherd, William G. "Can Capone Beat Washington, Too?" *Collier's*, October 16, 1931.
Sidran, Louis. "The Unmasking of Paul 'The Waiter' Ricca." *Reader's Digest*, November 1959.
Silverman, Joseph. "When the City was Paid to Smile." *Chicago Magazine*, October 1955.
"Sit-Back Guys." *Newsweek*, May 23, 1949.
Smith, Sandy. "The Charmed Life of Tony Accardo." *Saturday Evening Post*, November 24, 1962.
Smith, Sherwin D. "35 Years Ago." *New York Times Magazine*, February 9, 1964.
Stagg, Amos Alonzo. "The Coach as a Critic." *Saturday Evening Post*, November 14, 1936.
"The Stagg Saga." *Newsweek*, December 16, 1946.
"Stagg's Century." *Newsweek*, August 13, 1962.
"Stagg's 54th." *Time*, October 25, 1943.
"Stagg's Formulas." *Newsweek*, August 27, 1951.
Sullivan, Edward Dean. "I Know You, Al." *North American Review*, September 1929.
Sutherland, Sidney. "The Machine-Gunning of McSwiggin and What Led Up to It." *Liberty*, July-August 1926.

"The Thompson Defeat in Chicago." *The Literary Digest*, July 2, 1921.
"They Stop at Nothing." *Newsweek*, July 21, 1958.
Thompson, Lewis, and Charles Boswell. "Say It Ain't So, Joe!" *American Heritage*, June 1960.
Turner, George Kibbe. "The City of Chicago. A Study of the Great Immoralities." *McClure's Magazine*, April 1907.
Underwood, John. "Amos Stagg: A Century of Honesty." *Sports Illustrated*, August 13, 1962.
"The Untouchables." *Newsweek*, April 22, 1963.

Vanderbilt, Cornelius, Jr. "How Al Capone Would Run This Country." *Liberty*, October 17, 1931.
"Veeck . . . a New Bill for the White Sox." *Look*, August 4, 1959.
Velie, Lester. "The Capone Gang Muscles into Big-Time Politics." *Collier's*, September 30, 1950.
Votaw, Albert N. "Chicago: 'Corrupt and Contented.' " *New Republic*, August 25, 1952.
————. "Gangs and Goons." *New Republic*, September 24, 1951.

Wharton, Don. "The Case of the Moving Jaws." *Reader's Digest*, December 1947.
"When Ban Johnson Stepped Down." *The Literary Digest*, March 19, 1927.
Wilson, Frank J. "Undercover Man, He Trapped Capone." *Collier's*, April 26, 1947.
Wolfe, Edgar Forest [pseud. for R. H. Faherty]. "The Real Truth About Al Capone." *The Master Detective*, September 1930.
Wooley, Edward Mott. "The Business of Baseball." *McClure's Magazine*, July 1912.
Wrigley, William, Jr. "Owning a Big-Legue Ball Team." *Saturday Evening Post*, September 13, 1930.

Yoder, Robert M., and James S. Kearns. "Boy Magnate." *Saturday Evening Post*, August 28, 1943.

Bulletins, Documents, Pamphlets, and Reports

Better Government Association of Chicago: *Reports*, 1969–79.
Chicago Crime Commission: *Annual Reports*, 1919–79.

Chicago Police Problems. The Citizen's Police Committee, 1931.
Chicago Vice Commission Report, Chicago, 1912.
Citizen's Association of Chicago: *Annual Reports*, 1902–24.
Illinois Crime Survey, 1902–29.
Report of the Committee of 15 on Prostitution and Gambling in Chicago. Chicago, 1914.
Smith, Henry Justin. *A Gallery of Chicago Editors*. Chicago Daily News, 1930.
Social Evils in Chicago, A Study of Existing Conditions with Recommendations by the Vice Commission of Chicago. Chicago, 1911.

Newspapers

(The following Chicago newspapers were used extensively in research; years of reference are given in lieu of miscellaneous dates too numerous to cite here.)

American (1838–1948); *Commercial Advertiser* (1879–82) *Daily News* (1877–1977); *Democrat* (1840–1900); *Evening Journal* (1902–29), *Herald-Examiner* and *Examiner* (1904–38); *Inter-Ocean* (1891–1912); *Journal* (1879–95); *Record-Herald* and *Herald* (1904–17); *Republican* (1880–1917); *Sun-Times* (1960–80); *Times* (1854–1904); *Today, Evening American*, and *American* (1910–71); *Tribune* (1847–1980).

Index

Abbott, Willis, J., 10
Accardo, Tony ("Joe Batters"), 92, 96, 97, 245
Adams, Congress George, 180
Adams, Franklin P., 134
Adams, Thomas, 164
Ade, George, 24, 208
Addy, Bob, 100
Aiuppa, Joey, 97
Alcock, Tom, 88
Alda, Frances, 186
Alderisio, "Milwaukee Phil", 96
Alex, Gus, 97
Algren, Nelson, 224–225
Allen, Lee, 109
Allen, Lizzie, 67
Altgeld, Governor John P., 9
Altman, Vincent, 29, 32
Anti-Gonorrhea Club, 38
American Bicycle Company, 104
Anderson, Hunk, 154, 160
Anderson, Kate, 67
Anderson, Lois, 213
Anderson, Margaret, 210, 213–219
Anderson, Sherwood, 217, 220
Annenberg, Max, 27–30
Annenberg, Moe, 27–29
Annixter, Julius "Luvin Putty", 77
Anson, Adele, 108
Anson, Adrian Constantine ("Cap"), 105–112
Anson, Dorothy, 108
Aparicio, Luis, 130
Arlington, Billy, 64
Armour, Jonathan Ogden, 171–174

Armour, Mrs. Philip Danforth, 170
Armour, Philip Danforth, Jr., 171, 174
Armstrong, Louis, 205
Asbury, Herbert, 59, 77, 232
Attell, Abe "The Little Champ", 122, 123, 125
Audett, James Henry ("Blackie"), 243
Austin High Gang, 205
Axelson, G.W., 116

Baller, Charles E., 168
Banks, Ernie, 139, 225
Banyon, Judge Augustus, 18
Barbizon School, 203
Barclay, Sam, 64
Barnes, Ross, 101
Barrett, Charles, 31
Barrett, Edward, 29, 31
Barrett, Edward J., 246
Bartlett, Arthur, 104
Baum, Frank, 210
Beiderbecke, Leon Bix, 205
Beitler, Brooks, 33, 37, 38, 39, 40
Bellow, Saul, 224
Bennett, James Gordon, 10
Bennett, James O'Donnell, 42
Bever, Maurice Van, 76
Billington, John, 197
Bioff, Willie, 92
Blackstone Hotel, 47
Blaine, Mrs. Emmons, 184
Blaine, James G., 184
Blei, Norbert, 219

Briggs House, 32
Burr, Charlie, 70
Bodenheim, Maxwell, 213
Bodman, Albert H., 7–8
Boone, Levi D., 230
Bradley, George Washington, 101, 108
Brasch, Clarence, 246
Brennan, Mary, 59
Brickhouse, Jack, 225
Bridewell, 8
Brighton Race Track, 229
Britton, Shuler P., 127
Brooks, Gwendolyn, 224
Brown, John, 15
Browne, Francis, 213
Browne, George, 92
Brumbaugh, Carl, 157
Brundige, Harry T., 90
Bryan, William Jennings, 237
Buchalsky, "Issy the Rat", 77
Burnett, W.R., 224
Burnhardt, Sarah, 173
Burnley, James, 170
Burnside, General Ambrose E., 14, 15
Burns, Tom, 109
Burns, Walter, 47
Burns, William Thomas "Sleepy Bill",
122, 127
Bush, Earl, 246
Busse, Mayor Fred, 45, 240
Butkus, Dick, 162

Cadwallader, Sylvanus, 13
Caesarino, Antonio, 79
Calhoun, John, 1–2, 3
Calhoun, Mrs. John, 2
Calwell, "Speckled Jimmy", 59
Camilla, Frank, 79, 80
Campagna, Louis ("Little New York"),
92
Camp, Walter, 154
Canfield, Richard, 169
Capone, Al, 29, 80–91, 92, 93, 95, 99, 134,
190, 191, 224, 232, 239, 240, 242, 243,
244
Capone, Ralph ("Bottles"), 92
Carrozzo, "Dago Mike", 76
Carson, Frank, 49, 50
Caruso, Enrico, 77
Carver, William H., 99

Cassidy, Claudia, 189
Catherwood, Mary Hartwell, 210
Catlin, Mrs. Frank, 240
Cavarretta, Phil, 139
Central Music Hall, 208
Cerf, Bennett, 215
Cermak, Mayor Anton, 244
Cerone, Jackie "The Lackey", 97
Chadwick, Henry, 100
Chamberlain, Guy, 154
Chance, Frank, 131, 134, 141
Chatfield-Taylor, Hobart, 208
°Chicago Booster's Club, 242
Chicago Newspapers
American, 2, 4, 27, 29, 73
Daily News, 21, 22, 23, 24, 32, 181, 206,
208
Daily Socialist, 29, 31
Democrat, 1, 3, 4
Evening Journal, 33
Evening Post, 44, 89
Examiner, 29, 31, 32, 47, 48, 49, 50, 52,
54
Globe, 62
Herald-Examiner, 89
Inter-Ocean, 35, 45, 198, 207
Journal, 21, 238
Post, 41
Post and Mail, 21,
Republican, 21
Skandinavian, 21
Sun, 181
Times, 9, 10, 11, 13–19, 181
Tribune, 4, 6–10, 13, 15, 19, 27, 29, 31,
32, 40–42, 45, 47–49, 52, 70, 73, 83, 85,
87–89, 91, 95, 177, 182, 187–191, 198,
227, 238, 244
World, 31
Chicago Symphony, 205
Cicotte, Eddie, 122, 123, 124, 125, 130
Cimini, Pietro, 187
Citizen Hearst, 47
Citizen Kane, 22
Clarkson, John, 6
Clay, Clarence, 70
Clay, Henry, 2
Cleveland Leader, 4
Cleveland, Mrs. Grover, 143
Coats, Audrey, 181
Cochran, Alexander Smith, 186
Cohan, George M., 108
Collins, Eddie, 117, 124

°Collins, John "Shano", 124
Colosimo, "Big Jim", 73, 75–80, 81, 85, 88, 232, 239
°Colosimo's Cafe, 77
Colosimo, Victoria, 78–79
Columbian Exposition, 24
Colvin, Harvey D., 61, 62
Comiskey, Charles Albert, 113–122, 123, 125, 127, 130, 131
Comiskey, J. Louis, 127
Congress Hotel, 34
Connors, Red, 29
Controy, Jack, 224
Coolbaugh, William F., 195
Cooney, Dennis "Duke", 77
Cosmano, Vincenzo "Sunny Jim", 77
Couglin, "Bathhouse John", 73, 75, 77, 232, 237, 238, 239
Creel, George, 109
Cregier, DeWitt C., 232
Crisler, Herbert O., 148, 150
Crosby, Uranus H., 17
Cummings, Arthur, 100
Curtis, William E., 23
Cuscaden, R.R., 219

Daley, Richard J., 241, 245, 246
Dalrymple, Abner, 109
Daly, "Chicago Jack", 29
D'Andrea, Joey, 77, 92, 93
Daugherty, William E., 21
Davies, Parson, 63
Davis, Curt, 139
Davis, Jefferson, 13
Davis, Marc, 219
Davis, Thomas O., 2, 4
Day Book, 37
Dean, Jerome Herman "Dizzy", 139
Debs, Eugene V., 9
Dedmon, Emmett, 15
Dell, Floyd, 217
Dempsey, Jack, 155
Denslow, Arthur, 210
Depriest, Oscar, 241
DeStefano, Sam, 96
Detroit Free Press, 10
Dever, Mayor William, 242
Devlin, Jim, 102
Devol, George, 60
Dillinger, John, 136

Ditcka, Mike, 162
Dodge, Mrs. Dorothy Anson, 108
Dodge, Harriet, 18, 19
Doehring, John "Bull", 157
Donohue, Patrolman Florence, 63
Doubleday, Abner, 99
Douglas, Stephen A., 9, 10, 195
Drake Hotel, 200, 207
Draper, Shang, 210
Dreiser, Theodore, 62, 210
Dresser, Clarence, 23
Drucker, Charley, 62
Dryden, Charlie, 131
Duffy, Sherman Reilly, 33
Dunne, Finley Peter, 6, 24, 210
Durkin, Jimmy, 41, 42
Durocher, Leo, 141
Dyer, Mayor Thomas, 227

Eastland Hotel, 117
Eckersall, Walter, 147
Edison, Thomas, 103
Edward VII (King of England), 181, 230
Enright, Maurice "Mossy", 29, 32
Eric Dorn, 39
Evans, Nat "Brown", 122, 123, 124
Everleigh, Ada, 68–74, 75
Everleigh, Minna, 68–74, 75
Evers, John J., 131, 132, 134, 141

Fallon, William, 127
Farrell, James T., 224
Farrington, Madame, 44
Favorite, Calvin, 171
Feldman, Dora, 64–66
Felsch, Oscar "Happy", 117, 123
Ferber, Edna, 62
Fermi, Enrico, 146
Field, Ethel, 198
Field, Eugene, 24–25, 44, 109, 208
Field, Henry, 180
Field, Joseph, 177
Field, Marshall I, 177–180, 193, 194, 195, 198
Field, Marshall II, 73, 146, 170, 175, 180, 198
Field, Marshall III, 180–181
Field, Marshall IV, 181

Fischetti, Charles, 92
Fischetti, John, 162
Fischetti, Rocco, 92
Fitzgerald, F. Scott, 122
Fitzgerald, "Red Jimmy", 62
Fitzpatrick, Mac, 78
Fletcher, Art, 137
Flint, Sliver, 110
Foley, Tom, 99
Foreman, Milton, 42–44
Forest City Club, 100
Fowler, Nancy "Nettie", 182
Franche, Jim "Duffy the Goat", 78
Francis, Frederic, 59
Frank, "Dutch", 229
Frank, Stanley, 139
Freeman, Lawrence Bud, 205
Friedman, Louis "The Farmer", 31
Fuchs, Julius, 198
Fuller, Henry B., 208
Fullerton, Hugh, 125

Gaedel, Eddie, 129
Gallagher, James, 139
Gallantry, Charles, 29
Galli-Curci, Amelita, 77
Gandil, Arnold ("Chick"), 117, 123, 124,
  125, 130
Garden, Mary, 173
Gates, Charlie, 70, 167–168
Gates, John Warner "Bet-a-Million", 70,
  166–169, 175
Genker, Charlie, 77
Gentleman, Dutch, 29, 32
Gentleman, Gus, 29
George V (King of England), 41
Gest, Morris, 78
Giancana, Sam ("Mooney"), 92, 96, 245
Gleason, William ("Kid"), 122, 124, 125
Glorianna Gang, 224
Goldman, Emma, 213
Goldwyn, Samuel, 149
Gondorf, Charley, 62
Gondorf, Fred, 62
Goodsell, Jim, 13
Gordon, Archie, 17, 18
Gore, George, 109
Grabiner, Harry, 122
Grabiner, Joseph ("Jew Kid"), 78
Graceland Cemetery, 195, 197

Grange, Harold ("Red"), 154, 155
Granger, Bill, 219
Grant, Charlie, 117
Grant, General Ulysses S., 11, 13, 17
Griffith, D.C. Clark, 108
Griffith, D.W., 47
Griffith, E.H. "Ned", 34
Grimm, Charlie, 136, 139
Guerin, Webster, 64–65
Gullet, "Chicken Harry", 78
Gunsaulus, Reverend Frank, 208
Guzik, Jake ("Greasy Thumb"), 81, 92, 96

Halas, George, 150, 151, 154–158, 160,
  162
Hall, George, 102
Hamsen, Knut, 210
Hand, Johnnie, 198
Hankins, Effie, 68
Hanny, Duke, 154
Harding, President Warren G., 50, 108
Harley, Chick, 154
Harper, Lou, 67
Harper, William Rainey, 145
Harrison, Mayor Carter, Jr., 73, 193, 202,
  232, 234, 237, 238, 239
Harrison, Mayor Carter, Sr., 62
Hart, James A., 108, 131
Hartnett, Charles L., ("Gabby"), 134
Harvey, Col. George, 23
Haymarket Riot, 9, 24
Hay, Ralph, 152
Healy, Ed, 154
Heap, Jane, 213
Hearst, William Randolph, 27, 29, 31, 32,
  47, 48, 75
Heath, Monroe, 63
Hecht, Ben, 25, 33, 34, 35, 36, 37, 38, 39,
  42, 47, 206, 213, 219, 220, 224
Heitler, "Mike de Pike", 77
Hemingway, Ernest, 44, 217, 220–224
Herman, Billy, 139
Herrick, Robert, 208
Herschberger, Clarence, 148
Heston, Willie, 148
Hickey, Alexander, 31
Higinbotham, Harlow, 202
Hill, Horatio, 3
Hinkle, Clark, 158
Hinsdale Cemetery, 195

Hodes, Charlie, 99
Hodges, Mary, 59
Holbrook, Bob, 29
Hoover, President, 190
Hope Diamond, 202
Horne, William D., Jr., 220, 221, 223
Hornsby, Rogers, 137, 139
Howard, "Kid", 221
Howard, "Ragtime Joe", 81
Howey, Walter, 33, 41, 45–55
Hoyne, Mallay, 29
Hudson, Johnny, 139
Huggins, Miller, 150, 151
Hulbert, William A., 101, 102, 103, 105
    109
Hull, Paul, 23, 24
Humphries, Murray ("The Camel"), 92,
    136
Hunter, Capt. David, 3
Hunt, Sam ("Golf Bag"), 93
Hussey, Obed, 182
Hutchens, Martin J., 33

Illinois State Register, 3
Insull, Samuel, 194
Iroquois Theater, 42
Isham, Warren P., 11, 13

Jackson, President Andrew, 1
Jackson, Mose, 242
Jackson, "Shoeless Joe", 116, 117, 122,
    123, 125, 126, 130
Jacobs, Heinie, 81
Jenkins, Ferguson, 139
Jennison, Col. Charles, 15
Johnson, Bancroft B. "Ban", 115, 125
Johnson, Curt, 219
Johnson, Herbert, 187
Johnson, Jack, 74
Johnson, Walter "Big Train", 123
Jones, Bobby, 155
Johns "Canada Bill", 60
Joyce, James, 215
Jung, Carl, 199

Kansas City Star, 44, 221
Keane, Alderman Thomas E., 246

Keating, William H., 1
Keeley, James "God", 30, 40–42, 44
Keen, Tom, 96
Kelley, John, 41, 238
Kelly, Mike "King", 100, 104, 106,
    109–113
Kenna, Michael "Hinky Dink", 42, 75, 77,
    232, 234, 237, 238, 239
Kerner, Gov. Otto, 246
Kerr, Dickie, 124
Kinzie, Mrs. John, 210
Kirkland, Joseph, 210
Klem, Bill, 132, 134
Kluszewski, Ted, 130
Know-Nothing Party, 4

Lake, Frankie, 136
Landis, Judge Kenesaw Mountain, 126,
    136
Lardner, Ring, 42, 48, 108, 125
LaSalle Opera House, 131
Latman, Barry, 130
Lawrence, Harry, 62
Lawrence, "Long Green" Andy, 27, 29
Lawson, Victor Fremont, 21–25
Layne, Bobby, 162
Leathers, Billy, 78
Lee, General Robert E., 13
Lehmann, Lotte, 187
Leiter, Joseph, 169
Leiter, Levi Z., 22, 177, 178, 179, 194,
    195
Leiter, Mrs. Mary Theresa Carver, 194
Lennon, John, 181
Levin, Hymie ("Loud Mouth"), 92
Lewis, James Hilton, 65
Lewis, Lloyd, 17
Lincoln, President Abraham, 6, 7, 11, 13,
    15
Lincoln, Robert T., 180
Lindsay, Vachel, 217
Lingle, Alfred ("Jake"), 83–90
Literary Times, 219
Little Review, 217–20
Little, Richard Henry, 61
Little Squaw, 19
Lopez, Al, 130
Lorimer, Sen. Billy, 240
Lotshaw, Andy, 156, 160
Lovejoy, Rose, 67

262   INDEX

Lucia, Ellis, 145
Luckman, Sid, 161, 162
Ludlum, Lou, 62
Lujack, Johnny, 162
Lumpkin, Roy "Father", 157
Lundberg, Ferdinand, 29, 191
Lyle, Judge John H., 243

MacArthur, Charles, 34, 43, 44, 47, 48,
  52–55, 219
Mack, Connie, 109, 117
Mahary, Billy, 122, 123
Malloy, Jack, 36, 37, 39
Malone, Perce Leight "Pat", 137
Mangler's Saloon, 44
Marinuzzi, Gina, 187
Marion Star, 50
Markham, Pauline, 17
Marquard, Rube, 150
Marshall, Evelyn, 180
Martin, Morris, 62
Masters, Edgar Lee, 210, 217
Mathewson, Christy, 100
Mayer, Mrs. Elizabeth Churchill, 104
McCarthy, Joe, 136, 137, 139
McCormick, Mrs. Chauncey, 203
McCormick, Cyrus, H., 10, 182, 183–184
McCormick, Edith, 198–200
McCormick, Harold Fowler, 184, 186,
  187, 190, 191, 198, 200
McCormick, Jim, 219
McCormick, John, 109
McCormick, Leander, 183
McCormick, Medill, 27, 29, 31, 32, 75, 196
McCormick, Nettie, 183, 184
McCormick, Robert Hall, 191
McCormick, Col. Robert R., 6, 89, 95,
  175, 180, 181, 182–183, 187–92
McCormick, Robert Sanderson, 187
McCormick, William Sanderson, 184
McCutcheon, John T., 24, 42
McDonald, "Big Mike", 60–66, 232
McDonald, Mrs. Mike, 64, 65
McErlane, Frank, 29
McGraw, John, 117
McGuire, Phyllis
McHugh, Buddy, 48
McKinlock, Mrs. G. Alexander, 196, 197
McLaughlin, John J. ("Boss"), 86, 87
McLean, Evalyn Walsh, 202

McMullin, Fred, 123
McPartland, Dick, 205
McPartland, Jimmy, 205
McVey, Cal, 101
McWeeney, John, 29
Medill, Joseph, 4–9, 13, 19, 21
Meeker, Arthur, 73, 184, 203
Meggy, Percy R., 21
Merlo, Mike, 77
Metropole Hotel, 244
Meyer, Gustavus, 179
Millar, Ronald, 36, 37
Miller, Ernest, 220
Mills, Abraham Gilbert, 102, 103, 104
Moisse, Lionel, 44
Monroe, Harriet, 210, 219
Moore, Coleen, 47
Moore, Dinty, 125
Moore, James Hobart, 73
Moore, Nathaniel Ford, 73
Moran, George ("Bugs"), 81, 87, 96, 136,
  244
Moresco, Victoria, 75
Morgan, J. Pierpont, 167, 171
Morrison Hotel, 35
Motley, Willard, 224
Moysant, Father, 64
Murray Hill Hotel, 145
Musso, George, 160

Nagurski, Bronko, 158, 160, 161
Newberry Library, 195
Newberry, Walter Loomis, 195
Nichols, Al, 102
Nickel Plate Railroad, 23
Nitti, Frank ("The Enforcer"), 92, 95, 96
Nolan, Jack, 29
Noonan, Mary, 63
Norris, Frank, 210
North, Dave, 205
Norton, Johnny, 62
Norworth, Jack, 108
Novikoff, Lou, 141

Oaks, Dan, 61
O'Bannion, Charles, Dion "Deanie", 29,
  52, 53, 81, 88
O'Brien, Mike, 229

O'Donnell Brothers, 81
Ogden, Malvina Belle, 170
Ogden, William B., 182
O'Hare, Butch, 93
O'Hare, Edward J., 93, 95, 96
Owen, Steve, 160, 161

Palace Hotel, 64
Palmer, Bertha Honore, 201–203
Palmer, Potter D'Orsay, 175, 177, 196, 200, 202
Palmer, Mrs. D'Orsay, 196, 198
Palmer, Potter Jr., 202
Parker, Harrison, 220, 221
Pasley, Fred, 85, 224
Patterson, Joseph Medill, 42, 47
Patterson, Robert W., 9
Payne, William Norton, 23
Pearsons, Dr. D.K., 195
Pendergast, Patric Eugene, 234, 243
Pershing, General John, 42
Petrakis, Harry Mark, 219
Pfeffer, Fred, 107, 109
Phillips, Kenneth, 91
Phipps, Ruth Pryn, 181
Pieper, Pat, 142
Pilotto, Al, 97
Pinkerton, William, 111
Plant, Daisy, 60
Plant, Kitty, 60
Plant, Roger, Jr., 60
Poetry Magazine, 210
Police Gazette, 65
Poole, Ernest, 6, 177
Post, Emily, 166
Post, George W., 62
Powers, Alderman John, 219, 233
Pratt, Ernie, 37
Prince, Frederick H., 196
Prince Henry of Prussia, 72
Pullman, George, 180, 181, 197, 198, 202
Pullman, Harriet Sanger, 198

Quincy Number 9 Saloon, 53

Rasco, Burton, 34, 42, 217
Rath, Maurice, 124

Ray, C.D., 30
Read, Opie, 208
Ream, Norman B., 180
Reed, Col. Nate, 23
Reese, Bonesetter, 151
Reuther, Dutch, 124
Ricca, Paul ("The Waiter"), 92, 96
Richardson, Hadley, 223
Risberg, Charles ("Swede"), 117, 123, 125, 126
Robbins, Harold, 224
Robinson, Jackie, 117
Roche, Mayor John A., 230
Rockefeller, Edity, 184
Rockefeller, John D. Jr., 181, 200
Rockefeller, John D., Sr., 145
Rockne, Knute, 148
Romanoff, Harry, 48
Roosevelt, President Franklin D., 244
Roosevelt, President Theodore, 173
Root, Charlie, 141
Rothstein, Arnold, 122, 123, 124, 125, 127
Royko, Mike, 220
Russell, William, 83, 86, 87, 89
Russie, Amos, 100
Ruth, George Herman ("Babe"), 105, 109, 141, 155, 203
Ryerson, Arthur, 195
Ryerson, Mrs. Edward, L., 203

St. Louis Cardinals, 127
St. Louis Post-Dispatch, 89
St. Louis Star, 90, 91
St. Valentine's Day Massacre, 89, 244
Saltz, Irwin, 224
Saltis, Joe, 136
Sandburg, Carl, 37, 38, 39, 40, 210, 213, 227
Saratoga Club, 75
Sauer, Hank, 139
Sauganash Tavern, 3
Sayers, Gale, 162
Scammon, J. Young, 19
Schalk, Raymond ("Cracker"), 124
Scheuttler, Chief, 34
Schreiber, Belle, 74
Schlogl's Restaurant, 49
Scott, Nannie Douglas, 177
Secret Committee of Six, 91

Serritella, Daniel A., 243
Seymour, Horatio W., 16
Shaw, Dr. Albert, 23
Sheldon, Lolita, 173
Sheridan Plaza, 93
Sherman House, 88
Sherman, General William Tecumseh, 11
Shoun, Clyde, 139
Sinclair, Harry, 124
Sinclair, Upton, 210
Sisson, Edgar, 42
Smith, Al, 67
Smith, Henry Justin, 10, 32, 33, 37, 38, 39, 40
Smith, John D., 41
Smith, Kate, 223
Smith, Perry, 198
Smith, Wallace, 34
Smith, Y.K., 220
Smity, Harry B., 23
Snitzer, The Kid, 62
Soland, Vincent, 97
Sousa, May de, 237
Spalding, Albert Goodwin, 100–112, 131, 154
Spalding, J.W., 103
Spencer, D.D., 22
Sporting Life, 104
Sportsman's Park, 93, 95
Springer, Dr. Joseph, 88
Stafford, Annie, 67
Stagg, Amos Alonzo, 143–150
Stainback, Chuck
Staley, A.E., 152
Starrett, Vincent, 34, 36, 37, 217
Stead, William T., 60, 232, 234
Stein, Gertrude, 217
Stern, Richard, 219
Sternaman, Edward C. ("Dutch"), 152
Stevens Hotel, 85, 87, 88
Stevens, Walter, 29
Stewart, Annie, 67
Stichcomb, Pete, 154
Stillson's, 53
Stone, Melville E., 19, 22–25
Stopa, Wanda, 220
Storey, Mrs. Wilbur F., 17, 18
Stricklett, Elmer, 116, 117
Sullivan, Billy, 117
Sullivan, Edward Dean, 52
Sullivan, Helen, 84
Sullivan, John L., 208

Sullivan, Joseph "Sport", 122, 123, 124
Sulzberger, Ferdinand, 198
Sunday, Billy, 106, 107, 108, 109, 210
Swanson, Attorney John, 87
Sweet, General J.B., 14–15
Swift, Ann, 175, 176
Swift, Gustavus Franklin, 171, 174–176

Taft, Charles P., 131
Taft, Mrs. Charles P., 131
Taylor, Bert, 42
Taylor, John L. ("Tarzan"), 154
Tennes, Mont, 77
Terkel, Studs, 224
Teschemaker, Frank, 205
Thompson, Big Bill, 232, 240–244
Thompson, John R., 179
Thompson, Lidia ("Black Crook"), 17, 18
Tietjens, Eunice, 215
Tilden, Bill, 155
Tigley, Katherine, 104
Tinker, Joseph, B., 131, 132, 134, 141
Toney, Fred, 134
Toronto Star, 221, 223
Torrio, John, 78–81, 232, 239, 242
Tough, Dave, 205
Trafton, George, 155, 156, 157
Treach, Fred, 99
Troupe, Emerson, 64
Trude, Asa, 65

Union Station, 74
University of Chicago, 145, 146, 149, 150
Uptmas, George R., 6

Vanderbilt, Commodore, 19
Vanderbilt, William H., 23
Vanilla, Roxy, 78
Vaughn, ("Hippo Jim"), 134
Veeck, Bill, Sr., 152
Veeck, Bill, Jr., 129–131, 137
Vogel, Eddie, 93
Voronoff, Dr. Serge, 47, 187

Wade, Bill, 162
Wallace, John, 62
Wallace, Tom, 62

Walsh, Ed ("Iron Man"), 116, 117
Walska, Ganna, 184, 186
Walters, William, 3
Washburn, Charles, 71
Washburne, Hempstead, 232
Watson, Carrie, 67
Wayman, Charles, 29
Weaver, George ("Buck"), 117–122, 123
Webb, Teddy, 34
Weed, "Blackie", 35
Weiss, Earl ("Hymie"), 81, 88
Welles, Orson, 22
Wellington Hotel, 167
Wentworth, Long John, 2–4, 227, 229, 230
Wharton, George, 33
Wheeler, James, 8
Wheeler, Mrs. James, 8
Whipple, Harold C., 31
Whistler, James McNeill, 198
White, Jim ("Deacon"), 101
Wigoda, Alderman Paul I., 246
Wilde, Oscar, 206, 207
Wilderson, James H., 93
Wilkie, Franc B., 7, 18
Williams, Billy, 139
Williams, Claude ("Lefty"), 122, 123, 124

Williamson, Ed, 109, 110
Wilson, Frank J., 93
Wilson, Lewis Robert, 136, 137
Winter, Dale, 78, 79
Witt, Frank, 31
Wood, Jimmy, 99
Woodruff, Harvey, 42
Wrigley, P.K., 134, 139, 141, 165–166
Wrigley, William, Jr., 131, 163–165

Yale, Frankie, 80
Yerkes, Charles Tyson, Jr., 193, 210, 234
Yost, Fielding H., 147
Young, Cy, 100
Young, Edward, 137

Zangara, Joseph, 244
Zeigfeld, Florenz, 78
Zilborg, Dr. Gregory, 181
Zuppke, Bob, 150